Praise for *The Best New True Crime Stories: Crimes of Famous & Infamous Criminals*

"When famous people decide to commit crimes, the sheer evil behind the scenes becomes more apparent. A fascinating read that will haunt you, that will keep you up at night."

—**Aphrodite Jones**, author of *Cruel Sacrifice* and host of the ID series *True Crime with Aphrodite Jones*

"Author Mitzi Szereto has done it again. Her latest book, a true crime anthology titled *The Best New True Crime Stories: Crimes of Famous & Infamous Criminals*, includes stories from top crime writers that are wonderfully researched and compelling. Take the story of a popular World Heavyweight Championship winner who, once he hooks up with his future wife, grows increasingly mad, culminating in two murders. From small towns to the Big Apple, each story is titillating, making this book a must-read. You won't be disappointed."

—**Cathy Scott**, *Psychology Today* blogger and *Los Angeles Times* bestselling author of *The Killing of Tupac Shakur* and *Murder of a Mafia Daughter*

"Reading these true crime stories was like being given access to a murder investigator's secret notes. The clear, direct language used throughout serves only to heighten the gruesomeness and terror of these crimes. I highly recommend this anthology!"

—**Robert Kerbeck**, corporate spy and author of *RUSE: Lying the American Dream from Hollywood to Wall Street*

"The sport of watching celebrities get their comeuppance because of their own bad behavior seems to be an undying entertainment. We think of Bill Cosby, Harvey Weinstein, scores of politicians and movie stars, while the next idol to fall is just around the corner. But you know what they say about karma. One day it just sneaks up and bites you in the ass. And, as Mitzi Szereto's latest collection shows, it could happen to anyone, no matter how high or mighty. Sit back and enjoy this endlessly fascinating volume. And just be glad you're not on a pedestal like they are. Or were."

—**J. P. Smith**, author of nine novels including his latest, *The Summoning*

"This is a fascinating book, well written and engaging, which will appeal to true crime aficionados everywhere. Highly recommended."

—**Ron Chepesiuk**, bestselling author and host of the *Crime Beat* radio show

"Mitzi Szereto has done it again. *The Best New True Crime Stories: Crimes of Famous & Infamous Criminals* brings together cases that pull back the curtain on stories from the seamier side of the entertainment world. As with Mitzi's other true crime compilations, it is a compelling read that I could not put down."

—**Mike Browne**, host of the *Dark Poutine* podcast and author of *Murder, Madness and Mayhem*

Praise for Mitzi's Other Collections

"Conjuring the spirits of Truman Capote and Damon Runyon (with the ghost of Patricia Highsmith looking on), the stories in *The Best New True Crime Stories: Well-Mannered Crooks, Rogues & Criminals* thrillingly depict real-life misdeeds throughout history. An Ecuadorian Robin Hood, an art scandal in Paris, new insights into the life and death of a Depression-era bootlegger—what's not to love?"

—**Abbott Kahler**, *New York Times* bestselling author (as Karen Abbott) of *The Ghosts of Eden Park*

"What a fantastic collection of spellbinding true crime stories from around the world! Each one is deeply researched, thoughtful, and fascinating. This anthology is simply good reading for any fan."

—**Kate Winkler Dawson**, author of *American Sherlock: Murder, Forensics, and the Birth of American CSI*

"Here be monsters! This brilliant collection of gruesome small-town misdeeds spanning a century and four continents will have you running for the comfort and safety of the big city."

—**Peter Houlahan**, author of *Norco '80*

"This compelling collection of serial killer stories is more than its beautifully told parts—it adds up to a clear and startling portrait of murder as an addiction and the very human demons that haunt the lives of killers and victims alike."

—**Deborah Blum**, author of *The Poisoner's Handbook: Murder and the Birth of Forensic Medicine in Jazz-Age New York*

"An engrossing and multi-faceted anthology for a new era of true crime writing. This fascinating collection goes beyond the procedural to raise important questions about how man's darkest impulses both threaten and consume us—as individuals and as a culture."

—**Piper Weiss**, author of *You All Grow Up and Leave Me*

THE BEST NEW TRUE CRIME STORIES

CRIMES OF FAMOUS & INFAMOUS CRIMINALS

Also by Mitzi Szereto

THE BEST NEW TRUE CRIME STORIES

CRIMES OF FAMOUS & INFAMOUS CRIMINALS

MITZI SZERETO

Editor of *The Best New True Crime Stories: Small Towns*

mango
PUBLISHING

CORAL GABLES

For permission requests, please contact the publisher at:
Mango Publishing Group
2850 S Douglas Road, 4th Floor
Coral Gables, FL 33134 USA
info@mango.bz

For special orders, quantity sales, course adoptions and corporate sales, please email
the publisher at sales@mango.bz. For trade and wholesale sales, please contact Ingram
Publisher Services at customer.service@ingramcontent.com or +1.800.509.4887.

The Best New True Crime Stories: Crimes of Famous & Infamous Criminals

Library of Congress Cataloging-in-Publication number: 2022946595
ISBN: (print) 978-1-68481-124-3 , (ebook) 978-1-68481-125-0
BISAC category code SOC051000, SOCIAL SCIENCE / Violence in Society

Table of Contents

INTRODUCTION

"The greater the power, the more dangerous the abuse."

—Edmund Burke, British statesman and philosopher

People from all walks of life commit crimes. But when they're familiar faces and household names, it offers a new level of fascination. We keep hearing about celebrity criminals like athlete and actor O. J. Simpson, record producer Phil Spector, and punk rocker Sid Vicious, and even nonviolent celebrity wrongdoers, such as kitchen queen Martha Stewart and televangelist Jim Bakker. Yet there are plenty of others who have traveled down that murky pathway toward criminality, especially when they think they can get away with anything. Having a recognizable name and the status that accompanies it may work as a shield—at least for a while. But when the proverbial hits the fan, it hits big. And for those in the public eye, there's nowhere to hide.

These well-known personalities can end up being tried in the court of public opinion, condemned before the facts are even in—which was the case for at least one famous person in this collection. Or they can get away with criminal activity for years simply because no one wants to believe they're capable of committing such acts. There are accounts on these pages of beloved stars whose deeds were so horrendous that it's difficult to accept that these things went on and that everyone seemed to be blind to it.

Power, money, fame, and lineage—we've seen time and again how these elements can corrupt those to whom they're attached, often creating a monster. Although the seed of "badness" might have been there all along, these individuals' social standing and, with it, their sense of omnipotence, allowed it to sprout.

I'm pleased to welcome you to *The Best New True Crime Stories: Crimes of Famous & Infamous Criminals*, the seventh installment in my anthology series. You'll find all-new true crime accounts written expressly for this volume, featuring criminals ranging from actors, television personalities, rock stars, and other performers to celebrated sports figures, theater moguls, legendary entrepreneurs, and aristocrats. It just goes to show how easily fame can turn into infamy!

Mitzi Szereto

ROLF HARRIS: AUSTRALIA'S FORGOTTEN SON

ANTHONY FERGUSON

I remember it as if it were yesterday. January 1979. The tiny, sleepy backwater city of Perth, Western Australia, had barely woken from its small-town slumber. Officially recognized as the most isolated capital city in the world, it had quietly gone about its business, its denizens happy to avoid the glare of the global media, apart from the occasional outburst of attention—like when astronaut John Glenn, the first American to orbit the earth in the *Friendship 7* craft in February 1962, christened it the "City of Lights" after the state premier, David Brand, had ordered the streetlights kept on all night and encouraged every citizen to leave their lights on to salute the passing craft. Glenn duly noted that the lights of Perth were visible from space.

Founded in 1829, the city celebrated its 150th anniversary in 1979, a birthday that was to be marked by stellar events and by tagging itself, to its own future embarrassment, "The State of Excitement."

The year-long celebration began on New Year's Eve with a gala open-air concert on the Esplanade, an anomalous patch of long-green-grassed promenade separating the cusp of the tiny city center from the mighty Swan River, from which the original Swan colony had gained its name, taken from the presence of the unusually colored black swans that proliferated in the region.

The Esplanade, which is still there today, has long been a point of contention among those who tried (and tried) to liven up the sleepy, geographically isolated capital, involving radical ideas like redredging the land to allow the river to run its course and lap against the fringes of the buildings as it did in the nineteenth century or, even more outrageous to the conservative city council, a suggestion to run a cable car from the heights of the towering Kings Park, overlooking the city, down to the Esplanade.

However, all such talk was sidelined on this searing summer New Year's evening on the cusp of 1979, because one of Western Australia's most beloved sons had returned to grace us with his famous personality. Yes, "the boy from Bassendean," children's entertainer, admired painter, and alternative musical artist Rolf Harris had returned to the shores of his birth to anoint us colonial yokels with his presence, to let us bask in his mighty shadow for a few short hours.

Rolf, he of *Rolf on Saturday O.K.?* fame. English telly, no less. Rolf of the wobble board and the paint brush, respected artist and purveyor of popular whimsical tunes like "Tie Me Kangaroo Down, Sport," "Two Little Boys," and "Jake the Peg" (with his extra leg, *diddle-iddle-iddle-um*), was back among us. Rolf of the famous British Paints television ad—"Trust British Paints (*ba-dum-dum*), sure can!" And we were all so much richer for the experience. Sixty thousand denizens of Perth duly pulled their deck chairs up to the Esplanade and unfurled their picnic rugs to enjoy the entertainment on this warm summer evening.

Yet something grated, even then. Something didn't sit quite right about this ever-cheerful, smiling, bearded, curly-haired, National Health-bespectacled figure—even though he had penned a special new song for the occasion, titled "I Wanna Go Back to WA."

The lyrics of this song are imprinted on my mind even today. The gist of the song has Rolf singing whimsically about how much he misses Western Australia and his hometown of Bassendean, while simultaneously suggesting that the wonders of the rest of the world don't measure up to "home."

At this point, after hearing the song repeated on radio airplay for what seemed like the thousandth time, even sheltered, narrow-minded, clueless sixteen-year-old me thought, *Hang on, Rolf. You buggered off to live in London twenty years ago, and we haven't seen you since. So these whimsical lyrics make you sound like something of a hypocrite, old son.* I also had no inkling of how much the state government must have paid him to come for a visit and write that tune.

In one verse, Rolf reminisces about how the small town he was born in hasn't changed a bit over the years. He almost convinces us that he's actually stepped foot in the local pub at some point since the early 1960s.

Fast forward forty years from that balmy night, and Rolf Harris is *persona non grata* in his hometown. Unloved. Unmentioned. The plaque erected in Bassendean forcefully removed and stashed away. Unwanted. Unwelcome. How did it come to this?

The short answer is, Rolf fell victim to the #MeToo movement. It seems that Rolf had a touch of Jeffrey Epstein about him. Rolf got Harvey Weinstein-ed. Like so many older males among the privileged rich and famous set, Rolf used his power and influence to grope women and take advantage of children under the age of consent. They all got away with it for years and probably thought they would never be called to account. Once the cat got out of the bag and the dominoes began to topple, Rolf fell hard and fast.

However, before we go there, let's take a look at the unlikely meteoric rise of this affable entertainer from the unknown suburban backstreets of Perth, Western Australia, to the heady showbiz heights of London, England.

Rolf Harris was born in the little-known town of Bassendean in Perth on March 30, 1930. His parents had emigrated from Cardiff in Wales, and Rolf was named after his mother's favorite Australian author, Rolf Boldrewood.

Bassendean is one of Perth's oldest suburbs. Accessible by the original railway line and located in the northeastern corridor of the metropolitan region, it was settled in 1832 and originally known as West Guildford, since it sat to the immediate west of the town of Guildford, established three years earlier in 1829, the year the State of Western Australia itself was first settled. In 1922, West Guildford was renamed Bassendean.

Despite its long history, the town isn't really known for much. The handful of famous people who emanated from the area were all involved in state politics except for Rolf. Once happily dubbed "the boy from Bassendean," this humble painter and songsmith was for many years the town's most beloved son.

Rolf had an average middle-class childhood. He came from good stock with an old-fashioned protestant work ethic, and was a decent student who seemed to work hard. There was no indication of any behavioral issues. Young Rolf took an early interest in the fine arts, especially music (his mother arranged for him to get piano lessons), drawing and painting, and sport, becoming a particularly adept swimmer. In those far off days with very few public swimming pools, Rolf honed his strokes in the nearby Swan River, as did many children of that era. There was never any suggestion of the young man experiencing any kind of emotional or physical abuse at home or anywhere else. However, most of those things were swept under the carpet by polite society back then, so we'll probably never know if any incipient stressors led Harris to develop the predilections he would display in later life.

As a youth, he began to display his prodigious talents in the areas of art, music, and swimming. In 1946, Harris became the Australian Junior hundred-meter backstroke champion. Between 1946 and 1952, he became the Western Australian champion over a range of swimming distances. As he grew into adulthood, Rolf completed a Bachelor of Arts degree from the University of Western Australia, following it up with a Diploma of Education from the Claremont Teacher's College (which has since become a campus of Edith Cowan University). His art was considered good enough to be displayed at the Art Gallery of New South Wales in Sydney and entered in the annual competition for the prestigious Archibald Prize, which is still coveted today. He achieved all of these accolades while still a very young man.

Harris moved to England in 1952 to study at the City and Guilds of London Art School. He made his television breakthrough the following year, earning a ten-minute drawing segment on a children's television show called "Jigsaw." In 1954, he earned a regular spot on another children's show, "Whirligig."

Perhaps surprisingly, Harris grew disillusioned with art school and failed to complete his studies. He came under the influence of the Australian artist Hayward Veal, who became his mentor and influenced Harris' style. Veal was a Victorian painter who was seventeen years Rolf's senior. Veal had left Australia with his wife in 1951, and by 1952 had set up shop in London and earned high regard for his art. In 1953, Veal was elected president of the Australian Artists Association, London—hence his appeal to the young Rolf Harris.

Around the same time, Rolf got himself a weekly gig playing the accordion at an Australian expats bar called the Down Under. It was here that he would hone the performing and songwriting skills that would later produce his first hit, "Tie Me Kangaroo Down, Sport."

Harris continued his television work through the 1950s, perfecting his lighthearted patter while creating a series of pithy characters with his paintbrush, bringing them to life and interacting with them to amuse his audience. The key to Harris' success as an artist in the medium of television was that, not only was he good at it, but he could also draw very fast, and he could entertain with his banter at the same time. Rolf found his niche in children's television, which would later segue into adult light entertainment.

In 1958, he married Alwen Hughes, a Welsh sculptor and jeweler. They are still married today.

When television was introduced to Australia in the late 1950s, Harris was headhunted by network executives to appear on the new medium down under. This led to him returning to live and work in his hometown of Perth in 1959. As in London, Rolf earned regular gigs on Australian children's television shows, and he also had a weekly evening variety program of his own. It was at this time that he recorded his first song, "Tie Me Kangaroo Down, Sport," which became a surprise number-one hit in Australia and did very well in Britain. This was significant in that Rolf introduced his wobble board, a musical instrument he invented consisting of a thin piece of wood the size and shape of a painting canvas that can be manipulated to produce a variety of sounds—an instrument he became synonymous with as his fame grew.

Harris enjoyed a golden period through the 1960s. He got to tour Australia and the United Kingdom with his band, bantering with the audience and producing his art live on stage. Returning to England in 1962, he had an opportune meeting with famed music producer George Martin (best known for his work with The Beatles), who subsequently re-recorded all of Rolf's songs. "Tie Me Kangaroo Down, Sport" then became a hit in the United States, as did another Harris tune, the Indigenous-Australian-influenced "Sun Arise." Harris got to work and record with The Beatles, and compered their Christmas tour in 1963. In 1964, he and Alwyn welcomed baby daughter Bindi into the world. Life was sweet.

Rolf continued to get television gigs, presenting the shows "Hi There! It's Rolf Harris" and "Hey Presto! It's Rolf" in 1964; then, in 1967, he also scored his own eponymously titled variety show, which ran on BBC One until 1972. As well as featuring the usual 1960s lineup of guest comedians, singers, and magicians, Rolf got the chance to introduce a wide audience to his soon-to-be-exceedingly-popular signature tunes, often utilizing his wobble board or a didgeridoo, an Indigenous-Australian musical wind instrument. He also did a bush-tales segment in which he would gather selected audience members around him and, under subdued lighting, regale them with stories from the Australian bush often taken from Aboriginal mythology. While doing so, Rolf would paint a picture relating to the story on an enormous canvas some twenty feet across.

Harris was a natural storyteller and a visually striking individual, and he particularly captivated a younger audience. He had a way of aspirating rhythmically as he flitted around the stage, dabbing paint onto canvas. He'd be humming some nonsensical tune, breathing in and out, and looking for all the world like the Pied Piper of Hamelin.

Rolf became so popular that he was selected to commentate on the 1967 Eurovision Song Contest for British television. In 1969, he had his biggest hit single, a cover version of the 1902 song "Two Little Boys." Said to be inspired by his father and uncle's experiences of the Great War, Rolf's version occupied the number-one spot on the British charts for six weeks during the Christmas period in 1969 and sold more than a million copies.

Harris's career plateaued after this high point, but he remained a staple on British children's television throughout the 1970s and 1980s, particularly through the show *Rolf on Saturday O.K.?*, which I recall seeing my younger sister watching in my youth. He also had several other shows that highlighted his whimsical artistic ability. In the early 1980s, he had a weekly series on Australian television screens, *The Rolf Harris Show*. My personal experience of Rolf throughout this period was of a very familiar face that consistently appeared in the background. He became one of those personalities who are instantly recognizable. Rolf sported a unique look with his black curls, neatly trimmed beard, and thick, black-rimmed spectacles.

Harris was twice featured on the British edition of *This is Your Life*, in 1971 and again in 1995. Similarly, he was honored twice on the Australian version of the program.

In 1985, in an incident that would have ominous portent, he fronted a short documentary about preventing child abuse, called *Kids Can Say No!*

Harris continued to tour and perform and work with famous musicians on their albums, Kate Bush among them. In the late 1980s, Rolf was asked to perform a cover of the Led Zeppelin classic "Stairway to Heaven" with his wobble board on a popular Australian comedy show, *The Money or the Gun* (I remember this distinctly). Rolf's version was so well received it was released as a single a few years later, reaching number seven on the British charts. This led to him being invited to perform at the Glastonbury Festival in 1993. He went on to perform there in 1998, 2000, 2002, 2009, and 2010.

In 2000, Harris performed a version of his early hit "Tie Me Kangaroo Down, Sport" with the insanely popular Australian children's group, The Wiggles. (Thank God there have been no Wiggles scandals to date; I don't think the country would ever recover.) Harris was digitally removed from the DVD following his sexual assault convictions—that, my friends, is how popular and untainted the Wiggles's image is.

Between 1994 and 2003, Harris hosted *Animal Hospital*, a British reality TV show about veterinarians, which won five National Television Awards for factual programming. Between 2001 and 2007, he presented yet another television show called *Rolf on Art*, in which he waxed lyrical about some of his favorite classical artists. In late 2002, London's National Gallery hosted a selection of Harris's art.

In the mid-2000s, Harris hosted three series of a show called *Star Portraits with Rolf Harris*, in which he got to produce a series of portraits of famous celebrities. This led to the Australian being commissioned to produce a portrait of Queen Elizabeth II for her eightieth birthday in late 2005. The resulting work was very well received by the British public.

In January 2007, there followed a one-hour documentary on Harris's life as an artist, *A Lifetime in Paint*. Between 2007 and 2013, he continued to tour and appear on numerous television programs, keeping his image in the public eye. In November 2011, Harris was featured in a biographical show, *Piers Morgan's Life Stories*, in which he broke down and wept, admitting he was suffering from clinical depression. It's possible to conjecture that there may have been some rumblings behind the scenes about his personal life at this point. However, Harris remained a hugely popular public figure. A retrospective display of his major works was also very well received by the British public at the Walker Gallery in Liverpool in 2012.

In October 2012, Rolf began hosting a show called *Rolf's Animal Clinic* on Channel 5 in Britain. In March 2013, Harris was arrested as part of a police investigation called Operation Yewtree, and questioned on charges relating to historical sexual offenses. The show was immediately put on hiatus, eventually resuming with a different host and title. Harris vehemently denied the allegations and was subsequently released without being charged.

Harris resumed touring and thanked his audience for their support. However, he was arrested again in August 2013. This time there was no escape. He was charged with nine counts of indecent assault dating back to the 1980s involving dealings with two girls ages fourteen and fifteen, as well as four counts of making indecent images of children in 2012.

Harris pleaded not guilty. But in late 2013, three further charges of sexual assault were brought against him, this time for the assault of females aged nineteen in 1984, aged eight in 1969, and aged fourteen in 1975. Again, he pleaded not guilty.

The indecent-images charges related to items found on Harris's personal computer, namely thirty-three images of potentially underage models among thousands of pornographic images of adults. Harris's legal team argued successfully for these charges to be assessed separately from the sexual assault charges. It was later proved by the defense that the models were over the age of consent when the images were made, and those charges were subsequently dropped. However, the incident cemented in the public mindset that this beloved character they'd held in high esteem had a darker side. In contrast to his public persona, Harris was a man in his eighties who kept a large collection of pornography specifically relating to young girls.

Harris's trial began in Southwark Crown Court in May 2014. Several of the charges levied related to a sexual relationship Harris had entered into with one of his daughter's best friends. It was alleged that the sexual aspect of this relationship began when the girl was thirteen and continued until she was twenty-nine. Harris argued that he did not start having sex with the girl until she was eighteen. This occurred in the 1980s, when Harris had just turned fifty. The girl lived very close to the Harris family and spent a lot of time in the Harris home. On one occasion, the Harrises had even taken her to Australia on holiday with them. In other words, there was ample opportunity for Rolf Harris to groom her.

A letter was shown in court in which Harris had written to the girl's father long after the relationship had ended. In it, he stated that the relationship had progressed from mutual feelings of love and friendship. Harris seemed to still be under the misapprehension that the abuse had occurred with the full assent of a child who was too young, and probably too terrified, to afford her consent. This must have been cold comfort to the girl's father and to the victim herself, who would suffer the aftereffects of the abuse, to the detriment of her mental health, for the rest of her life.

There were several other charges concerning groping and sexual assault, involving girls under the age of consent as well as adult women. Harris denied every allegation. The defense team's main tactic was to suggest that every accuser was lying. Indeed, this refusal to accept any responsibility, and his apparent belief that he had done nothing wrong, worked to Harris's detriment. In particular, one accuser claimed that he had groped her in the town of Cambridge, to which Harris responded by insisting he had never been to Cambridge. The jury was then shown footage of a television program filmed in Cambridge at the time of the alleged assault, which clearly featured Rolf Harris. This was perhaps a turning point in the case, as it indicated that Harris was prepared to lie to try to deny his guilt. The jury found him guilty on every charge, and his public reputation went down the drain.

On July 4, 2014, Harris, now eighty-four years old, was sentenced to five years and nine months in prison. In the judge's summation, Mr. Justice Sweeney remarked to the defendant, "You have shown no remorse for your crimes at all. Your reputation now lies in ruins, you have been stripped of your honors, but you have no one to blame but yourself."

While Harris stewed away in prison, it became public knowledge that the police were investigating other alleged sexual offenses committed by him against young girls. Again, he did himself no favors when the details of a letter he had written to a friend were obtained by a British tabloid. The letter contained song lyrics he'd written that were highly abusive toward his female accusers.

It is clear from this response and his attitude in general that Harris has not accepted any responsibility for his crimes. Nor has he considered the ongoing emotional and psychological distress he has caused his victims. He displays an incredible arrogance and sense of entitlement, appears to think he is above the law, and has demonstrated utter contempt toward his accusers.

While he was in prison, several more women came forward with accusations against Harris of groping and indecent assault. As a result, a second trial began in January 2017, with Harris appearing by video link from his cell. He was considered too elderly and unwell to appear in court again.

Harris's defense team argued that the media frenzy surrounding his first trial had made him vulnerable to people making accusations against him. Three of the charges were dropped, and the judge discharged the jury from deliberating on the other four counts. The prosecution asked for a retrial, which was granted and took place on May 15, 2017. However, the jury was unable to reach a verdict, and the prosecution didn't pursue another retrial.

After serving three years in HM Prison Stafford, Harris was released on May 19, 2017.

Today, Rolf Harris is a broken man, living out his final years as a recluse in his Berkshire mansion. Practically housebound, he spends his days as the principal carer for his ailing wife, Alwyn, who is suffering the late stages of Alzheimer's disease. His only support appears to come from his daughter, Bindi Nicholls, now in her fifties, who is set to release a tell-all autobiography of life with her father. Nicholls claims her father is not a child molester, but rather just a relic from a bygone age when men were extremely patriarchal and considered it acceptable to openly flirt with women and get a bit touchy-feely.

Rolf Harris, who turned ninety-two in March 2022, suffers from diabetes. This is undoubtedly not how he envisioned spending his dotage.

Nearly all the honors bestowed upon him through his long public career have been rescinded.

Harris had been awarded an MBE in 1968 (Most Excellent Order of the British Empire), an OBE in 1977 (Officer of the Order of the British Empire), and a CBE in 2006 (Commander of the Order of the British Empire). These are ascending awards for outstanding contributions in the field of the arts and science. All were revoked by the Queen in March 2015. He had been a Member (AM) and an Officer (AO) of the Order of Australia, both of which were rescinded in February 2015. In July 2014, his name was removed from the list of people honored as Australian National Living Treasures. His two honorary doctorates from the University of East London and Liverpool Hope University were also rescinded. He was removed from the ARIA (Australian Recording Industry Association) Hall of Fame. His BAFTA Fellowship (British Academy of Film and Television Arts) was also annulled.

Harris is also *persona non grata* in the town of his birth, the place that once revered him and traded on his name. Bassendean is pretty much still the quiet suburban backwater it always once, a quaint old-world place worth visiting on a nice Sunday drive.

In July 2014, on the cusp of Harris being sentenced to prison in England, the Bassendean town councilors had a behind-closed-doors meeting during which they voted to remove all of "the boy from Bassendean's" artworks from their council chambers and lock them away in storage, strip his status as a freeman of the town, and pull up the plaque they had erected outside his childhood home, which remarkably still stands (*sans* plaque).

As quoted in *The West Australian* newspaper on July 3, 2014, then Bassendean mayor John Gangell said, "We ultimately decided to take a stance and draw a line in the sand. No longer is it tolerable if you hold a position or a special status to be allowed to have your artwork displayed or talent exhibited after a conviction … we have decided that the victims are first and foremost in this decision tonight."

A commemorative slab bearing Harris's name on St. Georges Terrace in the city of Perth was removed by that city's council.

As time passes and the end nears for Rolf, he finds himself unloved in his hometown, his home state, his home country, and his once-beloved adopted country. As more women are emboldened to come forward to reveal long-suppressed details of unwelcome attention by the former star, it is unlikely his reputation will ever be restored, despite the wishes of his one remaining supporter—his daughter Bindi.

Harris's reluctance to accept responsibility for his actions and his insistence on blaming his victims and accusing them of lying paint him as a sociopath, far removed from the image he presented to the world for decades as a beloved children's entertainer.

Back in the days when Harris and people like him in show business were allowed to get away with their abhorrent behavior, it is said that he was known within the television industry by a particular nickname pertaining to his wandering hands around women and girls: "the Octopus." As with many other privileged older-male media personalities in the 1970s and 1980s, this type of behavior was well-known, but was laughed off and brushed under the carpet.

In the more socially aware "woke" world of today, Rolf Harris is slowly being erased from history. This once-revered character, who seemed to be all over British and Australian televisions, who once had an entire episode of the smash 1970s comedy show *The Goodies* based entirely on him, who once was famously allowed to sit with Queen Elizabeth and paint her portrait, is now being removed from our cultural milieu.

Rolf Harris was once so ubiquitous that the briefly famous, foul-mouthed Australian comedian Rodney Rude penned a comedy song about him called "Why Won't Rolf Harris Just Fuck Off and Die?"—a tune ironic in retrospect, since it was written decades ago regarding Rolf seemingly being everywhere on television and of how beloved he was by his audience. Yet it now pretty much summarizes what most Brits and Australians wish of Rolf.

On a final, sad note, it is perhaps telling that nowhere across the
internet is it possible to find a recording of the song Harris presented as
a love letter to his hometown in Western Australia in 1979: "I Wanna Go
Back to WA." Nor will you find the lyrics. It's as if the song, much like Harris
himself, has been written out of history, a shameful and painful memory of
something once cherished that turned sour.

WRESTLING WITH DEMONS

JOE TURNER

Chris Benoit had the world in his hands.

He was a global superstar, an elite athlete, and one of the most respected performers in the world of professional wrestling. From humble beginnings in Montreal, Canada, Chris Benoit climbed his way to the peak of the wrestling world, eventually cementing his legacy as one of the greatest performers in history. In an industry known for its theatrics and overblown personalities, Chris Benoit was a fundamentalist and a tactician. He was a *wrestler's wrestler*, winning over fans and peers with his no-nonsense style and incredible ring work.

But Chris Benoit had demons he couldn't escape, that clawed away at his perceptions and his awareness of reality. These demons left him in a heightened state of paranoia and anxiety, and eventually led him into a spiraling blackness that consumed not only his own life, but the lives of those closest to him. Following a weekend in June 2007, Chris Benoit's reputation as a hero was stripped away, leaving behind a much more sinister legacy.

After Benoit failed to show up for several scheduled events, police descended upon his home in Fayetteville, Georgia, where he lived with his wife Nancy and seven-year-old son Daniel. There, in various rooms of the six-bedroom home, police found a scene that defied all sense and reason.

Despite the legacy Chris Benoit forged, all of his achievements would be forever overshadowed by the events of his final days. Chris Benoit's gradual descent into madness was a mystery that crippled an industry and left millions desperately searching for answers.

Early Days

Christopher Michael Benoit was born in Montreal, Canada on May 21, 1967, to parents Michael and Margaret Benoit. The older of two siblings, Chris soon moved to Alberta with his mother, father, and sister Laurie, where he spent the majority of his childhood and early adulthood.

Benoit was an ambitious young boy, unusually focused and determined. He was an intense character from day one, but he was ultimately a kind and likable student. Described by his father as "obsessive" about the things he enjoyed, this obsessiveness would become a staple of Benoit's entire life.

It was during his first year of high school that Benoit discovered weight training and bodybuilding, and throughout his school days, he completely immersed himself in athletic competition. Even at such a young age, he won awards for bodybuilding and amateur wrestling, and soon turned his eye to professional wrestling, at age sixteen.

Entering the unforgiving world of professional wrestling during the 1980s was a move that took incredible courage, but Benoit had no doubts about his decision. It was no secret that the life expectancy of a professional wrestler was one of the shortest of any industry, stemming from a combination of steroid and painkiller abuse and the physical toll of performing multiple times per week. However, Chris plunged headfirst into this world without a second thought, enrolling in the two harshest training camps in the industry.

It was here that Benoit learned to harness his intensity and to really flourish as a performer. However, it was also a grueling, nightmarish experience for Chris, drilling into him a sense of discipline that went far beyond mere self-control.

Benoit did the majority of his training in a system known as the Dungeon, a wrestling school run by legendary wrestling mind Stu Hart. The Dungeon was considered the harshest training school in the world, with Hart's training methods bordering on the cruel and sadistic. In addition to punishing workouts, Stu often placed his trainees in actual submission maneuvers as a way to expose them to prolonged periods of pain. But Chris endured the Dungeon and graduated in the mid-1980s, and then quickly rose through the ranks of the professional wrestling elite. He competed for several promotions in both the US and Japan, soon racking up championship victories and solidifying himself as a world-class performer. Around the same time, he met his first wife, Martina. They went on to have two children together: David, born in 1993, and Megan, born in 1996.

Around the same time, the Western wrestling industry had begun to cater to children as a means of financial survival, incorporating juvenile gimmicks and all-American heroes for characters. However, with his monstrous physique and brute-force style, Chris helped lend some legitimacy to a sport many considered "fake," as well as ushering in a new era of grittier, more adult-oriented wrestling.

But it wasn't without its hardships. Having gained a reputation as a hard-hitting technical wrestler, Benoit approached each of his wrestling matches as though it was his last. Concern for his own well-being came second to putting on spectacular performances, and over time, this took an incredible toll on Chris's body and mind.

A New Era

It was early in his career that Chris developed his signature finishing move—a diving headbutt from the top turnbuckle, which he delivered in every subsequent match he competed in. On average, Benoit was competing in 110 wrestling matches per year, meaning he was taking blunt trauma to the head more than twice a week. Combined with his insistence on taking unprotected shots from steel chairs as a way to depict legitimacy, concussions were a regular occurrence. Unbeknownst to Benoit, the sheer impact of this maneuver was gradually causing irreparable damage to his brain.

Showing no signs of slowing down as wrestling's boom period began in 1998, it was only a matter of time before Chris's reckless style caught up with him. Throughout his career, Benoit mostly kept to himself. Unlike many of his wrestling colleagues, he was an intensely private individual. Benoit was always the consummate professional, with few vices, although his gigantic physique made it clear he was a heavy steroid user. He conducted himself with the same self-discipline he'd learned from his days in the Dungeon, with behavior that often bordered on the neurotic.

In one bizarre instance, a colleague of Benoit's once discovered him backstage after a match between the two in which Benoit had made a small error. As an act of self-discipline, Benoit was in the middle of doing squats. He told his colleague he needed to do five hundred to purge himself of his mistake.

By 1997, Benoit had become one of the biggest attractions for World Championship Wrestling—the most popular wrestling promotion in the world at the time. He was just beginning an on-screen rivalry with a wrestler named Kevin Sullivan, and part of the rivalry involved Benoit becoming romantically linked with Sullivan's manager, Nancy, who happened to be Sullivan's real-life partner.

Soon, the lines between fiction and reality began to blur.

The Woman

In the ring, she was known only as "Woman." But in the real world, her name was Nancy Benoit.

Born in Boston, Massachusetts in 1964, Nancy Toffoloni came from modest beginnings. Her childhood saw her move from Boston to Daytona

Beach, Florida, along with her parents Paul and Maureen and her younger sister, Sandra.

As a teenager, Nancy married her high school sweetheart, Jim Daus, and took to working at an insurance firm to make ends meet. A strikingly beautiful brunette, it was Nancy's good looks that eventually led her into the world of professional wrestling.

On Sunday nights, she and Jim would head down to Orlando to watch local wrestling shows, and it was here that a chance photograph brought Nancy to the attention of a high-profile wrestling photographer. The photographer needed a cover model for a magazine shoot, and based on photos he'd seen of Nancy at the local Orlando show, he quickly enlisted her services.

Nancy then caught the attention of professional wrestler Kevin Sullivan, who convinced her to join him as his on-screen valet. At the time, Sullivan's wrestling persona was that of a cult-leading Satanist, and Nancy, with her dark features and stern but feminine beauty, made the perfect companion.

As Kevin worked for several promotions across the US, he and Nancy toured the country together. Soon, young Nancy had no time for married life. Her relationship with Daus fell apart, and Sullivan was there to pick up the pieces. Their relationship became personal, and by 1985, the two were married. Nancy's career quickly skyrocketed. She and Sullivan moved to World Championship Wrestling in 1989, where she went on to manage some main-event stars.

However, history soon repeated itself. In 1996, Nancy became involved with one of WCW's hottest commodities—Chris Benoit. They began an on-screen love affair that saw Chris take Nancy away from the clutches of Kevin Sullivan's satanic cult. But unbeknownst to many, there was an element of truth to the angle. Chris and Nancy's on-screen relationship evolved into a personal one, with many believing that the two were having relations while Nancy was still married to Sullivan.

As the storyline involving Benoit, Sullivan, and Nancy progressed, life imitated art. The relationship between Chris and Nancy flourished both in-ring and out, and before long, the two became romantically linked in real life. At the same time, Chris's marriage began to fall apart, brought on mainly by his demanding travel schedule. Likewise, Nancy's relationship with Sullivan also came to an end. The breakups took their toll on everyone involved, but Nancy and Chris found solace in each other.

Fame, Fortune, and Violence

At a wrestling event in 1997, Benoit and Sullivan were caught backstage in a genuine fistfight that had to be broken up by other wrestlers. It was believed that Sullivan had become aware of Nancy's deceit and lashed out at Chris. The relationship between Nancy and Sullivan was over, and their divorce quickly followed.

Somewhat mysteriously, Nancy then vanished from television with little explanation. She opted for a quieter life outside of the ring, acting as Chris's business manager from behind the scenes. The pair married three years later, and on February 25, 2000, Nancy gave birth to their son, Daniel Christopher Benoit.

Daniel was a happy young boy, full of life and personality, even from a young age. He was undoubtedly his father's son, the spitting image of Chris, and with the same short but stocky figure. Nancy's sister Sandra described Daniel as "a wonderful boy who kissed sweetly, hugged tightly, and laughed happily." He had a great fondness for animals, occasionally going horseback riding with his mother and neighbors.

It was only a matter of time before Daniel became curious about the world of wrestling, and by the age of four, he was already his father's biggest fan. Nancy taught Daniel about wrestling's history and told him stories of her and his father on the road as he listened with fascination. In his youthful naivety, Daniel still believed wrestling storylines and matches were non-scripted, so to him, his father was twice as heroic as he was to the rest of the world.

For Benoit's big matches, Daniel and Nancy would sit ringside to cheer him on. The most significant moment in Chris's career came at Madison Square Garden in 2004, when he won the WWE World Heavyweight Championship for the first time. It was an iconic scene for the wrestling world, and it saw both Nancy and Daniel joining Chris in the ring for a heartfelt celebration. Benoit embraced Daniel as tears ran from his eyes. Even through wrestling's lens of reality suspension, it was clear that Chris's love for his son ran deep.

It seemed Chris Benoit had forged the perfect life for himself. After a twenty-year career, he'd won the most prestigious prize in wrestling. He had a beautiful, loving family, and had certified himself as a future wrestling Hall of Famer, gaining the respect of his peers and colleagues in the process.

But things weren't all perfect for the Benoit family. Only a year before Chris's triumphant title win, Nancy had—shockingly—taken out a restraining order against her husband. It was a surprise to many, as few people could believe the mild-mannered Chris could be responsible for any kind of real-life violence. Nancy also filed for divorce, claiming "irrevocable differences" and that Chris often lost his temper and threatened to assault her physically. Nancy claimed she feared for the safety of herself and Daniel, and for several months in 2003, Benoit was banned from coming within a hundred yards of either of them.

But, strangely, all of these claims were dismissed by Nancy in August 2003, and the Benoits resumed their seemingly ordinary life. Precisely why she dismissed the claims has never been uncovered.

A sinister theory regarding the withdrawal is that perhaps Nancy believed the restraining order might incite further violence from Chris, and these fears would be valid, since just four years later, the legacy of Chris Benoit was left in ruins following a cruel act that sent shock waves through the wrestling world.

Bizarre Behavior

As the years went by, the consequences of Chris's lifestyle began to show. By 2007, not only was he injecting steroids far beyond the recommended levels, but many of his closest friends in the business had passed away. His best friend Eddie Guerrero, someone who also shared the ring with him during his triumphant title win, had died of heart failure only eighteen months before. Benoit's close friend and fellow wrestler Chavo Guerrero documented Benoit saying, "I can't take this anymore. I can't handle all of my friends dying."

The loss of Eddie Guerrero marked the beginning of Benoit's gradual separation from reality. He wrote letters to the deceased Guerrero in his diary, opening up about his addiction to painkillers and how he'd felt depressed for many years. He wrote lovingly about Nancy and Daniel, calling them the light of his life.

In mid-2007, Chris Benoit's behavior began to drastically change. The depression he'd talked about in his writings became noticeable, but more concerning was that he began to suffer frequent bouts of paranoia. He claimed to friends that he was being followed. By whom, he never said, but this resulted in Chris alternating his routes to gyms, airports, and grocery stores each time he left the house. Nancy's sister Sandra later claimed that Chris had memorized thirty driving routes to his local gym, and even went as far as making the trips in his friends' vehicles.

Similarly, he also pleaded with Nancy to stay home with Daniel as often as she could, claiming he was trying to protect their safety. He never said from what exactly, but around the same time, Chris became nearly convinced that he was about to lose his job with World Wrestling Entertainment.

The truth was almost the complete opposite. WWE management was planning on crowning Benoit with another championship in June 2007—something Benoit was undoubtedly aware of, but something he ultimately chose to distrust.

To outsiders, Chris's behavior was merely him being cautious and reserved—not entirely out of character for him. He remained a consummate professional on the surface, though to those close to him, these bizarre changes in his private life were evident. Both Nancy and her sister saw that Chris was struggling, but with what exactly, they didn't know.

On June 21, 2007, Nancy sent an ominous text message to a friend. It read: "I'm scared to death. If anything happens to me, look at Chris."

The next day, Friday, June 22, Chris returned to his Georgia home in the early afternoon, after visiting his doctor to pick up a supply of enhancement drugs. When he returned, he found Nancy and Daniel barbecuing in the backyard. For the next few hours, Chris played his usual role as father and husband.

But when nightfall came, and after Nancy tucked their son into bed, darkness also fell on Benoit.

Tragedy

While Nancy was in her upstairs office, Chris snuck up behind her and carried out the first of two vicious attacks that night.

Chris blitz-attacked Nancy from behind. Given Benoit's incredible strength, the blow was almost enough to knock her out cold. As she lay disoriented on the floor, Chris then restrained her hands and feet with black industrial tape. He reached for a nearby TV cable and wrapped it around her neck. With his knee lodged against her spine, Chris strangled Nancy to death.

With a small pool of blood below her face, Benoit wrapped Nancy's body in a towel. He then went to another room of the house, picked up a Bible, and placed it next to her. He left her where she died.

Meanwhile, on the other side of the house, Daniel Benoit lay fast asleep, unaware of the horror that had just taken place in the home office.

Friday evening turned into the early hours of Saturday morning. Exactly what time it happened remains unknown, but before the morning of June 23 arrived, Chris Benoit made his way to his son's bedroom.

The room was stacked with wrestling memorabilia—figurines, posters, and replica belts of the championships his father had won. Daniel was undoubtedly the biggest Chris Benoit fan in the world.

Chris woke Daniel, then sedated him with Xanax pills. As Daniel fell into a disoriented state, Chris strangled the boy to death. As he had done with Nancy, he also left a Bible near Daniel's body.

A few hours earlier, Chris Benoit had been a loving family man. Now, just before the sun rose on June 23, 2007, he had murdered the two people he claimed to love most in the world.

Yet Benoit's atrocities didn't end there. For the next two evenings, Chris was scheduled to perform at WWE shows in Texas. Maintaining his reputation as a consummate professional, he battled with the idea of leaving his home, boarding a plane, and actually attending the two shows he was booked for. Around four o'clock on the afternoon of June 23, Benoit called his friend Chavo Guerrero, who was also scheduled to perform at the same events.

Benoit told Chavo that Daniel was suffering from food poisoning, so he was running late for that evening's show, though he said he'd still make it there. In reality, Chris was sitting more than a thousand miles away while two dead bodies lay in two rooms of his home. Before hanging up, Benoit said to Chavo, "I love you."

Something seemed suspicious about Benoit's honesty. While Chavo had no doubt that Chris was being genuine, it was an uncharacteristic comment for the usually reserved Benoit. The show in Texas went on without Chris, despite WWE officials continually checking on his whereabouts. Benoit ignored their calls.

Between four and five o'clock on the morning of June 24, Chris sent a series of odd text messages to five of his coworkers. The messages simply listed his home address, along with: "The dogs are in the enclosed pool area. The garage side door is open."

Strangely, Chavo Guerrero received the exact same message from both Chris and Nancy's phones. Unbeknownst to him, it was actually Chris using both. Chavo put the incident down to a technological mishap and assumed Benoit would be showing up at the pay-per-view in Houston that evening. Benoit was scheduled for another championship victory. Once again, he didn't make it to the event.

With Benoit having now missed two shows, one of which was a high-profile televised event, WWE officials called Fayetteville police to conduct a welfare check on Benoit and his family. The first person at the scene was actually the Benoits' next-door neighbor, Holly Schrepfer. Police had knocked on her door after learning that she sometimes looked after the family's dogs while Chris and Nancy were on the road. After ushering the two German shepherds into the open garage, Holly crept up the stairs to the top floor of the house. She called out for Nancy or Daniel, but received no response.

Daniel's bedroom door was open, so Holly peered inside. There, in blue SpongeBob pajamas, lay Daniel Benoit on his bed, his head slightly turned against the pillow. Next to him was a copy of *My First Bible*, a children's edition of the New Testament. After leaning in closer, Holly could see that Daniel's skin was slightly discolored. Closer inspection revealed that he wasn't breathing.

Holly immediately ran to check every room for signs of life. In the home office, Holly found the second horror. In a white tank top and blue pajama bottoms lay Nancy Benoit, still with her hands and feet restrained and a television cable wrapped around her neck. Holly ran outside to inform police officers of the atrocities inside the home.

It was the police who made the next discovery. In the basement gym, they found the body of Chris Benoit. He was sitting upright on a bench, shirtless, and wearing red gym shorts and athletic shoes. Incredibly, Chris had engineered his weight machine into an amateur execution device by manipulating the pulley cable into a noose, then using the weight stack of the machine to lift him from the floor, snapping his neck in the process. It was an elaborate creation requiring extraordinary strength, clearly the result of much thought and planning. It seemed that even in his final moments, Chris Benoit still maintained the ferocious discipline he was famous for.

There was no suicide note. No clear motive. No apparent signs pointing to a deranged mind—at least not on the surface. Over the next twenty-four hours, tributes for the Benoit family poured in from fans and coworkers. The following evening's WWE show was a three-hour tribute to the man dubbed the "Crippler," showcasing highlights from Chris's outstanding career.

But less than forty-eight hours later, the truth about what had happened in the Benoit home became known.

Authorities officially labeled it a murder-suicide.

A Legacy Lost

Immediately, everything Benoit had worked for over his twenty-two-year career became overshadowed by the harrowing events of that weekend. Of all the tragic events that had occurred within the wrestling industry over the past fifty years, nothing came close to the cruel and perplexing nature of this case. Fans, investigators, and colleagues searched for a motive, but with little success. Why would Chris Benoit—the man who would come home in the middle of hectic touring schedules to spend a few hours with his family—do this to the people he loved the most?

Many theories were put forward, some plausible, some outlandish. Kevin Sullivan's name reared its head on many occasions, though any possible involvement by him was quickly ruled out by investigators. Benoit's true motives remained a mystery—and still are to this day. However, a shocking revelation was made by medical researchers in the months following the incident—a revelation that went partway toward explaining why Chris suffered such an extreme breakdown of his mental state.

The Sports Legacy Institute, an organization that studies the long-term effects of head injury in sports, carried out extensive medical tests on the brain of Chris Benoit. The SLI had studied the brains of deceased boxers, football players, and other contact-sport athletes many times in the past. However, SLI researchers found that Chris Benoit's brain was damaged beyond anything they'd previously seen.

A lifetime of head trauma—from diving headbutts to unprotected blows from fists and chairs—had reduced his brain to a condition resembling that of an eighty-year-old dementia patient. With such severe brain damage, the fact that Chris Benoit still managed to function in day-to-day life was nothing short of a miracle. While this didn't fully explain Chris's actions—or excuse them—it confirmed the belief that he was not of sound mind during his final days.

In the years since the incident, multiple pieces of information have been put forward in defense of Chris's innocence. All have since been debunked. Perhaps the most bizarre piece of information—and a coincidence bordering on the unbelievable—is the infamous Wikipedia entry. Fourteen hours before the police discovered the bodies, someone edited Chris Benoit's Wikipedia page to read: "Benoit was not at the show due to personal issues, stemming from the death of his wife, Nancy." Even stranger still, the edit came from someone located in Stamford, Connecticut—the home of WWE's headquarters. It later came out that the edit was made by a WWE fan who was playing a joke in light of Benoit's no-shows at the live events in Texas.

Similarly, other theories have been put forward in a futile attempt to rationalize Chris's actions, the most popular being that Daniel Benoit suffered from a condition known as fragile X syndrome, a genetic disorder that results in stunted growth, intellectual disability, and physical deformity. Some believed Chris had been plying Daniel with prescription drugs to increase his size, and on the night of the murders, accidentally overdosed him. However, it was later confirmed that Daniel suffered from no such condition.

Steroid abuse was another prominent theory. In a postmortem exam, Chris was found to have ten times the average amount of testosterone in his system, suggesting that perhaps he had suffered an outburst of so-called "roid rage." However, given that Benoit was methodical in his murders, including sedating his son, placing Bibles next to each body, and even creating a complex execution device, this was ruled out as a possibility.

Therefore, all that remains is to accept the most probable explanation: Chris Benoit murdered his wife and son because a lifetime of head trauma clouded his ability to think clearly. He may have planned out the attack in advance, or he may have suffered a bout of extreme paranoia and acted on impulse. Unfortunately, the only person who knew the truth also died that night.

The Day Everything Changed

Since the murders, Chris Benoit has been whitewashed from wrestling history. WWE have retroactively removed all footage and all mentions of him from their archived collection. Many of his awards outside of WWE have also been posthumously removed. In the eyes of his former employer and many fans, Chris Benoit never existed.

Despite all of the horrors of the Benoit family tragedy, the incident exposed some ugly truths about the wrestling industry. Behind its theatrics and larger-than-life characters is a real sport with real injuries. For decades, the welfare of performers had been a secondary matter to promoters, whose main concern was to draw crowds and make money. Luckily, performer safety within national wrestling promotions is now prioritized above everything else.

The WWE in particular currently operate a zero-tolerance policy to the type of in-ring abuse Chris Benoit subjected himself to and has thus forced other sporting leagues to open up serious discussion about head injuries. While professional wrestling takes the lead in concussion rates for contact sports, football and ice hockey closely follow. Research into head trauma has grown year over year since 2008, with all four major sporting leagues in the US having strict concussion policies in place.

A memorial service for Nancy and Daniel Benoit took place in Daytona Beach on July 14, 2007. They were both cremated, and their ashes placed in starfish-shaped urns. Seventy-five people attended the service, including many of Chris's former friends and those who knew Nancy during her time in the ring. Nancy's sister Sandra gave a eulogy that fondly remembered the two family members she had lost.

"Daniel was Nancy's whole world. They had a beautiful future," she said.

The service lasted a total of forty-five minutes. Chris Benoit's name was never mentioned.

THE RISE AND FALL OF THE DISCO KING

JANEL COMEAU

On West 54th Street in Manhattan, nestled between Eighth Avenue and Broadway, stands an unremarkable gray brick building.

Dwarfed by the nearby skyscrapers of Midtown Manhattan and hemmed in on either side by a twenty-four-hour parking garage and a burger restaurant, the building—which now houses a small theater and a basement supper club—blends into the backdrop of the bustling West Side. Tourists wandering by on their way to skate at the Rockefeller Center or catch a performance of *The Phantom of the Opera* on Broadway may not ever realize they're walking past a critical piece of New York history.

Because, in the late 1970s, this nondescript gray building wasn't just some place to be in Manhattan—for thirty-three glorious months, this was the home of Studio 54, *the* place to be in Manhattan.

On the surface, Studio 54—named for the street it was located on and the fact that the building had once been a TV studio—was simply a nightclub, one of dozens that popped up all over New York City at the height of the disco craze. Guests showed up every night to drink, dance, and try to catch the eye of an attractive stranger under the glittering lights. But for the people who made their way to the dance floor every night, there was so much more to Studio 54—it was a place that walked the line between fantasy and reality, where everything was permitted and anything was possible.

But the story of Studio 54 is more than just the story of a short-lived nightclub on West 54th Street. It is also the story of its founder, Steve Rubell, a man who brought an impossible dream to life and fell from grace alongside it. Without him, Studio 54 might never have existed.

And without him, Studio 54 might still exist today.

Steve Rubell was born on December 2, 1943, to a working-class Jewish family in Brooklyn. His father Phillip Rubell was a postal worker who managed to turn his passion for tennis into a professional career. It was at the country clubs where his father played tennis that Steve got his first glimpse of the wealth and status he would covet for the rest of his life. His was one of the few working-class families to frequent these country clubs, and he was astonished to learn that an entire class of people existed whose lives revolved not around work, but around luxury, leisure, and hobnobbing with the powerful and famous.

From then on, his path was clear: he would become one of them, no matter what it cost him.

As a teenager, Steve attended George W. Wingate High School in Brooklyn, where he showed the same aptitude for tennis his father had possessed. Ultimately, Steve chose not to pursue a professional tennis career. Instead, he packed his belongings and headed upstate to Syracuse University, where he would form a close friendship with a fellow student named Ian Schrager and take his first small steps down a path that ended with the birth of Studio 54.

From the outset, Ian Schrager and Steve Rubell appeared to be complete opposites. Schrager was introverted, timid, and studious—he spent much of his time huddled over his textbooks, studying hard to fulfill his dream of becoming a lawyer. Steve, on the other hand, was extraverted, vivacious, and well-connected; fellow students flocked to him for all their needs, whether they were trying to catch the eye of a pretty girl they'd spotted at a campus party or seeking advice on the courses they should sign up for in the following semester. There was also the matter of sexuality— Schrager was straight and Rubell was gay, a fact he would keep under wraps to all but his closest friends for the rest of his life.

Despite their outward differences, the pair found that they had a great deal in common. Both were from working-class families in Brooklyn. Both pledged the same fraternity—Sigma Alpha Mu. And most importantly, both shared a single-minded determination to rise above their station in life and achieve greater success than their parents had ever dared to dream of.

Steve eventually graduated from Syracuse with both a master's and a bachelor's degree in finance; Ian graduated from law school, just as he'd always planned. After returning home, Ian began practicing law. Steve, on the other hand, took his first baby steps into the world of luxury entertainment by opening a series of high-end steakhouses. He believed that becoming a steakhouse proprietor would catapult him to the life of wealth and status he'd always dreamed of.

His confidence was short-lived. Steve was too eager for success and attempted to expand his steak empire too quickly; the wheels began to come off his business venture, and his restaurants teetered on the brink of ruin. Desperate, he turned to his old school friend Ian to help shield him from the financial fallout of his businesses' collapse.

It was while they were working together to help Steve escape from his creditors after his steakhouses crashed and burned that the two friends came to a decision—one that would greatly impact the course of both their lives: they would go into business together as partners.

Their journey to Studio 54 was just beginning.

In 1975, Steve and Ian set out to uncover what kind of entertainment Americans wanted most and came up with one inescapable answer: the people wanted dancing.

In the mid-1970s, America was just wrapping up one of the bleaker moments of its recent history—namely, its involvement in the Vietnam War. After nearly two decades of horror, conscription, and anti-war protests, the last helicopters had left Saigon and the men had returned home. The American people were desperate to cut loose and forget the ordeal they'd just lived through—and if they happened to do so in a place where they could consume the sort of pills and potions that helped them focus on their fun, all the better.

Schrager and Rubell knew they wanted to open some sort of nightclub, and the pair took to the streets of Manhattan to research just what sort of club, exactly, they wanted theirs to be. Night after night, they hit the dance floors at clubs all over the island, all in the name of research.

The two quickly realized that they were most drawn to the city's gay clubs. It wasn't Steve's closely guarded sexuality that gave gay clubs their appeal; the pair were enthralled by the raw energy and fun that only the gay clubs seemed to have. In 1970s Manhattan, it wasn't just gay men who frequented those clubs—*anyone* who wanted to have a good time was there. Models and female celebrities would tag along with their gay male hairdressers and stylists at the end of the workday, packing the gay clubs with gorgeous young women. Once it became known that some of the most beautiful and famous women in New York were frequenting these clubs, straight men began to show up as well, hoping to try their luck. Soon, the gay clubs had become an all-out bacchanal where anyone was welcome. People of all gender identities and sexualities thronged the dance floors, worried less about who truly belonged and more about how to have the best possible night out on the town.

Steve Rubell found the energy infectious. And he wanted his club to have even more of it.

Schrager and Rubell also noted that gay clubs had another important thing their competitors did not: disco music. In the mid-1970s, disco music was considered "Black music"—far too Black for Manhattan's mostly White mainstream clubs. But gay clubs were far more progressive, wholeheartedly embracing the budding genre. And disco was a hit. Straight clubgoers packed the dance floors at gay clubs just to get their fix of Donna Summer's latest hits. Rubell knew that, if his club was going to be a success, disco needed to be a part of it.

It was during that time that Schrager and Rubell befriended popular disco promotor Billy Smith—who preferred to style himself as Billy Amato—and were soon introduced to John Addison, the South African owner of the popular Manhattan gay club, Le Jardin. They ended up starting their first club with Addison, going in together on a nightclub they opened in Boston.

Rubell wasn't satisfied with being one-third owner of a nightclub out in Boston, however—the greatest nightclubs in the world, he felt, were right there in New York City, and that's where he wanted to be. Schrager and Rubell set their sights on the New York club scene, knowing they would need to start somewhere.

For them, that somewhere was Queens.

In 1975, Schrager and Rubell opened a nightclub called The Enchanted Garden in the Douglaston neighborhood of Queens. The club was not unsuccessful. It was there, in fact, that they would meet their financial backer Jack Dushey, after he held his son's bar mitzvah party at The Enchanted Garden. But Rubell wasn't satisfied with owning a club in the far end of Queens that sometimes played host to bar mitzvah parties— he yearned for the city lights and the unrestrained, sexually charged energy he had found at clubs like Le Jardin and Infinity. The business partners set their sights on opening another nightclub, this time in Manhattan.

But first, they would need a building.

———————————

The New York City real estate market has long held a reputation for being fiercely competitive, and this still held true in the 1970s. As Rubell began the search for a building, he knew that finding the right combination of space, price, and location would be a challenge. A great building at a reasonable price in the wrong neighborhood could spell disaster. He needed a miracle if he was going to make his dream a reality.

His miracle came in the form of an abandoned TV studio on the lower floors of a nondescript gray office building in the central part of West 54th Street.

Built in the 1920s, the building that would become the home of Studio 54 had already served several purposes throughout its relatively short lifespan. The theater space had opened for the first time in 1927 as the Gallo Opera House. Shortly after opening, the Gallo Opera House had staged an expensive full-scale production of *La Bohème* that proved so disastrous it closed in less than three weeks. The opera house never financially recovered, and after failing to attract audiences to its subsequent productions, folded by 1929.

After that, the theater changed hands several times, being passed between several theatrical and entertainment companies before being purchased as a CBS television studio in 1943. CBS renamed the space Studio 52, to reflect that it was the fifty-second studio they'd purchased. For the next three decades, many of CBS's most beloved radio and television programs were recorded at Studio 52—*The $64,000 Question*, *What's My Line?*, *The Jack Benny Show*, and *Captain Kangaroo* were all filmed at the studio in its heyday, amid countless others.

But in 1976, CBS made the decision to close and sell Studio 52, relocating the filming of their popular shows to larger studio-owned buildings in New York and LA. There had been chatter on the art scene about potentially turning the space into a nightclub, but until Steve Rubell and Ian Schrager walked in to take a tour, no one had managed to come up with both the gumption and the funds to make this a reality.

From the moment they walked in the door, Rubell and Schrager were smitten with the building. It had everything they were looking for—the space was enormous by Manhattan standards, with plenty of room for a dance floor and pre-built offices on the upper level already prepared for club management to move into. Though they'd only come for a quick viewing, Rubell and Schrager were so taken with the overall look and feel of the place, they signed the paperwork on the spot.

They had their club.

The decision to open their flagship nightclub halfway along West 54th Street was a risky one. Today, Manhattan's Theater District is a squeaky-clean haven of family-friendly fun; tourists spill out of Broadway shows to dine at chain restaurants and purchase souvenirs at the enormous Disney and M&M stores. In the 1970s, however, the area was a haven for pickpockets and muggers. The sparkling lights of Broadway shared space with seedy porn theaters and peep shows, shamelessly advertising their lewd goods to passersby. The idea that clubgoers—let alone A-list celebrities—would brave the dangers of the grimy Theater District for a night out would have seemed far-fetched at best.

But Schrager and Rubell were certain—this was where they wanted to build their club. Against all odds, they knew they could make it a success.

From the moment the ink on the paperwork was dry, Schrager and Rubell were in a race against the clock to get the doors of their club open. Every day the building sat empty was akin to lighting a pile of money on fire—the costs of the building and renovations were astronomical, and the men knew their financial backer didn't have limitless generosity. They needed paying customers out on the dance floor, and quickly.

Unfortunately for them, turning an unused theater into a nightclub was no small feat. Neither of the partners was sure how long it would take to get the necessary permits or inspections they needed to make their dream a reality, and they didn't intend to find out—they simply went ahead and did the work. The club's floor presented a particular challenge; as a former theater, the building had a sloped floor that was unsuitable for dancing. Leveling the floor was no small undertaking, and required a permit before any construction could begin. But Steve and Ian needed their dance floor and had no patience for permits. They found sixty-five-dollar-a-day laborers willing to work without the proper permits, and got the job done.

The studio that had once occupied the space had left their lights and theater rigging behind when they vacated the premises, and the new club owners took full advantage. Anything that could be preserved from the club's theater days was saved, with a Tony-winning light designer brought in to optimize the lights for a night of disco clubbing, complete with laser light shows. Today, no self-respecting nightclub would operate without a lighting professional on staff. At the time, however, it was a groundbreaking idea, with Studio 54 being one of the very first pioneers to have a "lights guy" in the building.

The original theater balconies were also kept intact, allowing patrons to retreat to a more private space while still enjoying the festivities. For the more voyeuristic club regulars, the balconies would become a huge part of the draw. Pop artist Andy Warhol, still suffering from the long-term physical complications of his 1968 near-assassination, is said to have never set foot on the Studio 54 dance floor, despite being a frequent visitor to the club; he, like many others, preferred to watch from the famous balconies.

With the physical construction of their grand nightclub well underway, Rubell and Schrager set to the administrative work of opening their club, including preparations for the all-important opening night. The two men shared an office on an upper floor of the building, where Steve was fond of working from the couch. There, phone in hand, he would make the deals that helped make Studio 54 a raging success—he called publicists, promotors, and socialites, trying to drum up hype for the grand opening. Thousands of invitations were sent, with limos ordered to personally ferry VIPs to the front doors as they opened for the very first time.

Suddenly, there was nothing left to do but wait.

Rubell knew that opening night would be a make-or-break moment for the club. The first night would set the tone for all the nights to come. If the crowds showed up and had a good time, they'd be back with their friends night after night. If opening night was a bust, they'd have a hard time building up the momentum to make their club work. Opening night had to go well—the future of Studio 54 depended on it.

The big day arrived quickly, perhaps more quickly than anyone thought possible. All told, the renovations to the old theater had taken just six weeks to complete, at a total price tag of $400,000. As staff rushed about on the morning of the grand opening, putting the finishing touches on the space, Rubell and Schrager wondered if they were just hours away from realizing they'd made the greatest miscalculation of their lives.

———————

The doors of Studio 54 opened on April 26, 1977, to one of the greatest crowds New York City had ever seen.

Rubell had hoped for a good turnout, but the crowds that packed their small stretch of West 54th Street exceeded even his wildest imagination. The small staff was quickly overwhelmed. The entire security team that had been hired to control the atmosphere inside the club was placed outside, tasked with maintaining some semblance of order in the growing crowd. A nineteen-year-old bouncer named Marc Benecke—a teen with absolutely no prior club experience—was handpicked by Rubell to man the front door and do the all-important work of deciding who would be let into the club, and who was out.

Patrons lucky enough to make it past the front doors were greeted with décor that walked a fine line between "classy" and "gaudy," with a generous dash of 1970s disco flair. All the interior walls and windows had been blacked out. Glowing neon columns supported the ceiling over the parquet dance floors. Any surface that could be mirrored had been. The back wall of the club was lit up by an enormous Studio 54 logo emblazoned in gold neon; beneath that hung an enormous cartoon depiction of the moon, sniffing from an oversized cocaine spoon.

Studio 54 was never known for subtlety.

Crowds that first night were so enormous that the coat check was quickly overwhelmed; instead of hanging up coats, the staff quickly began piling them on the floor, many never to be reclaimed by their rightful owners. The challenge of controlling the enormous crowd outside on the sidewalk consumed much of the staff's attention, and would eventually lead Rubell and Schrager to put up a series of velvet ropes outside the club doors for crowd control, becoming the first club ever to implement such a system.

Clubgoers, fueled by a mixture of exhilaration and 1970s recreational party drugs, danced with wild abandon until the early hours of the morning. To Rubell's delight, the energy inside Studio 54 was exactly what he had hoped it would be—electrifying and sexually charged, with celebrities and ordinary people mingling freely under the disco lights.

Just like that, a New York City legend was born.

During the thirty-three months of its operation, a wild night out at Studio 54 always began with one near-impossible task: getting let into the club.

In the late 1970s, Steve Rubell became notorious in New York City for his habit of personally manning the door at his popular nightclub and handpicking the patrons who would be allowed inside. He was famously selective; though he often claimed that the rules for being allowed into Studio 54 were not arbitrary, club hopefuls and journalists alike struggled to determine exactly what they were. Some rules were consistent—he hated polyester shirts and would not allow them through the front doors, but other rules seemed to change arbitrarily from night to night. A person welcomed through the front doors on Thursday might be barred on Friday and welcomed back in on Saturday, even if they showed up in the same outfit three nights in a row.

The club maintained a nightly guest list, but its contents were every bit as arbitrary and indecipherable as the rules Rubell personally applied at the door. Guests on the list were divided into four categories. "PAY" denoted patrons who were required to pay regular cover charge, while "COMP" meant a patron should be let in for free. "NG," or "no goods," were people who weren't allowed to go inside the club at all, often due to their own poor behavior. And most importantly, some guests received coveted "NFU" status—this stood for "no fuck-ups," indicating the guest was a VIP and that mistakes like charging them a cover fee would absolutely not be tolerated.

The wealthy, famous, and powerful who showed up to party at Studio 54 without being on the list tended to be immediately ushered through the front doors—or they were, that is, if Steve Rubell happened to know who they were. He once accidentally turned away Warren Beatty after failing to recognize him. The 1978 smash hit song "Le Freak," written and performed by the band Chic, was about the performers' experience being turned away from the doors of Studio 54 on New Year's Eve despite having made the guest list.

Studio 54 also had its own celebrities made famous by their antics at the club. A crowd favorite was "Disco Sally," a seventy-seven-year-old retired lawyer and widow who frequently came out to show off her moves on the floor. Another notable face was that of Rollerena, an East Village drag queen who frequently turned up wearing roller skates and a lace wedding dress. Rubell defended his decision to let septuagenarian partygoers onto the dance floor—it was not what you looked like or who you were that mattered, he insisted; it was the energy you brought with you.

Once patrons made it past the doors, the club was a den of decadence, lust, and indulgence unlike anything the city—or, quite possibly, the world—has seen before or since. The club on West 54th Street quickly became one of the most famous nightlife spots in the world, fueled by wild and breathless stories about the things that went on within its walls.

Photographs taken at the height of Studio 54's popularity offer glimpses into a world in which anything was possible. Bianca Jagger rides a gleaming white horse in the middle of the dance floor. A beaming young Elton John firmly grasps the breasts of drag queen Divine. Male go-go dancers in curly blond wigs and delicate fairy wings haul empty trash buckets through the club. People in various states of undress—some ordinary people, some quite literally the biggest stars of their generation—sway beneath the lights, enthralled by whatever music was pumping through the club's speakers.

Rubell himself is captured in dozens of dance floor photos, mingling with the crowd. Ian Schrager was the shy one of the pair, and preferred to work behind the scenes in his office. Rubell, on the other hand, was the public face of the operation. He made it a point to be out on the floor each night, carefully ensuring that the energy in the club reached a fever pitch each and every night. In particular, he cozied up to his celebrity guests. He was at once fascinated by and obsessed with celebrities, and in time grew very close to celebrity Studio 54 regulars like Liza Minnelli, Bianca Jagger, Andy Warhol, Halston, and Michael Jackson. He aimed to create an environment where celebrities could cut loose and experience rare moments of freedom, and the stars flocking to the doors each night seemed to indicate he had succeeded.

Rubell was also not afraid to provide an artificial boost if he was concerned the club wasn't rowdy enough. He became fond of walking through the crowds in a trench coat, freely passing out party drugs from its pockets. He didn't like taking no for an answer. If a clubgoer turned down an offer of Quaaludes—Rubell's personal drug of choice—he would persist, pressing half of a pill into the clubgoer's hand and insisting they just take the half.

The balconies at Studio 54 became such a notorious hookup spot that they eventually had to be coated with rubber so that staff could easily hose off the accumulated bodily fluids at the end of each night. The club's basement also served a similar purpose, with clubgoers having intimate encounters on any of the dozen mattresses strewn across the floor. Rubell himself was said to have regularly snuck off into dark corners of the building with attractive male club patrons. If any of his late-right trysts were with celebrity patrons, Rubell was not one to kiss and tell. At least, not when it came to his own affairs.

When it came to the antics of others, however, Rubell couldn't tell often enough.

Rubell was in the habit of contacting publications like the *New York Post* on a daily basis to fill them in on all the antics celebrities had been up to at Studio 54 that evening—the more salacious, the better. Schrager and Rubell paid publicists to get their famous clients into the club and splashed across the pages of the paper.

By day, the people of New York City read about the outrageous antics taking place at Studio 54. By night, they flocked to the famous velvet ropes to try to see for themselves. At long last, Steve Rubell had achieved the dream he'd been chasing since childhood.

But it wasn't going to last.

Steve Rubell and Ian Schrager were the lifeblood of Studio 54; it was their vision and their passion that had brought the club to life, and it was the two of them who kept the magic of Studio 54 alive night after night.

They would also be the club's undoing.

Just as there had been no time for permits in the scramble to renovate and open Studio 54, there was no time to complete the lengthy process of acquiring an official liquor license. Instead, Rubell and Schrager devised a quick workaround—they incorporated their business as the "Broadway Catering Corporation" and sought a series of one-day catering permits that would allow them to serve alcohol. Though this was a clear abuse of the catering permit system, Schrager and Rubell were too preoccupied with other matters to spend time worrying about the scheme they'd devised. As the popularity and success of Studio 54 began to snowball, the issue of the club's liquor license would fall further and further down the owners' priority lists, until it dropped by the wayside entirely.

Steve Rubell and Ian Schrager may have forgotten about their liquor license, but the New York State Liquor Authority had certainly not forgotten about *them*.

A month after Studio 54 opened, the Liquor Authority denied the request for one-night catering permits and raided the club. Studio 54 was shut down by the state for abuse of the permit system and for selling liquor without a license. The one-day permits the club had been relying on were intended for single-day events like weddings—operating a nightclub night after night was not a legitimate use of the permits. Rubell and Schrager maintained that their use of nightly permits had not been a malicious intent to skirt liquor laws, but a simple misunderstanding, even as they were being arrested.

Studio 54 reopened the day after the raid, with fruit punch and soft drinks on the menu instead of cocktails. Rubell and Schrager had hired Roy Cohn, a defense attorney famous for defending members of the Mob, and he'd managed to secure their almost-immediate release. The club operated with nothing harder than fruit juice and sodas on the menu as they waited for their liquor license to come through.

Eventually, they got the news they'd been hoping for. With their license finally granted, they were free to carry on selling alcohol—and this time without the hassle of applying for daily catering passes. Rubell and Schrager felt invincible. They were young—barely out of their twenties— and they owned one of the most successful venues in nightclub history. In just one year of operation, their club in a tough part of town had raked in seven million dollars. Steve had money, status, and success, along with a star-studded Rolodex of the wealthy and famous who considered him a close personal friend. As far as the two men were concerned, there was nothing that could stop them now.

———————

As it turned out, it was Steve Rubell's overconfidence that would bring about the end of Studio 54.

In the months after the club opened, wait staff began to notice something unusual. Halfway through each night, the roll of receipt paper in their cash registers would be inexplicably changed by one of the owners, with no explanation given for the sudden swap. Staff came to the gradual realization that the owners were cooking the club's books—only the receipts from the first roll were being added to the club's official books, while the receipts from the second roll were whisked away by the owners.

Though they weren't reporting their full income, Rubell and Schrager did keep detailed business ledgers of all revenue and expenses, legitimate and otherwise—these ledgers would ultimately contribute to their downfall. Rubell carefully noted the costs of all the illicit drugs he purchased to hand out to club patrons, jotting down his handfuls of Quaaludes as business expenses. On one occasion, he had dumped eight hundred dollars' worth of dollar bills over the head of Andy Warhol to celebrate the artist's fiftieth birthday. This bucket of cash was carefully jotted down in Rubell's ledgers, denoted as a business expense. All of their decadence and drug-pushing was clearly spelled out in black and white in the lines of their financial records, waiting for the wrong person to come across them.

If Schrager and Rubell were clumsy at hiding their illegitimate business expenses and illegal purchases made with company money, they were even less competent at hiding the fact they had been skimming unreported revenue from the club. Their financial records made it easy for investigators to see how much money they were pocketing—they dutifully recorded every dollar they took, with the word "skim" jotted in the margin. The two men were skimming as much as 80 percent of the gross revenue, an amount that would raise the eyebrows of even the most seasoned embezzler.

And seasoned embezzlers, they were not.

In a 1977 article in *New York* magazine, Steve Rubell boasted about the overnight success of Studio 54, claiming that "only the Mafia does better." It was the sort of statement that drew the attention of authorities already inclined to be suspicious of a cash-only business that had once operated without a liquor license.

On December 14, 1978, Studio 54 was raided. Tipped off by a disgruntled employee, authorities knew exactly where to look—they found cash, receipts, and incriminating ledgers hidden in the ceiling of Rubell and Schrager's office. All told, the pair had skimmed a startling $2.5 million from the club, depriving the Internal Revenue Service of hundreds of thousands of dollars in taxes.

Skimming money from a nightclub's books was common practice for club owners in the 1970s. In the days before credit and debit card statements meticulously documented every transaction, it was easy for owners of cash-only clubs to pocket a few dollars here and there. Owners regularly got away with skimming small amounts of money; it was difficult for the IRS to notice, let alone prove, that a club owner had skimmed 5 percent of their revenue off the top.

But in true Studio 54 fashion, Rubell and Schrager had dared to go bigger and wilder than any club owner had gone before.

Steve Rubell and Ian Schrager were arrested in June 1979.

Both men faced charges of tax evasion, conspiracy, and obstruction of justice. The pair once again hired Roy Cohn—a favorite defense attorney of Mafia members, oligarchs, and Donald Trump—to defend them as he had when they were caught operating without a liquor license. The move backfired. Cohn had once been co-counsel with the trial judge on the famous Rosenberg espionage case, leading to public speculation that the judge would go easy on Schrager and Rubell. Perhaps anxious to prove the press wrong, the judge did the opposite. On January 18, 1980, the men were convicted of income tax evasion and sentenced to three and a half years in prison.

Rubell and Schrager were to report to prison on February 4, 1980. They spent their final night of freedom at Studio 54, throwing the grandest going-away party the club had ever seen. Club regulars Liza Minnelli and Diana Ross performed, with Farrah Fawcett, Jack Nicholson, Richard Gere, Sylvester Stallone, Mariel Hemingway, and a handful of other famous faces in the crowd.

Rubell and Schrager served fourteen months of their sentence before being paroled to a halfway house on April 17, 1981; they lived there for ten weeks before being released.

Studio 54 was sold in November 1980, while Schrager and Rubell were incarcerated, for a whopping $4.75 million. The two agreed to stay on as consultants for six months, and Studio 54 reopened under the ownership of Mark Fleischman in September 1981, until the doors closed for good in 1986. The building went through several new iterations as a nightclub until it was purchased by the Roundabout Theatre Company in 1998 to house a Broadway revival of the musical *Cabaret* while its regular Henry Miller's Theatre location was closed due to construction. The change stuck; Studio 54 is still the home of special performances by the Roundabout Theatre Company to this day.

After being released from prison, Schrager and Rubell decided to get back into the entertainment business, starting with a new nightclub. They purchased the Palladium, a former rock concert venue on East 14th Street, and reopened it as a nightclub in May 1985. Much like Studio 54, the place was an instant success. Palladium was a favorite of both celebrities and ordinary clubgoers, and was considered a crown jewel of the New York City party scene, until it was purchased and torn down by New York University in 1997 to clear space for a new campus dorm.

In addition to nightclubs, Rubell and Schrager dipped their toes into the hotelier business, opening the Morgans Hotel—the world's first boutique hotel—in 1984. Like nearly everything the pair attempted together, it was a runaway success. They went on to open the Paramount Hotel and the Royalton Hotel in NYC's Theater District, not far from Studio 54, and used their knowledge of socialization and entertainment to revolutionize the hotel experience.

Schrager would go on to become a giant of the hotel industry, sitting at the helm of the publicly traded Morgans Hotel Group and opening a variety of hotels and resorts around the world. His 1980 conviction for tax evasion led to a formal pardon by President Barack Obama in 2017, allowing Schrager to finally put the last remnant of his past behind him. As of 2021, he continues to operate and consult on a variety of hotels and residential projects in far-flung corners of the world and in his beloved New York City.

Steve Rubell was not so fortunate.

———

The nightclub craze was not the only thing sweeping New York City in the early 1980s—the city was about to become the epicenter of the American AIDS epidemic. The first cases of the disease were detected in 1981, and within a few short years, the virus would devastate the gay community in NYC, claiming thousands of lives while activists pleaded for medical institutions to take action.

Steve Rubell tested positive for HIV in 1985. If he knew how he'd contracted the disease, he kept it to himself. Although he'd worked hard to ensure that the wild escapades of Studio 54's patrons were splashed across the front pages of the newspapers, Steve kept the details of his own private life close to his chest. He spent the bulk of his life closeted, and preferred not to disclose details of his romantic and sexual encounters.

By the late 1980s, a rudimentary treatment regime was available for HIV-positive patients in the form of an antiretroviral drug called AZT. Rubell began taking it after his diagnosis. Today, HIV patients take AZT alongside a carefully timed course of several other drugs that work in combination to keep viral loads of HIV to such low levels the virus cannot be detected in regular screenings. In the mid-1980s, AZT was the only treatment doctors had. On its own, AZT is not enough to halt the progression of HIV; it can only delay the inevitable.

Rubell was also unable to give up his heavy drinking and drug use after his diagnosis, putting further strain on his weakening immune system. Eventually, he developed AIDS. In summer 1989, he checked himself into Beth Israel Medical Center in Manhattan under an assumed name and sought treatment for hepatitis, kidney failure, and peptic ulcers. He was not able to recover, and his condition quickly deteriorated.

Steve Rubell, the man who'd once been the undisputed king of New York City nightlife, died on July 25, 1989, at the age of forty-five. His official cause of death was a combination of hepatitis and septic shock, complicated by AIDS. A private funeral was held two days later at the Riverside Memorial Chapel in Manhattan's Upper West Side. Several Studio 54 regulars were in attendance, including Bianca Jagger, who'd once ridden a horse onto the dance floor while Steve Rubell looked on with delight.

Though he had a successful career after Studio 54, the legacy of Steve Rubell is inextricably linked with that of his first and most famous nightclub. Both Rubell and Studio 54 lasted only a short time. Both irrevocably changed the fabric of New York City, transforming celebrity culture and creating stories that would be whispered for decades to come.

And when they left, they vanished not into obscurity, but into legend.

THE VAMPIRE OF HOLLOWAY DRIVE

JILL HAND

They made an attractive pair, he with his tousled mop of curly, light-brown hair and retro-style horn-rimmed glasses, she with her piquant face and sleek, elegant body. Blake Leibel and Iana Kasian were a couple who seemingly had everything, until one day in May 2016 when it all turned very, very bad.

They came from vastly different backgrounds. Blake was born a child of privilege on May 8, 1981, in Toronto, Ontario. His mother, Eleanor Chitel Leibel, was an heiress to a plastics manufacturing fortune; his father, Lorne Leibel, a billionaire real estate developer and the founder of Canada Homes, specializing in low-cost, high-volume housing. The venture made Lorne a millionaire by age thirty.

In a black-and-white photograph, taken in 1980, on file with the Toronto Public Library, twenty-nine-year-old Lorne poses in front of a truck with his foot propped on the bumper and leg slung casually over its hood. Like his son, his hair is curly and tousled. He's dressed in the preppy style that was fashionable at the time: denim jeans, deck shoes, and a short-sleeved Lacoste polo shirt, the three mother-of-pearl buttons on the placket undone. He looks directly into the camera, his expression ambiguous, either questioning or challenging. In the background is a field, the only thing in it a small structure resembling an old-fashioned movie theater. Written with a flourish on the marquee are the words "Canada Homes Presents Bathurst Steeles."

Bathurst Steeles is a Toronto neighborhood, its residents primarily Russian/Jewish. The name comes from an amalgamation of two street names. Bathurst Street is the city's main north-south thoroughfare. It begins just north of the Lake Ontario shoreline and runs north to Steeles Avenue at the city's northern boundary, where it meets the southern limit of the York region. In 1980, when the photograph was taken, Canada Homes was building houses there.

Lorne Leibel is one of those flamboyant people who are described as larger-than-life. To Lorne's two children—Blake and his twenty-two-months-older brother Cody—he must have seemed dazzling and a bit intimidating. He refers to himself, unironically, as "Lorne Leibel Ferrari Man." He races cars and power boats and has acquired a reputation for being a playboy.

Generational wealth and its consequences form the backdrop of the story of Blake Leibel and the horrendous crime he committed. It is a tale of conspicuous consumption, and of yearning for success in the highly competitive world of the arts. To better understand him, we must first understand where he came from.

His paternal grandfather, Stanley Leibel, was the son of immigrants: William Zev Wolf Leibel, from Ukraine, and the former Lillie Lederman, born in rural Świętokrzyskie, Poland. He was a real estate developer in the Toronto area, eventually passing the business on to his son, Lorne. Stanley became active in yacht racing and represented Canada in numerous international sailing competitions, almost, but not quite, securing a berth on the 1964 Tokyo Summer Olympics team. Four years later, he succeeded in making Canada's roster for the 1968 Summer Olympics in Mexico City, serving as helmsman of a three-man crew. They came in sixth out of a field of fourteen in the 5.5-meter class sailing event.

At the time when Stanley began competing, yacht racing was primarily the domain of white, Anglo-Saxon Protestants. For someone like him, the son of Eastern European Jewish immigrants, his participation in the sport must have produced mixed emotions. He would have felt pride, but also a sense of unease, as if he'd entered into a strange country, one with customs he had to learn in order to be accepted, but which came instinctively to his competitors.

Stanley Leibel died on February 17, 2021, age ninety-three. Three years earlier, on June 20, 2018, his grandson Blake was sentenced to life in prison without parole for the torture-murder of his fiancée.

Yacht racing became a Leibel family passion. While Stanley's son, Lorne, eventually came to prefer the high-octane thrills of speedboat racing to racing under sail, another member of the family took up the sport. Stanley Leibel's nephew, racing sailor Allan Leibel, was the son of Stanley's brother, the late Dr. Bernard Saul Leibel, a senior diabetes researcher at the University of Toronto and colleague of Nobel laureate Sir Frederick Grant Banting, a co-discoverer of insulin and its therapeutic potential. Allan represented Canada in the 1976 Summer Olympics in Montreal. His partner in the two-man keelboat racing event was his cousin Lorne, still four years away from posing for that photograph in a Toronto field, about to break ground on a construction project that would help make him a millionaire. Their boat finished seventh among twenty-one. Lorne failed a urine test, testing positive for phenylpropanolamine, a nasal decongestant and appetite suppressant. He was the first Canadian Olympic athlete to fail a drug test.

Four years before, Allan Leibel had sailed in the 1972 Munich Summer Olympics. Its official motto was *"Die Heiteren Spiele,"* or "The Happy Games." It turned out to be an unfortunate choice of words. While gymnast Olga Korbut and swimmer Mark Spitz brought home gold medals, the Munich Games are best remembered for the massacre of eleven Israeli athletes and coaches and a West German police officer by Palestinian terrorists.

The shocking crime touched the Leibel family, although only peripherally. Forty-four years later there would be more bloodshed, this time involving one of their own.

Sailboat racing is a rich man's pastime. The closest Iana Kasian's father got to salt water was working as a laborer in a Ukraine naval yard. Her mother was a healthcare worker. Iana was born on January 27, 1986.

Iana studied law and took a job prosecuting crimes for the Ukrainian Tax Service in gritty Kyiv. In 2014, she left her homeland for the United States. Like Blake Leibel's grandparents, she was drawn by dreams of a better life. In her case, she hoped her beauty and determination to succeed would win her a high-paying career as a fashion model.

It was in Los Angeles that Blake and Iana first met.

At the time, Blake was married to Amanda Ruth Braun, a former actress and model. At age two, she had played Emily, a baby sold by her biological parents in the film *Broken Promise: Taking Emily Back*. Blake and Amanda married in March 2011. One month later, she gave birth to a boy. In the summer of 2015, she was pregnant with her second child, another son. But that didn't deter Blake from pursuing the dark-haired Ukrainian beauty. He moved out of the five-bedroom, six-bath, 5,393-square-foot Beverly Hills mansion his mother had bought for him and filed for divorce.

His new home was in West Hollywood—a two-bedroom, two-bath, 1,263-square-foot condominium with a large balcony on Holloway Drive. It was here that the gruesome mutilation-murder of Iana Kasian occurred.

The three-story building with its angular, Art Deco exterior is situated just below the Sunset Strip, where Alta Loma Road meets Holloway Drive. From here it's a one-minute drive and about a seven-minute walk to the Viper Room, the nightclub and music venue on the Sunset Strip popular with Hollywood's young elite. River Phoenix died from an overdose of cocaine and heroin on the sidewalk outside on Halloween night 1993. Tourists visit the original site, posing for selfies in front of the club's black-painted façade, standing where the twenty-three-year-old actor took his last breath.

Beneath its surface glitter, Los Angeles has always had a dark side. It's like a monster that beguiles and seduces the young and beautiful before devouring them. Elizabeth Short, known as the "Black Dahlia"; Thelma Todd, a former Miss Massachusetts who starred in films with Laurel and Hardy; *Playboy* model Dorothy Stratten; and actress Sharon Tate were just a few of those who found that out too late. Iana Kasian, blissfully soaking up the California sun after the bitter Kyiv winters, was about to discover the evil that leered and capered behind the city's smiling mask.

Blake and Iana got engaged, and she quickly became pregnant. They resembled a twenty-first-century version of Jay Gatsby and Daisy Buchanan, seemingly carefree, with everything they wanted within their grasp. They vacationed in Hawaii. Iana drove a Mercedes M-class SUV. She posed, smiling impishly, in front of the five-pointed brass and terrazzo stars on Hollywood's Walk of Fame, perhaps imagining the day when Blake, a screenwriter, aspiring producer, and fledgling animated-film director, would have his own star there.

That goal didn't seem impossible, though he'd met with initial failure. In 2009, Blake wrote and directed a comedy—a sex farce called *Bald.* Some films featuring juvenile humor, such as *Porky's* and its various spinoffs, manage to achieve a cult following and make a respectable return on their investment. *Bald,* however, bombed. Scott A. Gray, writing for *Exclaim!,* panned it for "bad acting, bad directing, bad writing, bad editing."

The previous year, Blake got a shot at directing/codirecting three episodes of *Spaceballs: The Animated Series.* It was an adult animated TV show based on the 1987 sci-fi/comedy directed by Mel Brooks. It ran for fifteen episodes and wasn't renewed for a second season.

Success—the kind of A-lister success he craved—kept eluding him.

Like Blake, his big brother Cody had moved to Los Angeles in 2004, along with a coterie of their Toronto friends. Almost immediately, Cody Leibel's name was in the news for starting a short-lived record label called

C-Note Records. At twenty-three, he was living like a rock star, playing in high-stakes underground poker games and throwing boisterous parties at a huge house in Bel Air, the music cranked up to ear-splitting volumes. As if that wasn't enough excess, Cody purchased a bright-red $1.2 million Ferrari Enzo, one of only a few hundred in existence. He owned another Enzo, a yellow one, which he kept in Canada. He also had a Ferrari 550 Barchetta Pininfarina and was about to take delivery of a Maserati MC12, all while contemplating buying a Rolls-Royce Phantom, according to an interview with John Jarasa in the Oct. 1, 2004, issue of *MotorTrend*. Despite complaining that it wouldn't fit in his garage, he went ahead and bought the Phantom.

F. Scott Fitzgerald nailed it: the very rich *are* different from you and me.

Cody's name was linked in the gossip columns with Hilton Hotels heiress Paris Hilton, and with actress Tara Reid from *American Pie* and *Sharknado*. Meanwhile, Blake wasn't being talked about except as someone who could be counted on to pick up the check after an evening out.

Money wasn't Blake's problem, not exactly. Both he and Cody had trust funds. Every month, $18,000 was deposited into each of their bank accounts. It was a gift from their parents, who had separated many years before, though they still remained married. What nagged at Blake was a sense of injustice derived from his belief that his father favored the athletic, outgoing Cody over him.

When Blake was ten years old, the rift between his parents deepened. Blake went to live with his mother in a grand Georgian-style home on Burton Road in Toronto's upscale Forest Hill South neighborhood. Cody stayed with their father at Lorne's three-hundred-acre estate nearby.

On June 4, 2011, Eleanor Leibel died of cancer at age sixty-one. Blake sued to have her will overturned, insisting he had a right to her entire estate, valued at twelve million dollars in property, cash, and stock.

A legal battle ensued. Blake, in his personal capacity along with his brother Cody, as trustees of the Eleanor Leibel Family Trust, sued their father, Lorne. The suit also named their aunt, Roslyn Chitel Lewis and her husband Herb Lewis, as well as Chitel Enterprises Ltd.; Alros Products Ltd.; Cody Leibel; Blake Star Holdings Inc., owner of a condominium in Florida; and Lee Corp. Inc., owner of a condominium in Los Angeles.

Leibel v. Leibel presents a close-up view of a bitter grievance between members of an extraordinarily wealthy family. At the heart of the issue was Eleanor's fortune, derived largely from the success of Alros Products, a plastic sheeting company founded in 1957 by her late father, inventor Paul Pinchas Chitel. The Ontario-based company currently does business as Polytarp Products.

Alros grew from humble beginnings into a multimillion-dollar company that supplies a variety of plastic products, including vapor barriers for the construction industry, food packaging, reflective plastic for backyard ice-skating rinks, and polyethylene multipurpose film used in agriculture. Dun & Bradstreet reported Polytarp's annual revenue as $23.83 million in US dollars.

Not only were Blake and Cody suing their father, but Cody was also, in effect, suing himself as a beneficiary of his mother's estate. At issue were Eleanor's primary and secondary wills, both dated April 9, 2011. Secondary wills involve assets that do not require probate, such as shares of stock held privately, or personal effects such as jewelry or antiques. Eleanor left Blake her Toronto home on Burton Road, which he later sold for $5.5 million, as well as her art collection and two condominiums, one in Florida, the other in Los Angeles.

According to the suit filed in Ontario Superior Court on June 19, 2014, Blake claimed his mother's wills were not valid. He stated that she had changed her will several times in the past, and that she intended to do so again, naming him as sole beneficiary. He insisted she would have written another will, making her intentions known, but by then the cancer in her lungs had metastasized to her brain and she wasn't thinking clearly.

In the suit, he is described as having expressed concern that Cody would inherit the lion's share of their father's estate, worth far more than Eleanor's. His fears stemmed from his claim that his relationship with his father was acrimonious, with Lorne favoring Cody over him. He complained that Lorne had funded his elder son's wildly extravagant lifestyle while at the same time ceasing to pay his—Blake's—credit card bills.

The court ruled against him. The decision involved several factors, one of which was that he had waited too long to contest his mother's wills. The two-year period from the date of her death allowed by law to file an objection had expired three months previously.

So Blake turned his attention to becoming famous.

He wanted to become known as a creator of illustrated (or "graphic") novels—ones that would create a buzz and, with luck, get turned into a video game or a TV series. To that end, he tried to project the image of a brilliant nerd, one too caught up in whatever project he was working on to care about what he wore or whether he combed his hair. Among a certain set of young creative artists, being geeky is a badge of honor. It proves that they are dedicated to their craft, and that they know every little detail about superheroes like Batman and Captain America, and about role-playing games and comic books.

In August 2004, not long after he moved to Los Angeles, Blake paid a seventy-dollar filing fee and formed a corporation called Fantasy Prone LLC. He named himself as director and set up an office in a condo on South Oakhurst Drive in Beverly Hills. It was there that he prepared to become a comic-book publishing mogul.

In 2008, Fantasy Prone released the first in a series of comics called *United Free Worlds*, written by Blake and illustrated by well-known comic-book artist Patrick Blaine. The storyline has humans pitted in warfare against space aliens and their dinosaur army. Blake had hopes of the series becoming a video game. He was into video games and was proud of his high score in the first-person-shooter online video game *Half-Life*, at one point claiming to be world champion.

A Hollywood producer who knew Blake Leibel spoke anonymously about him to the *Toronto Sun*. "He wanted to be a respected comic-book guy and he used his money to create that image," the producer said. "He wanted to be cool and edgy—and he wasn't. But you could tell, he wasn't right in the head."

Blake stood out, the producer told the *Sun*, even among people who embraced being different. "With movie and comic geeks, that world attracts a lot of weirdos, but even in that world of bad hygiene and general weirdness, Blake was on the outer fringe."

Blake joined Soho House, a private club located in a fourteen-story, glass-walled building on Sunset Boulevard at the West Hollywood gateway from Beverly Hills. Its members work in the creative industries. The club's name comes from the first Soho House, which opened in London's Soho in 1995. There are twenty-eight Soho Houses throughout the world.

Soho House West Hollywood boasts an atmosphere that's young and casual. It makes an attempt to encourage individuals under the age of twenty-seven to join by offering them a 50-percent membership discount until they reach thirty. Members who pay the full price of $4,191 plus an additional "initiation fee" of $680 (as of 2022) are given access to all the Soho Houses. The club has a tree-shaded rooftop garden with a splendid view of the city and a bar equipped with comfy vintage sofas. Members must adhere to a strict code of conduct. No photos taken are to be shared on social media, and no tweeting about celebrities spotted hanging out there is allowed.

It was at Soho House, acquaintances said, that Blake liked to smoke marijuana and pitch his ideas, one being a graphic novel called *Syndrome*, which he published in 2010. It poses the ancient question of what causes people to commit horrific acts of evil. The cover features a smiling, blue-eyed baby doll on a pale blue background. The top of the doll's skull has been peeled off, displaying a realistic-looking brain.

Syndrome opens with a television news reporter stationed outside a prison where a serial killer is about to be executed. As in *La Femme Nikita*, the execution is faked. The serial killer is whisked away in an ambulance to the Nevada desert. At great expense, a huge film set has been meticulously crafted there. Like the setting for *The Truman Show*, it appears to be a real town.

A neuropathologist is making this the culmination of his life's work. He is determined to fix the brains of sociopaths, allowing them to feel empathy. That way, he hopes, murders and attacks stemming from violent rage can be almost eliminated.

In one panel, a woman's decapitated corpse lies sprawled on a blood-soaked bed. The doctor muses, "Used to be, a person did something like this, the experts would call him evil. Possessed. It must be some kind of spirit that stole into his body, forced him to do the Devil's work."

The serial killer awakens, thinking he has escaped from prison. He stalks an actress who has been hired based on her experience in improvisational theater. She knows nothing about the project other than that she must play along with whatever happens.

Syndrome is beautifully illustrated, the plot flowing quickly through 104 pages. The introduction asks the question, "If you loved hurting things, what would you do?" It warns, "In the end, we ALL become monsters."

Prosecutors in Blake's trial claimed he used the book as a blueprint for the torture-murder of Iana Kasian.

No matter how one feels about fictional portrayals of extreme acts of violence, *Syndrome* is a striking work. But it wasn't entirely Blake Leibel's own, according to the producer, who spoke to the *Toronto Sun* on condition of anonymity. "It was a clever idea, but what was unusual is that he paid other people to write, draw, and design the book," the producer said. "That's never done."

It's no secret that writers Daniel Quantz and R. J. Ryan, as well as illustrator David Marquez, are credited with being the graphic novel's co-creators. Their names appear on the cover after Blake's, but apparently, he caught flack for it not being entirely his own work.

So committed was he to making his graphic novels a success that he would walk into comic bookstores with a stack of copies, offering them for free to anyone who wanted one, a friend of his told the *Daily Mail*.

Three weeks after Iana gave birth to their daughter, the façade of her enviable Instagram life split wide open. To her horror, Blake's dark and twisted secret life was revealed in the most shocking way possible.

Just after midnight on May 20, 2016, Blake was arrested and charged on suspicion of sexual assault. The victim was a woman he knew, storyboard artist and producer Constance Buccafurri. She worked on the animated films *Frozen* and *Aladdin,* starring Will Smith. Not only did Blake know her, he'd purchased a house for her. They'd been having an affair. He was released on $100,000 bail.

Reporter Scott Johnson interviewed Constance Buccafurri for a December 18, 2017, article published in the *Hollywood Reporter.* She said she and Blake's wife, Amanda, had joined forces against Iana, who they perceived to be their common enemy. She showed the reporter text messages she and Amanda had exchanged, criticizing Iana for being a gold-digger and wondering if they could contact the US Citizenship and Immigration Services and have her deported. "She's the nastiest person," Amanda wrote of Iana.

Whatever friendly feelings there were between Blake's wife and his mistress eventually vanished. On December 1, 2016, Amanda Leibel filed a harassment lawsuit against Constance Buccafurri in Los Angeles County Superior Court.

Amanda was granted a temporary restraining order against Constance after she claimed Constance was stalking her, much like the obsessed woman in *Fatal Attraction.* She said she feared for her safety and that of her sons. The harassment case was later dismissed.

Shattered by the news of Blake's arrest, Iana took their three-week-old baby, Diana, and moved out of the Holloway Drive condo she shared with Blake into another one down the street, which she'd rented for her mother. Diana had been born on May 3, Olga Kasian's sixtieth birthday. One month previously, in April 2016, Olga had made the journey from Kyiv to Los Angeles. She was excited about the upcoming birth of her granddaughter, but her joy would be short-lived.

After going shopping with Iana for a baby stroller on May 23, Olga never saw her daughter again. A seven-minute phone conversation on May 24 was their last contact, according to testimony at Blake's trial.

Days after his arrest for sexual assault, Blake apologized to Iana. He begged her to come home, promising to explain. She went, leaving the baby in the care of her mother.

Surveillance videos from the Holloway Drive complex that were entered into evidence showed Iana going into the building at nine-thirty on May 23. She wouldn't leave again until May 26, when her mutilated body, scalped and drained of nearly all its blood, was removed.

May 24, 2016, was a Tuesday. The day started out gloomy, the sky a dull gray with clouds obscuring the sun. By noon, the clouds had blown away and the weather in Los Angeles had turned sunny. It was a perfect day for a trip to the beach—colorful Santa Monica, perhaps, with its landmark pier, or bohemian Venice or pristine Zuma, where dolphins and sea lions play in the surf.

But Blake and Iana didn't go to the beach that day. They remained inside Blake's condo, where he was slowly torturing her to death.

Later, blood-soaked mattresses, blood-splattered walls, and carpet stained with bloody footprints would provide mute testimony as to what went on inside the condominium unit on Holloway Drive.

After repeated telephone calls to Iana went unanswered, Olga Kasian went to the building with a friend around 1:44 p.m. on May 25. According to court documents, she saw the Mercedes Iana drove parked in the complex's garage. Olga then went to the front of the building, where she saw the sliding glass door to the balcony of Blake's condo was open. She called out, "Blake, open the door for me!" He didn't respond. Instead, she saw his silhouette as he silently pulled the door closed.

Hours earlier, at 1:48 a.m. on May 25, Blake had used Iana's cell phone to order some food. He'd left instructions to leave the delivery outside the door after being buzzed into the building, and not to ring the doorbell. The delivery was made at 2:11 a.m. Blake would place another food delivery order using Iana's phone shortly before three in the morning on May 26.

He'd evidently worked up an appetite torturing and mutilating her.

Two sheriff's deputies had visited the condominium on May 25, summoned by Olga Kasian, who was frantic with worry over not hearing from her daughter despite calling and texting her at least twenty times. At 5:49 a.m., she had an English-speaking friend call 911. The call to the dispatcher was recorded and can be heard online. Olga expressed fear for Iana's safety. Iana had delivered a baby by C-section three weeks before, she said through her interpreter, and she might need medical assistance, adding that she feared her daughter was being kept inside against her will and to please send someone at once.

When the deputies arrived, no one answered the door. All appeared calm. The deputies left voicemails telling Blake that they urgently needed to speak with him. Then they went away, having found no justification to force their way inside. Iana wasn't a minor. She was thirty years old, an independent adult. There was no reason to believe she was in danger. Perhaps she and Blake had gone away for a few days.

On May 26, unwilling to give up hope that Iana was alive and being held prisoner, Olga went to the building's front door and again called 911. This time, Deputy Micah Johnson arrived and spoke with a neighbor in the hallway, though the neighbor said he hadn't seen anyone enter or leave the condo for a couple of days. Johnson knocked on Blake's door. When there was no response, he left a voicemail telling Blake it was urgent that he contact him.

Minutes ticked by with no call from Blake. That's when Johnson made up his mind that something was wrong. He obtained a key to the condo unit and tried to use it to open the door, but it was latched from the inside. Deputy Todd Mohr arrived and called their sergeant, who gave the go-ahead to kick in the door.

The scene that met them inside was eerily calm. It was dark, the lights off, the curtains pulled shut. The deputies checked the living room, dining room, kitchen, and balcony, finding no one.

Next, they turned their attention to the locked door leading to the hallway. They tried to force it open, only to find that a mattress had been pushed up against it. Mohr managed to push it over, and the search continued. Other deputies followed as they cautiously checked the guest bedroom and bathroom. In the guest bedroom, they found bloodstains on the headboard of the bed.

At that point, it was no longer a case of a young couple who weren't returning phone calls because they didn't want to be bothered. The condo on Holloway Drive had now become a crime scene.

The door to the master bedroom was closed and locked. The deputies called out, announcing their presence. Receiving no reply, they tried to kick in the door. Again, they found the door barricaded by a mattress. The deputies called out for whoever was inside to come out. A male voice responded, saying that he wouldn't come out and that he was afraid they'd beat him up.

The deputies assured him they were only there to check on his girlfriend. The man replied that she was fine; she was at Cedars-Sinai Hospital, adding that he was waiting for his father, who would be there soon. He'd come out then.

But Blake wasn't referring to Lorne, from whom he was estranged, but to Steven Green, his accountant and mentor. He had called Green around noon that day, after Green had been trying for months to contact him without success. Green had left a voicemail on Blake's phone on May 23, saying he was worried about him and that he loved him.

When Green arrived at the condo, he explained to the deputies who he was. He spoke to Blake through the partially opened bedroom door and then phoned him from the living room.

With Green coaxing him, Blake finally emerged from the bedroom, wearing only a pair of white boxer shorts. He asked Green to pass him some clothes from the living room. The deputies searched the clothing, finding four thousand dollars in cash and Blake's passport, indicating he had plans to flee the country.

Entering the bedroom, the deputies stopped in their tracks. Iana Kasian was lying motionless on the bed, her naked body covered with a red Mickey Mouse blanket. It was obvious she had been subjected to savage violence. Her head was on a pillow and her scalp, starting from above her eyebrows, had been removed down to the bone. Two paramedics waiting outside came in and pronounced her dead.

Blake seemed strangely detached. Sergeant Robert Martindale later testified in a deposition that Leibel claimed he didn't know Iana was dead. "He just held firm that she wasn't—he wasn't even aware that she was dead," Martindale said. "And very callous when I told him—I think very striking—well, I pointedly said, 'She's dead in that bed.'

"And he's like, he looks at us and goes, 'Well, I guess you'll find out who did it then.'"

An autopsy showed Iana had been drained of nearly all her blood. A portion of one of her eyebrows was found on the floor near the bed. There were bloodstains on a second mattress in the room and on the mattress that had been blocking the door, and on the walls as well as on the headboard of the bed in the guest room. A trash can contained a clump of her hair and a razor. There was blood in the kitchen garbage disposal. A paring knife with a green handle was found in a drawer in the master bathroom with blood on the blade.

Iana's left ear was discovered in a dumpster under a trash chute located in the hallway outside the condo. Some of the skin on her face had been torn away. There were bite marks on her left jaw and left bicep, the kind an enraged animal would make, except these were human bite marks.

Jonathan Lucas, chief medical examiner for the Los Angeles County Medical Examiner-Coroner's department, testified at Blake's trial that the cause of death was blood loss due to head trauma. He estimated it had taken eight hours for Iana to die, and that part of the time it appeared she had been placed in a bathtub with her head lower than her feet, with water running over her. For what purpose was unknown, unless it was to prolong her suffering. The level of violence she sustained is almost unimaginable and must have been excruciatingly painful.

Warm water had been running in the bathtub of the master bathroom when the deputies first entered, and they turned it off. Bloodstains and hair could be seen in the tub. The drain in the bathtub in the guest bedroom also tested positive for blood. What had taken place in that condo were extreme acts of carnage, carried out on a victim who was alive through most of it.

Iana had fought desperately for survival. When he was taken into custody, Blake showed signs of having been in a fierce fight. The tip of the little finger on his right hand was missing. He had severe bruising to both eyes and across the bridge of his nose. There were scratches under his left eye and long, red scratches on his neck and chest. Both his shins were bruised, as was his right ankle. There was also an injury to his right bicep consistent with a human bite mark.

Those injuries attested to the fact that Iana had refused to go down without a fight. But at five feet four inches tall and weighing 152 pounds, she was no match for six-foot-three, 210-pound Blake.

Blake was escorted from the building and locked up. Unlike his arrest for sexual assault six days earlier, this time he would be denied bail.

On June 20, 2018, a jury of eight men and four women found Blake Leibel, scion of two of Canada's wealthiest families, guilty of first-degree murder, mayhem, and torture. Iana's mother, who was present in the courtroom throughout the proceedings, burst into tears. Her family and friends, some of whom had flown from Ukraine to attend the trial, surrounded her and held her close.

Blake's older brother Cody was the only member of the Leibel family to attend every day of the trial. When the verdict was announced, he sighed and stared straight ahead at the back of his brother's head as he stood with his attorneys.

Blake's ex-wife entered the courtroom after the verdict was announced. Blake left, escorted by a bailiff, without looking at her or his brother.

During the week-long trial, the prosecution displayed illustrations from Blake's graphic novel *Syndrome*. They called it a blueprint for Iana's murder.

Much of the prosecution's case consisted of presenting a barrage of forensic evidence, illustrating the acts of violence that occurred throughout the condo. There was blood in the kitchen drainpipe and in the dining room. Pieces of flesh were torn from Iana's body and flung behind the mattress and onto the floor of the master bedroom. In the building's basement were eleven trash bags containing bloody sheets, towels, and bathmats, as well as chunks of Iana's hair and scalp and pieces of her flesh.

The jury found no doubt as to what had happened to her, or who did it.

An appeal was filed in the California Court of Appeal, Second Appellate District, on April 29, 2020. Blake's lawyer, Sarah H. Ruddy, argued that by entering the cover, the credit page, and five pages of illustrations from the graphic novel into evidence, the prosecution had violated his constitutional right to due process. She argued that the acts described in the novel were irrelevant to the facts of the case and only served to inflame the jury. The appeal was denied.

Blake Leibel will spend the rest of his life behind bars. He is incarcerated in the California Correctional Institution in Tehachapi. While he lost his freedom, Olga Kasian lost a daughter. Diana Leibel will grow up without her mother.

One final question remains: Why?

Why would a man brought up in the lap of luxury and given every advantage in life commit such a heinous crime? The answer is unknown. Perhaps heredity played a part. Blake's maternal grandmother, Leona Leah Chitel, was bipolar, according to a lawsuit she filed against the Bank of Montreal in 1998. Perhaps Blake was too.

Bipolar disorder is considered a very common mental health condition. More than three million cases are reported in the US each year.

Its relationship to violent crime is uncertain, according to the *Journal of the American Medical Association*. A 2010 study of 314 individuals with bipolar disorder showed that 8.4 percent committed violent crimes resulting in convictions for homicide, assault, robbery, sexual assault, or arson, as compared to 3.5 percent in a group of the same size selected from the general population. The study found the risk was mostly confined to bipolar individuals who abused drugs. Without a comorbidity of drug abuse, the risk of someone with a bipolar diagnosis committing an act of violence was minimal, the study found.

Blake smoked marijuana and took mushrooms containing psilocybin, according to his friends. Neither drug typically causes users to become violent.

Was it jealousy over Iana paying more attention to the baby than she did to him? That was a theory the prosecution presented at his trial. Was it frustration over failing to make it big as a comic-book publisher that pushed him over the edge?

No one knows. Blake may not even know. Sometimes people just snap. Sometimes a slap or a punch seems to flip a switch in the brain, making a howling blood-beast take over, clawing, tearing, destroying. When that happens, it's left to the survivors to try to pick up the pieces.

LORD LUCAN: THE TWICE-DEAD ARISTOCRAT

CHARLOTTE PLATT

Lord Lucan, given name Richard John Bingham, was the seventh Earl of Lucan, a British peer, almost one of the men to play James Bond and, curiously, one of the few people to be declared dead twice.

Both times without a body.

The mystery of Lord Lucan's disappearance, lack of reappearance, and the decades-long debate about his actions, survival, and title have been part of the British social psyche since his disappearance on November 8, 1974. Alleged sightings of him stretch from Ireland to Australia, and he has been a household name up to the late 2010s, when his second declaration of death was officially given.

To understand why the somewhat clichéd circumstance of an obsessive ex-husband, bitter custody battle, and murdered nanny came to be such a continuing interest, you have to consider the rise and fall of the bright young star that was Richard John Bingham.

Lord Lucan, known by his middle name John, was born on December 18, 1934, the eldest son of George Charles Patrick Bingham, then the sixth Earl of Lucan. He had one older sister, and both a younger sister and brother. Throughout his father's life, John was known as Lord Bingham, as Lord Lucan is a peerage title which would not pass to him until his father's death.

Peerages are a UK-based title system, which can be both hereditary and, more recently, lifetime, where an individual is nominated. The sitting government can make such nominations, though appointment is only by the monarch. The hereditary nature of the Lucan peerage, and the complications it wrought, will be returned to later.

Because of his tender age at the outbreak of the Second World War, John was evacuated from London into the British countryside, as were most children who could be. He spent time in Wales and in the United States, as did his siblings. As a member of the aristocracy, he studied at Eton College, once he returned from his safe isolation after the war ended.

He served as a member of the Coldstream Guards—the longest-serving regular regiment in the British Army, having been founded in 1650 and never amalgamated. This regiment is part of what's known as the Household Division, a selection of elite and historically important military units throughout the British Commonwealth that offer protection for the British Monarchy. Membership in the Guards is a significant undertaking and honor, even for the British aristocracy, which, at the time, often held an expectation that the eldest son would join some form of military service.

John was placed with them in West Germany from 1953 to 1955 at the rank of second lieutenant, a short term, but a notable position to have held. It's believed that this is where he developed his taste for professional gambling, as he was a skilled player in both backgammon and bridge, though he was noted as attending horseraces during his studies as well.

After leaving the army, John joined William Brandt's Sons and Co. Ltd., a London-based merchant bank. This was a respectable job that also offered continued networking and development for him, given his background. Here he met Stephen Raphael, a skilled gambler and stockbroker, with whom John forged a strong friendship. They holidayed together, traveling as far as the Bahamas, and were frequent companions for golf, water-skiing, backgammon, and card games such as poker.

Games of skill like backgammon and bridge were a firm favorite of John's and he often won at them, but he also suffered significant losses.

At times assisted by family members to pay off the debts he accumulated, including the notable army officer John Bevan, who was his uncle through marriage, he nonetheless continued to pursue gambling as a professional endeavor.

In 1960, John quit his job at Brandt's, both buoyed by a recent significant win and frustrated that a colleague had been promoted ahead of him. He was noted as saying, "Why should I work in a bank, when I can earn a year's money in one single night at the tables?" despite his turbulent luck in card games. After a period in the United States, he returned to set out on his own, leaving the family home to establish himself.

John was known for his lavish lifestyle, a common element of British high society and the aristocracy at the time. He raced (then named) power boats during holidays in the US, drove a recognizable Aston Martin, and was an original member of the Clermont Set, an exclusive gambling club that met at the Clermont Club, which was based in a renowned townhouse at 44 Berkeley Square in the Mayfair district of London.

Infamously started with "five dukes, five marquesses, almost twenty earls and two cabinet ministers," it was founded in 1962, and was the first London casino after new laws on gambling were introduced in the UK. The property also housed the controversial—but ever popular—Annabel's nightclub from 1963 onward. Other members included novelist Ian Fleming, as well as Peter Sellers, David Stirling, and Lucian Freud. This familiarity and camaraderie with Fleming was how John later came to be tied to the James Bond franchise. He was being considered as one of the many men to bring the popular character to live action, though he was beaten to the position by the often-overlooked George Lazenby.

During this period of relative success and high living, John met Veronica Mary Duncan. The daughter of Major Charles Moorhouse Duncan and Thelma Duncan, Veronica had been raised in South Africa and England following her father's death and her mother's subsequent remarriage. Veronica studied art at Bournemouth, and worked as a model and secretary while sharing a London flat with her sister, Christina. She was introduced to London high society after her sister married into the wealthy Shand Kydd family, resulting in Veronica attending more society events to accompany Christina.

At one such event, at a golf club in 1963, she met John. Their subsequent engagement was announced in October 1963, featuring in both respectable and tabloid papers. This was not uncommon at the time; marriage announcements for prominent society members were a social event, and attendance at the wedding could be hotly contested.

Such was not the way for their marriage on November 20, 1963, for which the only notable attendee was Princess Alice, Countess of Athlone, the last surviving grandchild of Queen Victoria. It was commented at the time that Princess Alice only attended because one of her ladies-in-waiting was related to Veronica, which would have been a social embarrassment for John.

They honeymooned on the Orient Express, touring Europe through the journey. John's father gave him a marriage settlement to allow the couple to buy a larger property for their future family, and for any further renovations. This was a common practice at the time, since it was felt it would be better to pass on familial wealth when a new family was starting out, rather than hoard funds until inheritance after elder family members died. It also meant that the dowry payments brought in by a bride were matched by her husband, ensuring her dowry would be used to maintain her throughout womanhood or passed on to the children should a tragedy befall their mother. Such practices have now become old-fashioned.

Unfortunately, this consideration was short-lived. John's father died in January 1964, just two months after the couple's wedding. This left him with a substantial inheritance, even after division of some assets between his other siblings and his father's various titles vested in him. These included the title of Earl of Lucan, thereby allowing John to become Lord Lucan, but also Baron Lucan of Castlebar, Baron Bingham of Melcombe, and Baronet Bingham of Castlebar. Veronica became Countess of Lucan, known more commonly as Lady Lucan; she would be called by this title until her death in 2017.

The couple went on to have three children: Lady Frances Bingham, born in 1964; George Bingham, the now eighth Earl of Lucan, born in 1967; and Lady Camilla Bloch (previously Bingham), born in 1970.

A nanny assisted with the day-to-day care of the children, with Lillian Jenkins helping with the care for Frances from early 1965. The Lucans still led very public lives, with Lord Lucan attending the Clermont Club throughout the day, often taking lunch there before playing backgammon over the afternoon. He would return home to change into evening wear, generally black tie, and frequently returned to gamble late into the night.

Earning the nickname "Lucky Lucan," he was a skilled player and ranked among the top-ten backgammon competitors in the world. He won the well-recognized St. James's Club tournament and held the American West Coast championship. There was no question that in games of skill he performed well, his quiet demeanor and easy-to-enjoy company allowing him access to many high-end and private clubs. He would spend to excess beyond gambling, hiring private planes to fly friends to horseraces and importing premium Russian vodka of his preference.

The couple purchased and moved to the now-infamous property of 46 Lower Belgrave Street, in the exclusive Belgravia area, in 1967, financed in part by Lord Lucan's inheritance, and extensively redecorated. This was a substantial house in a very desired area of London, large enough for the family to expand into as they had more children and still had staff, including live-in, to assist with childcare.

However, Lucan's public façade was a sham—he lost more than he won, and his finances were drained. Not having learned from his previous embarrassment with family help against his losses, he continued to gamble professionally across card games, casinos, and racetracks. In 1968, he was alleged to have paid more in race entry fees than he made back in winnings, and the continued stress strained his marriage.

This strain was made worse by Veronica's own deteriorating mental health. She suffered substantially with postnatal depression after the birth of both George and Camilla, to the point of John trying to have her committed to a psychiatric clinic in 1971. She refused to be admitted, but consented to medication and home visits by a psychiatrist.

While these treatments seem to have helped Veronica, they did not help the marriage. The family went on holiday to Monte Carlo in summer 1972, but Veronica returned to England early, bringing Camilla home with her and leaving Lucan with Frances and George. The couple remained together for the rest of the year, but Lucan moved out of the family home in early January 1973. He first moved to nearby Eaton Row, then later to a larger property in Elizabeth Street, which would allow him better accommodation to see the children.

The separation was a struggle for the entire family, but Lucan suffered great emotional turmoil from not being around his children. He became obsessive about seeking custody, and despite some attempts by Veronica to reconcile, he focused solely on getting the children from her. This devolved into what would now be acknowledged as stalking. He recorded phone calls between himself and Veronica; he looked for doctors to declare her mad; his car was often seen on the street of the family home; and he hired private investigators to track her. He canceled the regular food delivery to the home and delayed payments to the childcare agency and amenity payments like the milk delivery. At one point, Veronica took a part-time job to ensure she could meet the bills independently, working at a local hospital.

Lucan also began more erratic behavior, such as calling the home and asking for people who didn't live there or simply breathing heavily down the phone. This unsettled many of the live-in nannies, who frequently left after a short time. One nanny reported being told by Veronica that Lucan had previously pushed her down the stairs, and not to be surprised "if he kills me one day," which, while prescient, may not have been comforting for a young woman assisting with childcare.

Lucan did not keep this struggle private either. He would play tapes of the recorded phone calls to mutual friends, even including Christina, Veronica's sister. He told acquaintances that no one could work with Veronica and that the turnover of nannies was because of her unreasonable behavior. Again, this would now be recognized as coercive behavior, but at the time this was simply considered an unfortunate public spectacle.

Matters came to a head in March 1973, when Lucan abducted the children. He and two private detectives confronted the nanny, Stefanja Sawicka, claiming the children had been made wards of the court and had to be handed over. Wards of the court are children or other incapacitated parties who are under the protection of a court until a decision can be made about their care or future, and removal from parents or carers is a common aspect of this position. Accordingly, though erroneously, Sawicka handed George and Camilla over, and Frances was collected from school by Lucan later that day. It was, of course, a ruse by Lucan, but given the ongoing separation and the allegations, Sawicka's mistake may be looked at sympathetically.

Veronica fired Sawicka and sought a court order to return the children to her care. Parental abduction of children has been a contentious and complex area of law in many jurisdictions, and the court expected this would be no different, so a hearing date was set three months in advance to allow both parties to prepare their arguments.

Knowing Lucan would seek to rely on claims about her mental health, Veronica booked herself into the Priory Clinic, a still well-known private mental health facility that's often frequented by celebrities. During this stay, while it was acknowledged that she was still somewhat psychologically fragile and would benefit from support, she was not considered to be mentally unwell. Her anxieties and depression were manageable, and it could be said they had a reasonably obvious source given the abduction of her children and the bitter separation.

When the hearing went forward in June 1973, it did not go as Lucan desired. He was focused on presenting Veronica as unfit to care for the children, but the judge focused on his unreasonable behavior, which put him at an unexpected disadvantage. The hearing went on for weeks, with numerous witnesses and lengthy legal arguments, but Lucan could not recover from the judge's view that his behavior had been unreasonable. This cast him as the unfit parent of the couple in the eyes of the court. This perception would haunt Lucan, even to the point of him mentioning it in letters immediately before his disappearance.

At the advice of his representatives, Lucan eventually conceded the case at great emotional and financial cost. The judge, Mr. Justice Rees, awarded custody to Veronica, and Lucan was given fortnightly weekend access—a decision that reignited his obsessive behavior.

He stalked the family again, hired more detectives, and even tried to befriend some of the nannies who worked through the childcare agency Veronica had had to employ following the court decision in her favor. This resulted in hundreds of pounds' worth of detective fees, but nothing he could use to challenge Veronica's custody of the children. It continued to drive some of the nannies away, though, and by late 1974, Sandra Rivett was employed by Veronica.

At the same time, Lucan began to spiral. He was in debt for tens of thousands of pounds from the court case, overdrawn on all his domestic accounts, and still gambling. His addiction ran rampant, and though the stakes he entered were much diminished from his previous encounters, he was still losing continuously. Lucan drank excessively and smoked constantly, worrying friends in terms of both his lack of care about himself and of how out of character it seemed. During drunken rants, he would discuss how killing Veronica might save him from bankruptcy, and how he would dispose of her body, bragging that he would never be caught. He went as far as describing how and where he would dispose of her body—by throwing it into the Solent, the twenty-mile-wide strait between mainland UK and the Isle of Wight. No one reported this behavior to any authorities, though some friends gave statements to the police about it after Lucan's subsequent disappearance.

In late October 1974, Lucan's debts were catching up with him, but his demeanor changed. He began seeking help through loans and applying to discretionary charitable trusts. He no longer spoke openly of seeking to have the children returned to him and seemed to be more like his old self, engaging in discussions about politics and partaking of social outings. He even broke his now-habitual late sleeping—a risk of the gambling life, as casinos in the UK at the time could only operate between two in the afternoon and four in the morning due to licensing laws. Lucan was invited to write articles for the Oxford University magazine and consulted with well-appointed friends for feedback and advice on his writing, including Michael Hicks Beach, a literary agent. This change of behavior seemed to be an attempt to get back on track with himself, but it didn't last.

He missed several appointments with friends on Thursday, November 7, resulting in some going to check on him, as this was entirely out of character. He did not answer the phone when called, did not answer the door to his flat, and his car could not be found locally.

Lucan was noted as having visited a pharmacy in Lower Belgrave Street, close to the former family home, that afternoon, asking for a small capsule to be identified. He had apparently done this several times since the separation and the chemist indulged his curiosity, presumably because of Lucan's position. It was confirmed that the capsule was a form of amitriptyline (Limbitrol in this instance), a drug approved to treat anxiety and depression as well as nerve pain and migraines.

What happened through the rest of the evening of November 7, 1974, is still a matter of debate, though the findings in the 1975 inquest set out a largely agreed-upon timetable.

Sandra Rivett did not habitually work on Thursday evenings; it was her usual evening off to see her boyfriend. This unfortunate week she had seen him the day before, so she was at 46 Lower Belgrave Street. At around nine o'clock, having put the younger children to bed, she went to the basement kitchen to make herself and Veronica a cup of tea. Basement kitchens were not uncommon in London properties, which often had (and still have) restrictions on how far they can expand the property—this results in expansion down rather than up, as may be expected. This continues to be controversial even today.

When Sandra entered the kitchen, a short turn off the basement steps, she was bludgeoned to death with a piece of lead piping. The inquest went on to confirm that she had been killed by a combination of blunt force injury to the head and inhalation of blood contributing to asphyxiation. Her body was then placed in a large canvas sack, believed to be a mailbag.

It would later be confirmed by police that the bulb had been removed from the light fixture at the bottom of the stairs and left on a chair in the kitchen. This not only showed premeditation by the attacker, but that the attacker had a reasonable knowledge of the property.

Veronica came down to the ground floor to investigate why the tea was taking so long and was accosted at the top of the basement stairs, being struck with the lead pipe after calling out to Sandra. While she was being attacked, she screamed, and her attacker shouted at her to shut up. Veronica claimed she recognized her husband's voice and fought back against him. She bit his fingers and clawed at him, and when she was thrown down onto the carpet in an attempted strangulation, she twisted around to grab his testicles and squeeze them. This caused the attack to cease.

Lucan was initially unclear about what had happened to Sandra, though when pressed, he admitted he'd killed her, leaving Veronica terrified. Not only had her husband tried to kill her, but he had also killed the only other adult in the house, leaving Veronica alone with the children upstairs. She bargained with him, saying she would help him escape from the inevitable murder charges if he let her live, but he had to stay there with them for a few days so her wounds would heal and not raise suspicion. She was bleeding from her head, and would later bruise significantly in her face and neck.

The couple returned upstairs to find Frances had got up at the sound of screaming. They sent her back to bed before going to another bedroom to clean Veronica up. Lucan told her to lay a towel on the bed to avoid staining the sheets, then asked if she had any barbiturates to help with the pain. He went to the bathroom to get supplies for cleaning her face and, seeing her chance, Veronica ran from the home, fleeing to a nearby pub called the Plumbers Arms.

The pub landlord described Veronica, when she had rushed in, as covered in blood and clearly distressed, shouting that someone had tried to murder her and saying, "My children, my children, he's murdered my nanny." She seemed to fall into a state of shock, and the police were called, as well as an ambulance.

Testimony later read at the inquest by a police officer who had interviewed Frances—delivered by Detective Constable Sally Blower due to the girl's young age—confirmed that Frances had heard her father shouting for her mother, and she had seen him exit the bathroom and go downstairs.

It's believed that Lucan visited the nearby Chester Square home of Madeleine Florman, the mother of one of Frances' school friends, after bloodstains were found on her doorstep. She reported having heard someone banging on her door at around ten o'clock, though she had ignored it as she was alone in the house. She also received an incoherent phone call, which she'd hung up on.

It is known that Lucan called his mother, the Dowager Countess, between ten-thirty and eleven that evening, asking her to collect the children from the family home and saying there had been a "terrible catastrophe" at the property. Lucan presented a story of driving past the house when he saw a mysterious man attacking Veronica in the basement and stopped to intervene. He claimed that, upon entering the home, he had found Veronica hysterical and screaming. It's unknown where he was when he made this call.

Next, he drove the Ford Corsair he was using—not his notable Mercedes-Benz, which was left at his flat with a dead battery—down to Uckfield, a town in East Sussex approximately forty miles from London.

There he visited family friends, the Maxwell-Scotts. This meeting with Susan Maxwell-Scott is the last confirmed sighting of Lord Lucan.

Susan later commented to police that Lucan seemed disheveled, with his hair "somewhat ruffled," which was out of character for him. He told her a similar story to what he had told his mother—that he was passing the house when he saw Veronica being attacked and had gone inside to intervene, but had slipped in a pool of blood, and that Veronica had accused him, during a hysterical reaction, of hiring a hit man to kill her.

Lucan again called his mother at around twelve-thirty, but refused to speak to the police constable who was now with her, saying he would call the police directly in the morning. He did not.

While with the Maxwell-Scotts, Lucan penned three letters—two to his brother-in-law, Bill Shand Kydd; and one to the owner of the St. James's Club, Michael Stoop, a close friend and the owner of the Ford Corsair Lucan was driving. Two of the three letters, those to Bill, were bloodstained. Forensics at the time showed that the blood appeared to match Sandra Rivett's and Veronica's blood types.

The letters to Bill alternatively set out financial matters and begged Lucan's brother-in-law to take in his children so they would be well cared for. Lucan discussed fees for private school and how much Veronica hated him, and that he could not stomach the idea of the elder children having to live through him going on trial for murder. These letters were posted to Bill's London address. When Bill learned of the letters through Ian Maxwell-Scott, he drove up from his East Sussex country house to intercept them. Noting the bloodstains, he handed them over to the investigating officer, Detective Chief Superintendent Roy Ranson.

The letter to Michael Stoop was a brief note of despair. In it, Lucan referred to "a traumatic night of unbelievable coincidence," and that all he cared about was that his children should be looked after. In retrospect, and with a modern understanding of mental health, the letter to Michael reads very close to suicide ideation. Michael destroyed the envelope the letter had come in, so it wasn't possible to tell where Lucan had been when he posted it, but the Ford Corsair was found a few miles away in Newhaven on November 10. The trunk of the car contained a bottle of vodka, lead piping similar to that used in the attack, bloodstains, hairs from Veronica, and a writing pad.

Newhaven is a port town in southeast England, with a regular ferry service. This ferry service, and Lucan's reference to "lying doggo for a bit" in his letter to his brother-in-law, have fueled speculation that he escaped by buying his way onto a ferry despite the fact police were looking for him. His description was provided to Interpol, the international police facilitation service, in case this was what had occurred.

Detective Chief Superintendent Ranson suspected that Lucan had killed himself, but considered a search of the likely area—Newhaven Downs—to be impossible because of its enormous size. Sniffer dogs were brought in, though they found nothing other than the skeletal remains of a previously missing judge, long deceased and under dense undergrowth; later searches of the harbor by police divers also found nothing. Lucan was simply gone.

Lucan's children spent several months with their aunt, Lady Sarah Gibbs, until Veronica had recovered enough to take them back home. This took several weeks, and given the level of press attention, the family eventually moved to a friend's property in Plymouth for a while.

The inquest into Sandra Rivett's death opened initially in November 1974, and was adjourned after a short hearing when her ex-husband confirmed that he had identified her body, and a pathologist testified that Sandra had died from beating around the head with a blunt instrument.

An inquest is a type of formal inquiry into the circumstances of a death—it is not the same as a trial. The aim of an inquest is to find out who the deceased was and the broader circumstances of their death (how, where, and when they died) to allow the death to be formally registered. An inquest is held automatically if a death occurs in police custody or prison, if it is violent or otherwise unnatural, or if the cause of death is unknown despite initial investigations. It's not unusual for the basic facts of a death to be established and the inquest adjourned to a later date to allow for further police investigations, as these investigations would assist with the fact-finding needed in the inquest.

When the inquest went ahead in June 1975, after two further adjournments, it was expectedly controversial. The press had been rabid for as much detail as possible since the attack became public, and they attended in droves. The Dowager Countess hired a Queen's Counsel on Lucan's behalf, and the QC was entitled to question the thirty-three witnesses being called by the inquest. This naturally included Veronica, who was questioned extensively on her marriage, the family's financial struggles, the night of the attack, and her employment and working relationship with Sandra Rivett. Veronica was questioned at length, though the coroner sought to ensure that questions remained relevant to the inquest.

Lucan's supporters were highly critical of the investigation and inquest, as they felt it was a one-sided affair. They were uncooperative with police, earning the nickname the "Eton mafia" with police officers, even threatening libel actions against newspapers that condemned Lucan or their own behavior concerning the attack. The satirical magazine *Private Eye* was successfully sued by one of Lucan's friends when it claimed he'd attended a meeting on November 8 that became the focus of wild speculation about hiding Lucan or assisting in a coverup.

While it's clear there was resistance to blaming Lucan, or an indulgence in the idea that he was innocent or simply a "man driven to the edge," so many members of high society being actively unhelpful with the police investigation fueled speculation regarding Lucan's escape.

When the inquest eventually returned a verdict that Lord Lucan had killed Sandra Rivett, it was not a shock to many involved in the matter. Lucan would be the last person committed by a coroner to the Crown Court for unlawful killing, with the coroner's power to do so being removed by the Criminal Law Act of 1977. While some conspiratorial discussions at the time viewed these circumstances as linked, there was never an acknowledgment of this. Lucan also became the first member of the House of Lords to be named a murderer since 1760—the previous being Laurence Shirley, fourth Earl Ferrers, who was hanged for killing his steward.

Many of Lucan's friends continued to proclaim his innocence, but the British press openly reported him as Rivett's killer. His defense of having seen his wife being attacked in the basement did not hold up to inspection; police reenactments showed that he would have had to be staring into the basement windows to see this. While he had been stalking his family, this coincidence seemed unbelievable, especially combined with the blood and lead pipe in the borrowed car, the forensic evidence, and the drunken discussions about murdering his spouse. It must be noted, however, that his fingerprints were never found at the scene. His supporters focused highly on this.

Being declared a murderer was not the end of the matter, though. Lucan's debt had not disappeared as he had. His creditors sought to have him declared bankrupt, and given that he could not defend the action himself, his family had to deal with the outcome. The family silverware was famously sold off in early 1976, which raised enough money to pay off the most immediate debts; the Lucan family trust gradually paid the remaining sums in the years following his disappearance.

It was only in late 1999, some twenty-five years after his disappearance, that Lucan was initially declared dead in the courts to allow the granting of probate—the English court process that allows a trustee to wind up matters of the deceased. This was Lucan's first death, but it did not yield a death certificate, which meant that his son could not inherit his father's title or take up his place in the House of Lords. The hereditary nature of the title meant that assumption of Lucan's death was not sufficient. There needed to be a recorded death, which could be evidenced by a death certificate. This vexed George, who felt he should be able to take up the title, now that he was an adult and it was clear to him that his father would never return.

This certainty was not shared by everyone. Sightings of "Lucky" or "Loopy" Lucan, as he had become known, were prevalent. He became something of a true crime legend, with reports of his "new life" coming from South Africa, France, Colombia, Goa, and Australia. Several unfortunate innocent gentlemen, and some who had been faking their own disappearances, have been mistaken for Lord Lucan. More speculative theories have also been floated: that he was killed and fed to tigers in a private zoo; that he had been smuggled out of the country by a cohort of underground financiers before being judged too great a risk, then killed and buried in Switzerland; that he was homeless and living rough in Australia. Even police detectives involved in reinvestigations have commented that Lucan may have escaped the UK to live abroad for several years.

Factually, Lucan's last confirmed sighting was leaving the driveway of the Maxwell-Scotts before the car he was using was found near the English Channel. Several of his friends, as well as Veronica, felt that Lucan had killed himself using the Channel, either by drowning or crashing his boat, rather than face an insufferable investigation and trial. Veronica was somewhat warm in her description, commenting that he had killed himself "like the nobleman he was." Veronica also unfortunately took her own life, though this was much later, in September 2017, and was suspected of being due to her concerns about her health.

Lucan's second declaration of death came on February 3, 2016. This time it resulted in a death certificate, thanks to the passing of the Presumption of Death Act 2013. This law brought England more in line with surrounding jurisdictions, and meant that a death can be considered as having occurred either on the last day the presumed deceased could have been alive, if the court is satisfied that they are dead, or on the day seven years after the date the presumed deceased was last seen alive, if death is presumed by the lapse of time. Given the circumstances of Lucan's disappearance, these requirements were met, and his death was recorded on the Register of Presumed Deaths, which has the same effect as a registration of death. This finally allowed George to become the eighth Earl of Lucan and take up the seat within the House of Lords forty-two years after his father disappeared.

Despite his twice-dead position, sightings of Lucan continue to be made. In 2020, it was reported that he was living in Australia, a claim that is seriously entertained by Neil Berriman, the adopted-out son of Sandra Rivett. He only discovered his identity in the late 1990s, and has spent considerable time and funds trying to track Lucan down. Lucan's surviving family has commented that such sightings are fanciful. If he were still alive, Lucan would now be nearing his nineties and bearing the complications that age brings.

It is easy to see why the case of Lord Lucan, Lucky Lucan, caught the public eye so enthusiastically. He was a poster child for the "old boys' club," a man who golfed and gambled and lived the high life to great excess. He was charismatic and engaging, and even with his addictions, he was a popular man, with both power and powerful friends. Such a public and bloody fall from grace, and the lurid details of a fragmenting family revealed through his desperate letters, were an intoxicating look behind the high-society curtain of 1960s and '70s London. The legend refused to die just as thoroughly as Lucan himself refused to, brought back to life with sightings and speculation even decades later. Given the inevitable passage of time, maybe his ghost will no longer haunt the British psyche, especially given that at least his familial matters have been resolved, though there is no guarantee they have been laid to rest.

LIFE OF THE PARTY

ALISHA HOLLAND

A new term has come to the forefront of American conversation of late: "cancel culture." Should an entertainer, politician, or anyone in the public eye do something deemed offensive, be it a minor misspeaking offense or a major transgression such as making racist remarks or being charged with a crime, response from fans can end that person's career. It may seem like a new concept, but it is far from that. The film industry has spanned more than a century, and in that time many celebrities have found their careers curtailed through their behavior and the subsequent public outcry.

Some feel "canceling" is for the betterment of all—it keeps those who are seen as role models in check and protects victims. Others feel it goes too far by not only limiting freedom of speech, but hindering the creative expression of those too frightened of ramifications to convey their true feelings.

Whatever you believe, there's no denying the conversations surrounding political correctness have done some good. Paired with the #MeToo movement, not only has "canceling" brought what happens in the dark to light, but we've also seen actual progress. Sexual predators have been sent to prison. Even those whose behavior might not permit legal action are still being held accountable, facing personal and professional consequences, all in hope of creating safer, more inclusive spaces.

In 1921, Hollywood's first superstar was also the first to be canceled and the focus of the first celebrity scandal. Now the question remains: was he deserving of such treatment, or was there a mob and tabloid mentality thirsty for juicy gossip, morbid entertainment, and an unjust punishment?

Roscoe Conkling Arbuckle was born on March 24, 1887, on a sod farm in Smith Center, Kansas, to parents Mary and William. He wasn't famous for the nickname "Fatty" just yet, but even at birth he was notably larger than other infants, weighing in at a whopping thirteen pounds, with some reports even claiming sixteen. It was his concerning weight that not only caused injury and health problems for Mary, but also led his father to believe that Roscoe was not his biological son.

Since Mary and William were of a smaller build, there was instant animosity between father and son—so much so that William decided to name his newborn Roscoe Conkling, a moniker that was already well-known, as it belonged to a former state representative and senator. It makes you wonder what William Arbuckle was like, considering he loathed the senator who had supported rights for ex-slaves, approved of President Lincoln, and even assisted in drafting the Fourteenth and Fifteenth Amendments, which supported citizenship and the right to vote for ex-slaves, respectively.

William transferred the detestation he had for Senator Roscoe to his newborn son, the first, but far from last, degradation Roscoe would endure. It was William who gave Roscoe the nickname he would grow to loathe so much: "Fatty."

The farm wasn't a quiet home, Roscoe being one of nine children. William didn't love farm life, so he sold it and moved the family to California. The Arbuckles officially settled on the West Coast just before Roscoe's second birthday. When he was eight, he had his first performance in a role that would most certainly get him canceled today. The young but not-so-little Fatty took the stage in full head-to-toe blackface. That was all it took to fall in love with performing for an audience.

By age twelve, Roscoe was growing into his Fatty moniker, as his weight approached two hundred pounds. In addition to his size, he was about to become motherless. Whether because she was in her later years when having children, because she had given birth nine times, or because Roscoe's size had caused permanent injury and health issues, Mary Arbuckle passed away at the age of fifty. William never forgave his son for the damage he believed he'd caused his wife. By then, William had abandoned the family, and Roscoe was on his own.

After Mary's death, her family put the boy on a train to go and live with his father. Upon arrival, Roscoe learned that his father had heard he was en route and once again skipped town, leaving his young son to fend for himself. On his own as a pre-teen, Roscoe found odd jobs, usually as an errand boy in hotels. When he was a teenager, a manager overheard him singing while at work, and it was suggested that the now fifteen-year-old enter a talent show.

As Fatty, he didn't do well at first. Nowadays we can vote from the comfort of our homes for our favorite acts in reality show competitions, but in the days of vaudeville, it was the live audience's reactions of laughter, clapping, or booing that would dictate the fate of the performer. Cheers would get you a career, boos would get you dragged from the stage with a shepherd's crook. Roscoe's singing voice was lovely, though his song choice was not what the crowd was interested in. Spotting the hook coming for his neck, he had to think fast. He made a dramatic escape by rolling forward and somersaulting off the stage. This extreme display of physical comedy and agility won the crowd over, and Roscoe survived the humiliating hook of the crook.

That roll off the stage was the inception of a massive career. By seventeen, he soon had consistent jobs, working in theaters owned by Sid Grauman. Now involved in vaudeville acts all along the West Coast, Roscoe ended up in Oregon, where a fateful encounter would knock over one more domino on his road to fame. After getting work in some of Grauman's productions, Roscoe stopped at the Star Theater in Portland while on tour. After performing, he met Leon Errol, the manager of the Orpheum Theatre. They quickly struck up a business relationship, and Leon taught Roscoe the ropes of show business.

Over two years, Roscoe bettered his acting abilities while touring and performing. In 1909, he got his first chance at the big screen—a new concept, as films had been in existence for less than twenty years. At the start, he had smaller, even uncredited, roles in the short films in which he appeared. But that didn't matter, as Roscoe was sharing the screen with his wife, actress Minta Durfee.

Minta and Roscoe first met in 1906, when she was a seventeen-year-old chorus girl. In 1908, they married in a location that was special to both—on stage after a show. Both pursued careers in show business, having worked in vaudeville and with Mack Sennett's comedy troupe. Joining the troupe just as movies became part of the job was Charlie Chaplin, considered the greatest silent film performer of all time. Minta's talent earned her the highly coveted role of Chaplin's first leading lady in his premiere film, *Making a Living*.

Through his work with the troupe, Roscoe became an extra with Keystone Pictures Studio. It didn't take long for executives to realize Roscoe was not meant to be hidden in the peripheries of their films—he was clearly a star. The special *something* noticed was the *Fatty* part of Roscoe. He had a way of using his weight; it was never to make fat jokes, but to break boundaries and turn expectations upside-down with his physicality.

His speed, flexibility, and strength were unexpected for someone his size. His weight of 275 pounds was jarring to audience members who had an average weight of 150 pounds. Like the actors who followed in his footsteps, such as Chris Farley and John Candy, Roscoe's weight was not damaging to his image or a hindrance to his success. He had perfected a way of presenting his weight so that it was never the punchline. In subsequent years, he appeared in dozens of one-reel comedies, usually playing a police officer. To everyone he worked with, he was a kind, gentle, and delightful man who made everyone laugh and had no qualms about sharing the screen. We have Roscoe to thank for Charlie Chaplin. The pair worked on bits together, with Roscoe teaching the newbie everything. Those lessons were not only about filmmaking, but about comedy as well. Roscoe helped create the iconic bowler-hat-and-baggy-pants costume for Charlie's "The Tramp" character, and he even let Chaplin use the iconic routine he created, known as the "Dance of the Dinner Rolls."

His popularity growing, Roscoe was eventually featured in longer, more prestigious productions. Besides dancing rolls, he also gave us the classic comedy routines of a pie in the face, pratfalls, and female impersonation. This led to Keystone Pictures giving him more creative control over his pictures and the ability to play leads. He was now greeted with "Fatty!" in public. As much as he appreciated his fans, he still didn't appreciate the nickname, and would remind them that his name was Roscoe.

After his success with Keystone, Paramount stepped in. They saw how his talent and affability filled theaters consistently, and they wanted in. Roscoe's current pay of nearly $1,500 a week was not of concern for the studio. To make sure they got him to sign, they offered an incredible, record-breaking contract. For his three years with Paramount, he would not only be given complete creative control, but he'd be making one million dollars a year. In today's money, the contract would be about $46,500,000—an unheard-of amount for the time.

Roscoe was the talk of Tinseltown with his $5,000-a-week salary ($78,000 today), an impossible amount to spend.

Not that he didn't try! There were many hands in the pot when it came to that kind of cash. Roscoe's agent of sorts, Joseph Schenck, took a thousand off the top. His manager, Lou Anger, took another 10 percent. From what remained, Roscoe gave five hundred dollars to Minta and set some aside for taxes. The rest went to Roscoe and his spending habits. Besides his $100,000 mansion ($1.5 million today), he had a love of cars. The large garage in his residence was filled with them. He owned at least six, including a $25,000 car that was believed to be the most elaborately equipped vehicle in the state of California.

His financial success also allowed him to invest in his passion. He had developed a close relationship with an up-and-coming comedian named Buster Keaton. Before finding fame on his own, Buster had been discovered by Roscoe, and just as he had with Chaplin, he took Buster under his wing, showing him all the tricks and tips of surviving their ruthless business. Roscoe then created the Comique Film Company. When it was time for him to fulfill the Paramount contract, he trusted Buster to take over production at Comique.

Roscoe wasn't focused just on helping his friends' careers. He had been busy acting in his own comedies, and had fallen in love with directing. This had him behind the camera nearly as often as he was being filmed. Writing, performing, directing—Roscoe could do, and was doing, it all.

Being a comedian, especially a physical one, doesn't come without risks. Sometimes falling bodies or a flung object can lead to injuries. In 1915, Roscoe was injured by a pitcher that was thrown from a second story, which he had been unable to dodge. The following year, he developed an infection in his leg that nearly led to amputation. Doctors were able to save the leg, but the morphine used for pain management was alleged to have remained a habit of Roscoe's. Similar whispers surrounded his alcohol use.

When September 1921 rolled around, the actor was ready for a break. So far, he hadn't been having the best week. His car was in the shop and, adding insult to injury, he'd accidentally sat on an acid-soaked rag in the garage while waiting for the repairs. The acid had burned through his pants, leaving second-degree burns on his buttocks. The pain had Roscoe wanting to cancel the ten-plus-hour drive to San Francisco he had planned for the weekend with friends Lowell Sherman and Fred Fishback, but Fishback wasn't having it; they got Roscoe a cushion and headed north. After what had to have been a painful drive, the three arrived at the St. Francis Hotel (now the Westin St. Francis) in Union Square. They settled into their connected rooms and began to enjoy their luxurious suite.

The drinking they were partaking in alone could have led to legal troubles, since this took place during Prohibition. In January 1920, the United States implemented the Eighteenth Amendment to the Constitution, which prohibited the sale, creation, and transportation of alcohol. The booze ban became one of the government's most difficult laws to enforce, due to bootleggers, speakeasies, and crime syndicates that found great financial success in providing illegal drinks to the masses seeking them. It wasn't until 1933 that the Twenty-first Amendment came along, repealing the Eighteenth and making drinking legal again.

Twenty-one months into Prohibition, the three men were enjoying their time in the hotel, making the most of the Labor Day weekend. More guests arrived on Monday. They were Alice Blake, Zey Prevost, Al Semnacher, Ira Fortlouis, Bambina Maude Delmont, and Virginia Rappe. Roscoe knew most of the attendees, and he also knew the women's reputations for being ladies who partied a little harder than he cared to. Not wanting to rain on the festivities, he didn't fight too hard against their entrance to room 1219. Lowell Sherman turned on the music, drinks were served, and the day of dancing and laughing carried on.

So who were these players in what would place Roscoe in the starring role of a personal horror? Alice Blake was in her mid-twenties at the time of the hotel party. She and Roscoe had been friends and coworkers for about a decade, costarring in comedies like *The Cook* and *Oh Doctor!* before she ventured into dramatic acting. She didn't fare so well in that genre, or when silent films transitioned into talkies; after nearly a hundred roles, her career would come to an end in 1935 with *Frisco Kid*. At the time of the party, she was the mother of a seven-year-old child conceived out of wedlock—a fact that would be used against her in the future.

Zey Prevost was a showgirl and actress as well, and was part of Mark Sennett's productions. Al Semnacher was the manager of Virginia Rappe, and he was rumored to be more than friends with some of his clients, including Virginia and Delmont.

Virginia Rappe (born Rapp) was an actress who was always working toward that big break. Her mother was from Chicago, but had gone to New York when she became pregnant with "illegitimate" Virginia. Eleven years after Mabel Rapp gave birth to her daughter, she died. Virginia was moved back to Chicago to live with her grandmother. At fourteen, she started a career in modeling, and within a few years, she moved to San Francisco, where she continued modeling for artists.

Those years in between were not kind to the young girl. A childhood filled with trauma and loss left Virginia struggling to make healthy decisions and connections. It's been reported that she'd had five abortions by age seventeen. It's also been rumored that she may have had a child whom she allowed to be placed in foster care, with variations saying that she did have a child, or that it only lived for a short while, or that she never gave birth at all.

In her early twenties, Virginia became engaged to fashion designer Robert Moscovitz. Shortly afterward, he was killed in a trolley accident. The loss of Robert was devastating, and Virginia left for Los Angeles, moving in with her aunt. The new location provided a fresh start for Virginia, who then added an "e" to her surname. Perhaps Rappe had more show business style, as she started to find more work, and even love. This time it was with director Henry Lehrman.

Virginia's relationship with Henry didn't provide peace, however. They would fight, break up, get back together, and repeat the cycle. There were whispers around town about them having lice (possibly crabs) and sexually transmitted infections, leading to them being kicked off movie sets out of fear of contamination. In September 1921, they had their final break-up.

Then there was Bambina Maude Delmont, or "Maude" as she preferred. She too was well-known, but infamous rather than famous. Maude had no qualms when it came to extortion, blackmail, or retrieving private information regarding celebrities. She had a rap sheet that included charges of fraud and bigamy, and it was her unexpected presence that was most concerning to Roscoe, giving him pause before allowing her to join the party. Dressed in his bathrobe and pajamas, all he could hope was that his other guests wouldn't be alarmed at the sight of them, or that the gossips wouldn't alert authorities to the alcohol-laden gathering.

On Monday, September 5, at three o'clock in the afternoon, Roscoe was planning to leave his own party to visit a family friend who lived in town. But before he could do so, he claimed to have found Virginia on his bathroom floor, passed out and ill. When he lifted her up, she wheezed one word: "Water." Roscoe provided the water, assuming she was drunk. He then placed her on his bed and went about getting ready. By the time he was dressed and back in the bedroom, Virginia had rolled off the bed onto the floor. Picking her up, he placed her back on the bed, recalling a trick taught to him by his friend Buster Keaton. If you aren't sure if someone is faking being unconscious, you place ice on their thigh and their response will provide the answer. With that in mind, Roscoe retrieved some ice. It would serve two purposes: Virginia could use it for hydration, and he could test her legitimacy. Now at her side, he took a piece of ice and placed it on her thigh (some later reports say he placed it on her vulva). He realized she was genuinely unwell when she didn't react.

Just then, Maude Delmont entered the room and saw the ice being held to Virginia's intimate areas. Assuming Virginia had simply passed out in response to the alcohol, Roscoe and Maude weren't overly concerned until Virginia began screaming, writhing, and tearing at her clothes. Knowing his career could be over if he was caught with booze, Roscoe wanted her removed from his room.

Virginia was taken to another room, then placed in a cold bath in hope that it would calm her out of the frenzy of pain she appeared to be experiencing. The hotel doctor was called, but since he wasn't available, another doctor was brought in. He too felt there was nothing more going on than intoxication. Virginia was returned to bed, and her friends returned to drinking.

Roscoe was finally able to leave to meet up with his friend. Returning later, he found the hotel doctor had arrived to check on Virginia. She was still in pain, so he treated her with morphine. The next morning, the doctor returned with more morphine and a catheter. Virginia had not been urinating, which concerned him. Another doctor was called. This one wasn't through the hotel, though—it was Maude's friend. Seeing no other issues besides her pain and urination problem, he too tried to alleviate both.

The next day, Roscoe and his friends checked out of the St. Francis Hotel. He was ready to put both the party and the city behind him.

Now back in Los Angeles, Roscoe didn't give Virginia's welfare another thought—that is until ten-thirty in the evening on Friday, September 9. As he was leaving his home, he was swarmed by reporters inquiring about an orgy he had held at a hotel. He was unaware that as early as Tuesday, rumors of a booze-filled, raucous, raunchy orgy having taken place in his hotel room were already swirling.

Wanted for questioning in San Francisco, Roscoe made the trip again to meet with investigators, assuming he would be on his way as soon as their questions were answered. That's when he learned the fate of twenty-five-year-old Virginia Rappe.

After being sick and in pain for days, she was finally taken to a hospital on Thursday, the 8th. By Friday, she was dead from an unknown cause. What *was* known was that there had been a party with the world's biggest film star, and one of his guests had expired under suspicious circumstances.

Reporters soon found Maude Delmont—who was still under doctor's orders as "recovering"—and she had information to share. According to Maude, her friend Virginia was not only dead, but she had also been murdered, and there was no mystery as to the culprit. It was Roscoe "Fatty" Arbuckle who had killed Virginia Rappe.

After Maude was questioned by investigators, she went on to tell this harrowing tale at the coroner's inquest. The woman known for hanging around celebrities in order to sell dirt on them had suddenly become the only witness to what would be the most scandalous trial in Hollywood.

According to Maude, she was friends with Virginia, and the two of them, along with Al Semacher, met up in Los Angeles on Sunday, September 4, with alcohol and a plan to drive to San Francisco. On the morning of the 5th, Roscoe called their hotel room, requesting the presence of Virginia. After she arrived, another call was made for the pair to join her. Maude agreed that yes, Roscoe did initially exhibit some hesitation when it came to their attendance. In the room was a table, with guests Sherman,

Fortlouis, and Fishback seated around it. It being early in the day, two of the men, including Arbuckle, were still wearing pajamas and bathrobes.

Maude's memory, she insisted, was perfectly clear, even if she had been drinking. She was certain the ten whiskey drinks she'd consumed had not affected her ability to recount the events that took place. She was also certain Virginia didn't drink, but later said her friend had three gin-and-orange-juice cocktails.

Later in the day, two more guests arrived: showgirls Alice Blake and Zey Prevost. As music was being played, Virginia used the bathroom connected to Roscoe's room. When she came out, he was standing there and grabbed her. Dragging Virginia into his room, Maude claimed he said, "I've waited for you for five years, and now I've got you!" before slamming the door.

Ever the loyal friend, Maude said she used the heels of her shoes to kick at the door, screaming for it to be opened and for her friend to be freed. It wasn't until an hour later that she was finally let in. By then, the silk pajamas Roscoe was wearing were drenched in sweat, and he was wearing Virginia's hat. Virginia was lying on the bed, also soaked in sweat—be it her own or run-off from "Fatty"—and screaming, "I am hurt! I am dying! Roscoe did it!" That's when the remaining partygoers removed her clothes and placed her in the cold bath.

When this story was told, it was William Randolph Hearst, the media tycoon, who was first to show no hesitation in printing what he felt would sell papers with no concern regarding the validity of any information. Headlines about an "orgy" with Hollywood's biggest star were selling papers faster than they could be printed. This only encouraged the smear campaign against Roscoe. It also swayed the public—so much so that, by the time he returned to San Francisco to meet with investigators, he was guilty of murder in the public's eye.

The grand jury heard from nurses from the hotel—Vera Cumberland, Jean Jameson, and Martha Hamilton. Vera withdrew herself from the treatment as she felt the doctors were not providing Virginia with adequate care. Jean made contradictory statements about what Virginia had said. Doctors involved claimed Maude stepped in as a sort of power of attorney for the sickly Virginia. Al Semnacher, the manager, claimed not to have heard screaming, but that he did hear her say "Roscoe hurt me."

The grand jury almost didn't hear from two star witnesses, Alice Blake and Zey Prevost. Alice had gone missing in the time between the party and the inquest. After Virginia's death, both women were put in the voluntary custody of a Mrs. John Duffy, who noted that while they were out in town, men would approach Alice, trying to get information about the case. When they learned her chaperone would have to be present for a conversation, the men retreated. At some point Alice got a ride to her mother's. As officials searched for her, it was announced that, if she didn't appear by ten o'clock the morning of the interview, the district attorney would issue a warrant for her mother and hold Alice on bond. This was enough motivation to get her to return.

Zey Prevost was also a reluctant witness. She didn't deny that Roscoe had been in the room with Virginia, but this information came only after the threat of a perjury charge. Getting both women to testify was quite the undertaking, but nothing was too much for District Attorney, and promising candidate for California governor, Matthew Brady.

DA Brady didn't just want the governorship; he knew a case of this magnitude could get him on a path to the White House. This was less than two years into Prohibition, and at the start of the public's desire to censor the "filth" they felt was coming from the motion picture industry. Brady knew his case was entirely dependent on the questionable testimony of Maude Delmont, but that didn't deter him from seeking murder charges.

Brady was smart enough to not have Maude testify before the grand jury, which is why Alice and Zey were so important to the case—so important that Brady had investigators break them down. Alice was the first to crack. Though she and Zey held firm that they felt no wrongdoing had occurred at the party, when authority figures threatened to have Alice's "illegitimate" son taken away, she agreed to sign a statement. Even then she pushed back, as the first statement claimed Virginia had said, "Roscoe's hurting me." Alice only agreed to sign when the statement read, "I am dying. *He* hurt me."

For Zey, it was Alice folding paired with the threat of perjury that pushed her into testifying. She would later say that she and her family were removed from their house in the middle of the night, during which the threat of perjury charges was made. Even after all that, she refused to agree with Maude's statement, also holding firm that Virginia was fully dressed on the bed.

On September 13, Roscoe "Fatty" Arbuckle was indicted for the manslaughter of Virginia Rappe. The judge hadn't felt there was enough evidence for a murder charge, perhaps not even enough for manslaughter. His reasoning for not throwing out the case was that he felt there had to be some sort of consequence for the public figure who had broken the law and perhaps believed he was above it.

That same day, Maude and Al were at San Francisco's detective bureau for questioning, and they made quite a scene. Getting into a shouting match about her hotel room bill, she hit Al in the face with her purse before leaving. No charges came of it, and she was soon kicked out of the St. Francis due to lack of payment.

When the medical examiner's report came back, it was bad news for District Attorney Brady. Dr. William Ophuls found Virginia's cause of death to be the result of a ruptured bladder—a bladder that had been cystic since Virginia was young. Even though there had already been tales of Virginia thinking she was pregnant by her estranged fiancé and that she had been seeking abortion assistance from Roscoe, there was no physical sign of a pregnancy, abortion, or sexual assault. No bruises. No external injuries. Just a ruptured bladder that went untreated for days.

This put a huge wrinkle in Brady's plan. It was believed Roscoe hadn't killed Virginia, but perhaps his weight or physical treatment had led to the bladder issue. Thus began the multiple-trial saga of *The People of the State of California v. Roscoe Arbuckle*.

Before the first trial could commence on November 14, 1921, Roscoe was already watching his star fall. Movie theaters pulled his films, especially one of his newer releases that was currently playing: *Life of the Party*. He was interviewed by the federal Prohibition director and investigated by the Anti-Saloon League for Prohibition-related charges. He was voted out of the exclusive Los Angeles Athletic Club by his peers. Knowing he had done no wrong, aware of the lack of evidence, and with his wife Minta at his side, he faced the judge, jury, and public with unflappable stoicism.

Although Brady knew this case could make his career, he was keenly aware there wasn't a strong case against Arbuckle, so he had his assistant district attorneys handle the trial. During the three weeks of testimony, more than sixty witnesses were called to the stand, none of whom was Maude Delmont. Eighteen of the witnesses were doctors. They focused on Virginia's health history, including the rumored abortions from when she was younger, her chronically cystic bladder, the possible gonorrhea she was dealing with at the time of her death, and the wounds she was believed to have suffered. Just as with the medical examiner, there was no sign of rape by Roscoe or from any foreign objects. By the time the trial was underway, the story had transmogrified into a tale of Roscoe not only grabbing Virginia and pulling her into a room, but raping her with a Coca-Cola bottle or chunk of ice (depending on who was telling the story), and as he attempted to rape her on the hotel bed, his abundant weight had crushed her, causing the explosion of her bladder.

On December 4, 1921, after forty-four hours of deliberation, the jury was declared deadlocked. This was thanks to two jurors. After the first vote of 8–4 in favor of acquittal, the next vote was 10–2. Juror Thomas Kilkenny just couldn't decide, and went back and forth on his vote. In the end, he claimed to have received phone calls from people related to the case, telling him to acquit the actor.

For juror Helen Hubbard, it was a much different scenario. She refused to look at the evidence. She would not discuss the case with her fellow jurors, simply saying, "I'll vote guilty until Hell freezes over." She didn't believe the stories told by witnesses. There was a conversation about a fingerprint on one of the doorknobs, which she felt was Roscoe's because the defense didn't dispute it. Interestingly enough, Hubbard's husband was a lawyer who did business with the San Francisco district attorney's office, and her mother-in-law was the first California Regent of the Daughters of the American Revolution. Both facts raised eyebrows, and questions as to why the defense allowed her to remain on the jury, causing speculation as to what her biases might have been. San Francisco wouldn't have concerns about her serving on future juries, though. She told newspapers that being involved in this case was "the most trying ordeal of my life," suggesting that no sane woman should leave her home to deal with the horrors of the judicial system.

Going to trial again on January 11, 1922, both sides hoped for a different outcome. Besides Virginia's health issues, there were witnesses who spoke about her very peculiar habit when she drank. A neighbor of Virginia's took the stand, sharing that on multiple occasions she had gotten drunk, stripped off her clothes, and run outside, claiming to be hurt. There was more information uncovered by the defense, but Roscoe wouldn't allow his team to disclose it as he wished only to clear his name, not to smear Virginia's.

Unlike the first trial, Roscoe didn't take the stand in his own defense. His team now knew just how weak the prosecution's case was, so they stayed focused on Virginia and the discrediting of the fingerprints found in the hotel room. As with the first trial, Maude was not invited as a witness, even though her testimony had led to there being an investigation in the first place. After closing arguments, the jury took the case to deliberate, this time taking forty hours.

The initial vote was 9–3 in favor of guilt. On February 3, the final vote was 10–2, with jurors Lee Dolson and Clem R. Brownsberger holding out for acquittal. Frustrated to have to dismiss yet another case, Brady had to stand firm. He even went so far as to say that, if the vote had been in favor of acquittal, he would have dropped the charges. One can only assume that by this point, Brady hoped that would be the end of the case and he could leave the mess behind him.

March 13, 1922, saw the start of the third trial against Roscoe Arbuckle. He again took the stand, telling the exact same account as he had before. He had found Virginia and attempted to aid her until Maude excused him. When both sides finished on April 12, it took the jury a mere five minutes to reach a verdict. Not guilty.

Not only did the jury feel Roscoe didn't have any involvement in Virginia's death, but there was also no evidence whatsoever that warranted the arrests and public destruction that resulted. Those five minutes were not even spent deliberating. They used that time to construct a statement:

"Acquittal is not enough for Roscoe Arbuckle. We feel that a great injustice has been done to him. We feel also that it was only our plain duty to give him this exoneration, under the evidence, for there was not the slightest proof adduced to connect him in any way with the commission of a crime. He was manly throughout the case, and told a straightforward story on the witness stand, which we all believed. The happening at the hotel was an unfortunate affair for which Arbuckle, so the evidence shows, was in no way responsible. We wish him success…. Roscoe Arbuckle is entirely innocent and free from all blame."

A lot has changed surrounding this case in the last hundred years. It was learned that Maude had sent two telegrams to friends when Virginia had fallen ill. They read: "We have Roscoe Arbuckle in a hole here. Chance to make some money out of him." And Al Semnacher, the manager, was a lover not only to Virginia, but to Maude as well, and it was believed that his invite to the women was all part of a plan to blackmail Roscoe. Perhaps this was something just he and Maude concocted, or perhaps someone at the studio was concerned about the money they were spending and needed Roscoe's value to drop. As for Maude's claim of kicking at the door for an hour to save her friend? She had actually been locked in a bathroom herself—with Lowell Sherman—for that hour. What exactly they had been doing is unknown, but one could assume they were enjoying the lack of inhibition the alcohol was providing.

History has also taught us that William Randolph Hearst wasn't too fond of facts if they didn't sell newspapers. Seeing record sales thanks to the multi-layered scandal consisting of sex, stars, and spirits, the stories of Fatty crushing a virginal girl after raping her (the ironic scenario not being lost on reporters covering the death of Virginia *Rappe*) and the possible use of Coke bottles or ice were all that mattered. Even when Roscoe's charges had been initially reduced from murder to manslaughter, the papers continued to exhibit the shock and horror of a murder.

In the end, Roscoe said he would be planning a return to the cinema, should the people show interest. But the damage had been done. Master copies of his films were destroyed. Boycotts continued. The plea of the jury to recognize the wrongdoing fell on the deaf ears of a public who had already held a court of opinion and found him unforgivably guilty.

Roscoe was now thirty-five, out of work and out of money. He owed $700,000 ($11.5 million today) to his legal team and had a five-hundred-dollar fine to pay for transporting alcohol from Los Angeles to San Francisco. This was all transpiring as the public outcry for censorship in films was nascent. Not wanting the government to control what could be released, the Motion Picture Producers and Distributors of America (MPPDA) was created as a means of self-governance. Roscoe "Fatty" Arbuckle was blacklisted and seen as the poster child for what can happen when you have money, are a star, and drink alcohol.

Now seen as inappropriate, all of Roscoe's films were banned. Using the pseudonym William B. Goodrich (a name believed to be chosen as a joke or perhaps a reminder—Will B. Good), he was able to find work behind the camera as a director.

Desperate to perform for an audience, Roscoe returned to his roots in vaudeville, touring and receiving the love and applause he craved. Although estranged from him, his wife Minta had been by his side throughout the scandal, one report even claiming she had been shot at while outside the courthouse due to the extreme public disdain for her husband. She filed for divorce in 1923. The two remained friends, and she only ever declared him to be kind and caring. The divorce was due to Roscoe meeting and falling in love with Doris Deane while on the vaudeville circuit. They married in early 1925, divorcing in 1929 on grounds of desertion and cruelty.

Through the years, Roscoe continued to work with his close friends Charlie Chaplin, Buster Keaton, and others who still supported and believed in his innocence. He loved writing and directing, but struggled with depression and alcohol, as he still couldn't do what he really loved— perform. In 1932, he married his third wife, Addie McPhail. As it had been a decade since the scandal, Warner Bros. was willing to take a chance, and signed Roscoe to a six-short-reel deal after a trial "talkie" showed he still had fans willing to watch his work. This was not to say his comeback would be easy. These new comedies weren't allowed in British cinemas due to his perceived continued indecency.

With four of the six comedies released and doing well, things were looking up for Roscoe. On June 28, 1933, he wrapped the final film in the series. Warner Bros. had been so pleased with the performance of the films they invited him to sign a contract for a starring role in a feature film. Celebrating the conclusion of filming, his new contract, and his one-year wedding anniversary, Roscoe, Addie, and friends went out to dinner. It's reported that Roscoe's excitement was palpable as he said, "This is the best day of my life."

That was June 29. After the jubilee, he and his wife arrived home and went to bed. Suffering a heart attack in his sleep, Roscoe never woke up. He was forty-six years old.

Historians and film lovers alike have tried their best to keep Roscoe "Fatty" Arbuckle's memory alive. For those who feel he was wronged, they celebrate him for not only the work he did on screen, but what he taught those we consider the greatest of the time. Yet after all these years, so much footage has been lost and jokes about "Fatty" crushing a girl to death remain, tarnishing any hope that he may be remembered for his humor, not his size and his scandals.

Parts of this story can feel distant—Prohibition, the silent film era—but there are so many aspects that remain prevalent today: trials being held by a public that has been informed by media outlets only looking to scandalize and sell; political motivations ignoring calls for justice; movies and alcohol being demonized and blamed for tragedy; a woman's history being used against her in a trial that's supposed to protect her; a star being canceled before the truth surrounding the situation can be clarified.

Virginia Rappe was more than just the girl who was at the "wild hotel orgy" with a big star. She was a fashion designer and feminist. She was one of the first women to wear a tuxedo as part of women's fashion. She made "peace hats," hoping the dove wings adorning her headwear would inspire the wearer to find peace in a world that never offered her any. She was so much more than her health history, and more than "the story that sold more papers than the sinking of the Lusitania."

Roscoe was more than "Fatty." He was known as a caring man who would use his success to do what he could to help fellow artists find success. His comic genius will resonate for generations, even if we don't realize he's the one who deserves the credit.

JIM FIXED IT:
THE SHOCKING CRIMES
OF JIMMY SAVILE

MARK FRYERS

"You're not the only one," Savile responds to a journalist telling him that he scared him as a child.

One of my earliest childhood memories involved the television set and abject fear. A show was aired on a Sunday evening, *Play It Safe*, designed to show children and their parents the dangers encountered in everyday situations, particularly around the house and home. It featured graphic pictures of children who had been horribly burned, maimed, or otherwise injured, accompanied by eerie and dramatic music that made household objects take on a sinister character. It terrified me like no other program I saw on TV at that age, and I had to either look away or ask to be removed from the room while it was on.

Play It Safe was presented by one Jimmy Savile, with his name in the opening titles suffixed by OBE (Order of the British Empire) to remind viewers of his status as a trusted national institution. He also contributed to the "Stranger Danger" campaign, warning children not to speak to or go off with strangers.

Like many children who grew up in 1970s and 1980s Britain, Jimmy Savile was a constant public presence in my childhood, mainly through his successful TV show *Jim'll Fix It* (1975–1994), itself something of a national institution. In this series, this odd-looking and odd-sounding, aging, platinum-haired Yorkshireman would present the show sitting in an armchair like the kindly avuncular figure he was projected to be, distributing medals to children lucky enough to be on the show and to have their wishes granted by him. Jim made children's dreams come true on the show—he literally "fixed it" for them.

Yet the man who made children's dreams come true lived a dual existence. He "fixed" a lot of other things. As one of the most prolific serial sexual predators in British history, and certainly the most high-profile, Jimmy Savile is now a figurehead for all that is evil in society—the stuff of true nightmares. Following his death in 2011, revelations about his "private" life erupted in a stream of allegations that could scarcely be believed. These earth-shattering revelations sent ruptures and reverberations throughout every institution that had seemingly allowed him to get away with his offenses, from the NHS, the BBC, and the police force to the Royal Family. These ripples continue to be felt to this day.

James Savile

"Nobody will ever know what you have done for this country, Jimmy."
—Prince Charles, eightieth birthday message to Jimmy Savile, 2005

"Jimmy, I and millions more salute you. God bless you."
—Margaret Thatcher

A middle-aged man in swimming shorts, sunglasses, and gold chain stood at the entrance of Rampton Secure Hospital, waiting to make a beeline for any of the psychiatric facility's young female patients or their visiting relatives and entice them into a "trip" in his motorhome, also parked on the secure grounds. He was not qualified to be there, had no right to be there, and certainly shouldn't have been allowed to do what he was doing there. But the man was a celebrity, a charity worker, and later, a national institution with links to the most powerful in society, so whatever he did to these underage and vulnerable children in his van was both an open secret for many and ignored by others. It was only after his death that this country *did* know what Jimmy had done.

In England, we are known for loving eccentrics, and there was no more eccentric individual in the latter part of the twentieth century than the man born James Wilson Savile. A constant fixture on TV and radio, and in newspapers and other media, everyone could recognize the bleached-haired, cigar-chomping ex-disc-jockey, usually attired in tracksuits or other attention-grabbing garb. Even on radio, the northeast accent accompanied by verbal tics, halting speech patterns, vocal gymnastics, noises, and catchphrases ("How's about that, then?" and "jingle, jangle"), he was unique to such a degree that many comedians routinely had a "Savile" in their repertoire of impersonations, which made him an even more ubiquitous presence.

In common with many British "stars," Savile was virtually unknown outside the British Isles, especially in America. But Savile claimed to be fine with that—a big fish in a small pond.

Savile was born on October 31, 1926, to a mother who turned forty the next day. He remained very close to her for the rest of her life, and claimed that the reason he didn't try to "crack" America was so that he wouldn't be too far away from the woman he called "the Duchess." Others attest that she had a domineering presence over her son, one that he later held over others.

Savile would later romanticize his life to journalists, but it was clear to others that it was marked by sickness and unorthodoxy. An early encounter with death came about due to a serious injury that initially refused to heal. Savile would look back at this survival as an indication that he was somehow divinely "chosen."

Having few friends, and with his mother being a devout Catholic, he spent a lot of time at the St. Joseph's Home for the Aged with sick and dying patients. This morbid curiosity intensified during World War II, where the teenaged Savile witnessed death and maiming in the streets caused by German bombing raids. He later claimed to struggle to empathize with those who had lost loved ones during the conflict, exhibiting sociopathic tendencies that were to punctuate his adult life. Indeed, this early preoccupation with death, while remaining distant from the emotions that usually accompany it, puts him in common with many serial murderers.

Savile also claimed to have been shaped by his experiences allegedly working in the mines as a "Bevin Boy" during the war, in which there was a shortage of adult workers to mine coal for the war effort. Here, he worked a solitary job which he claimed afforded him time to read books that he smuggled in inside secret compartments in his coat. He also claimed to have started attending work in outrageous and incongruous attire, which got him noticed as being an eccentric and "different"—a tactic he was to deploy successfully throughout his subsequent career. An accident in the mine left him temporarily bedridden—a chance to reflect on his mortality.

Doubt has subsequently been cast on Savile's own accounts of this period, and indeed as to whether he was a Bevin Boy at all. It is believed that this was a smokescreen for his actions making money on the black market during the war, a rumor he didn't deny.

Either way, eccentricity and sharp practice were to lead Savile on a successful career that entwined with the cultural "big-bang" moments of postwar Britain—through youth culture, pop music, radio, television, and beyond.

Power

Following his recovery from whatever injury he did, in fact, sustain, physical fitness became one of the guiding principles in Savile's life (aside from his immoderate intake of cigars). His next steps were into the world of professional cycling, and he ended up taking part in the first official Tour of Britain cycle race in 1951.

Yet cycling itself became a distraction from the attention Savile could gain from publicity stunts, something that got him noticed by the newspapers. By his own admission, he once threw away the opportunity to win a race when he spotted some young ladies having a picnic and insisted on joining them. It was an early sign that his libido and opportunism overrode any other concerns.

Seeing the craze for dances and the emerging rock-and-roll phenomenon making its way across the pond, Savile experimented by putting on dances in local halls in which patrons could dance to the latest records, rather than to a live band, as was customary. Moving on from this, he was appointed assistant manager of the Mecca Locarno Dance Hall in Leeds. Mecca, a chain that owned some of the biggest dance halls in the country, quickly saw the potential of Savile's experiments with record dances. Promoted to take over the Mecca Palais-de-Danse, Ilford, located in London's East End, Savile made the bold claim that he employed the first twin turntable in history. He later moved to manager of the Mecca Manchester Plaza Dance Hall before a triumphant hometown return as manager of the Leeds Mecca Locarno, where he established a Sunday dance club for teenagers. He also introduced a period of the evening in which young lovers could nuzzle each other—labeled "smooch time," which was likely mildly scandalous at the time.

It was no doubt an exciting time to be young. At the Plaza, he ran a talent competition for young bands. One group, the Fourtones, was allegedly cautioned by Savile to only enter the competition once a month, as they were guaranteed to win. The Fourtones would later become The Hollies.

The maverick, uniquely attired Northerner was also attracting attention. It was here that he started to bleach the color out of his hair—a signature look that set him apart from the crowd. It was also here that Savile got his first taste of real power—first by controlling the rhythm and tempo at which the patrons danced on the dance floor, and second, by building a powerful entourage of bouncers and minders to do his bidding. Savile also made it a point to get friendly and on good terms with all sections of society. Another thing he established was something he called the "Friday Morning Club"—a meeting of high-profile local figures at his flat, including many senior police officers. These associations were key in keeping lurid accusations at bay, as was his schmoozing of senior police on Saturday nights.

With this power and security, Savile began his alternate career as a prolific sex offender.

Despite this, or perhaps because of it, Savile's star ascended. Several appearances on television, including the popular *Juke Box Jury* music show in 1959, led to a DJ slot on the new Radio Luxembourg. As the BBC had a monopoly on radio broadcasting at this time, pirate broadcasters found ingenious ways of circumventing these rules by broadcasting outside of UK territory in international waters, at old military forts on the Thames, or on ships anchored off the British coast. It seems appropriate for Savile to find his natural home on a station that was based on subterfuge, evasion, and illegality—or at least, a bending of the rules.

The brash Northerner was an instant hit in an era known for clipped Southern accents. Savile was quite literally a new and unique voice to spearhead the invading pop music and youth culture, anticipating the winds of change that were to sweep through the British establishment and herald the "Swinging Sixties."

Icons

By this time, Jimmy Savile was rubbing shoulders with the twentieth century's biggest icons, or those who were to become so. In 1960, he flew to Los Angeles to present Elvis Presley with a gold record on behalf of

Decca Records. Never one for modesty, he had a photo taken with himself and "the King" enlarged and placed outside the Mecca Locarno in Leeds.

With his ascending fame coinciding with the attendant rise of the Merseybeat bands, Savile appeared as himself in the Gerry and the Pacemakers 1964 film *Ferry Cross the Mersey*. More importantly, he worked with The Beatles on several occasions. He was the compere for their Christmas shows at the Hammersmith Odeon in 1964. A year prior, Paul McCartney had spotted Savile in the crowd at their Christmas show in Bradford and dedicated a song to him. They shared tea the next day at the Empire Theatre in Liverpool. Everyone seemingly had a strange tale to tell about Savile, and McCartney was no different. McCartney recalls the band giving Savile a lift home in their van after one of their early gigs, where Savile proudly regaled them with stories of his black-market exploits during the war. When they dropped Savile outside his home, they asked to be invited in for a coffee, but were refused—something McCartney regarded as "suspect." It certainly sounded like a man with something to hide.

Savile also worked with The Beatles' supposed rivals in those days, the Rolling Stones. They have an even more sinister story to tell about the then-DJ and "personality." As he was an early champion of the band on his radio show and in print columns, the Stones arrived to play for Savile at the Top Ten Club at Belle Vue in Manchester. When Savile was informed that the band refused to play due to their instruments being lost in transit, he revealed his true colors. With two of his biggest minders alongside him, he hissed at the band, "You've got the time it takes this stage to revolve to make your mind up…. If you're not going to play, you're going to be unconscious because my minders are going to chin [punch] all of you…. And I'll throw you to the fucking audience. I guarantee you that." The Stones ended up performing.

His success eventually led to the BBC calling. Keen to capitalize on the zeitgeist of pop music, executives decided to launch a show that showcased the charts and the artists in front of a young studio audience. The show, *Top of the Pops*, was to become one of the longest-running and most successful programs on British television—a national institution in itself.

When it came to selecting a host, Savile was a name that naturally was put forward to front the show. Tellingly, there was a lot of objection at the BBC to Savile's name at the time, and he was not the producer's first choice, with some suggesting that he was both "dodgy" and "heavy" in his methods. Regardless, Savile was selected as host, and went on to present the show intermittently until the mid-1970s. The first show was recorded in Manchester, and featured The Beatles and the Rolling Stones. With first-night nerves, the show's recording was said to be somewhat "ramshackle," but it was the Stones themselves who suggested Savile was the glue that bound the show together, with Keith Richards claiming that he "energized" it and kept it all running smoothly.

Savile was to become known for his energy, be it marathon-running, raising money for charity, or otherwise. Indeed, he led an itinerant and nomadic lifestyle, something that was showcased in his long-running BBC radio series *Savile's Travels*, which he recorded between trips down to London to tape *Top of the Pops*. Although Savile kept several residences, he was very rarely in one place at one time and preferred to live out of his specially outfitted motorhome, which he parked everywhere—from King's Cross, BBC Television Centre in London, and Broadmoor psychiatric hospital to outside Buckingham Palace itself. Something that was seen as merely another offshoot of Savile's eccentricity was actually a smokescreen for his opportunistic offending. In Savile's own words, "I tramp around the country like a gray timber wolf," selecting an aptly predatory simile.

Savile continued to be a popular face on television, and increasing rumors of wrongdoing, even on BBC premises, did nothing to derail his TV career as it continued its ascendancy. The time eventually came for him to stop representing the nation's youth on *Top of the Pops*, and he switched from this to the program that was to define him, in my and many others' eyes: *Jim'll Fix It*. In 1972, Savile was awarded an OBE by the Queen. He was even described as the "spearhead" of the BBC's Christian attack on upholding standards, serving on numerous watchdog panels. It marked the move toward Savile becoming something of a national institution, a fact that was to buffer him from an attendant groundswell of suspicion.

Charity Champion and National Institution

Jimmy Savile presented *Jim'll Fix It* from a specially made armchair, giving him the appearance of a kindly uncle or grandfather, his long, bleached hair now making him look like something of an aging beatnik. Although he was described as the nation's "Santa Claus," he had very little interaction with the children who went on the program (something he engineered himself), instead simply handing out special *Jim Fixed It For Me* medals to the children who got to drive steam trains or meet their favorite pop idols in the studio (or in pre-filmed sequences on location). These medals passed into popular British culture, becoming coveted playground items.

Savile's first major foray into charitable as well as health institutions originally began in the early 1960s, when he was invited by the chief porter of Leeds General Infirmary to help promote the launch of the hospital radio station. He was soon volunteering as a porter himself, wheeling the bodies of deceased patients to the mortuary, often in the early hours of the morning. If this seemed like strange behavior for a celebrity, it was a whisper rather than an open rumor and viewed as a rare example of a celebrity "giving something back." For Savile, it firstly provided continuity with an obsession with death that had begun in childhood—"I've got an aptitude for dead people"—and secondly, provided access to vulnerable patients he could manipulate.

Savile also had access to Rampton, another secure psychiatric hospital in the Midlands. Here he would organize trips out for the patients. At the same time, he began visiting Duncroft, a school in Surrey for gifted but troubled young girls, offering presents, rides in his car, and tickets to TV shows.

Stoke Mandeville was likely Savile's greatest public triumph. The hospital, which sits in the Home County of Buckinghamshire, was famous for being the originator of the Paralympics with the Stoke Mandeville Games. It was also my local hospital, where I and my family frequently visited for treatment at a time when Savile had the run of the place. There were, we now know, definite suspicions of wrongdoing among the staff, but at the time I only heard about the good Savile had done for the institution, where he began volunteering as a porter in 1969.

It was hard to deny. Savile was almost single-handedly responsible for the successful fundraising and building of a world-leading spinal injury clinic at Stoke Mandeville, opened by Prince Charles and Princess Diana in 1983, at a cost of more than ten million pounds. Beginning in 1980, at a time of economic austerity and funding cutbacks to healthcare, Savile took the initiative and galvanized all his contacts and "clout" (including, according to his secretary, threats and intimidation on occasion) to launch a three-year national fundraising campaign that included convincing the Secretary of State for Health to part with half a million pounds. The campaign was the definition of success by every measure, nudging Savile from national institution toward national treasure.

It seems strange, then, that nurses were privately instructing children to pretend to be asleep when this bleach-haired messiah prowled the wards late at night.

National Treasure

Savile's charitable endeavors at Stoke Mandeville had gotten the attention of some very powerful people. In the early 1980s, Britain's new prime minister, Margaret Thatcher, was looking for examples of personal enterprise and achievement, and she began to view Jimmy Savile as the very embodiment of the "virtues" she wanted to instill in her new "Enterprise Britain." Appearing a few years earlier on *Jim'll Fix It*, she had asked him to "fix it" for her to become prime minister. In return, she campaigned tirelessly on his behalf for a knighthood. Again, it is interesting that for several years her efforts were knocked back by the Honours Committee who, for whatever reason, just felt that he wasn't fit to be a Knight of the Realm.

There were plenty of others who did, it seemed, from the higher echelons of British cultural life. Savile's first introduction into the Royal Family was via his charity endeavors with the Royal Marines. He became the first civilian to be granted an Honorary Royal Commando Green Beret after he completed the grueling training in 1969. Savile claimed that Lord Mountbatten didn't know who he was, but they quickly developed a rapport, and Mountbatten saw Savile as someone who likewise had a good rapport with the public. Being the "favorite uncle" of Prince Charles, the heir to the throne, Mountbatten was likely responsible for introducing the unlikely pair, seeing Savile's charisma as something that might rub off on the publicly awkward Prince of Wales.

Savile was moving in elevated circles. In 1990, he would receive an honorary Papal knighthood from the Vatican for his charitable work. Likewise, Savile's reputation went into a higher gear, mainly thanks to the ceaseless charity work he embarked upon, which wedded his avuncular image from *Jim'll Fix It* with that of a tireless campaigner for the sick and infirm.

Similarly, back in 1975, Savile piggybacked on a location sequence for the *Jim'll Fix It* Christmas special to Israel to make similar overtures for peace in Palestine, something he clearly exaggerated. In his 1979 book, *God'll Fix It*, Savile appears to compare himself to Jesus Christ; it is clear that he felt his fame put him on another level, something helped by being officially designated an "Official Friend of Israel." It's also clear that this feeling of invincibility was even more of an incentive to abuse the unprecedented power it now seems inconceivable he could have been given.

By the 1980s, it would have been difficult to argue. As Dan Davies points out in his 2014 book *In Plain Sight: The Life and Lies of Jimmy Savile*, Savile's ascendance into elevated circles can be evidenced by one day in July 1981, in which he spent the day at Royal Ascot organizing Prince Charles' showjumping endeavors for the Stoke Mandeville appeal, and then spent the evening as a guest of Prime Minister Margaret Thatcher and her husband Dennis. Later that year, he was invited to spend Christmas at Chequers with the Thatchers. The following year, he was extended the same invite for New Year's.

Meanwhile, Savile's association with the Royals continued apace, mainly by virtue of his association with Stoke Mandeville. If the Green Berets had hastened his entry into the inner circle, then the hospital allowed for him to consolidate it. After Prince Charles visited Stoke Mandeville in 1977, the two became "friends" through their mutual concern for charities for the disabled. Princess Diana would later describe Savile as her husband's "mentor," but it didn't stop there. He and Diana would go on long walks around the wards discussing matters, and she wrote to him regularly. He successfully persuaded her to appear on television as part of the anti-drugs "just say no" initiative. Janet Cope, Savile's private secretary at the hospital, claimed "Princess Diana was very fond of him."

So close was he to the royal pair that when their relationship hit the buffers, it was Savile who helped try to reconcile them. He invited them to Dyfed, Wales, in May 1989 to publicly comfort the victims of flooding. Here he managed to get the two speaking to each other for the first time—"an unlikely Royal peacemaker," in trusted royal journalist Andrew Morton's words. He also referred to Charles as "His Nibs," an incredibly colloquial way to speak about the heir apparent, but demonstrative of the sway Savile now held in powerful circles. He would frequently break protocol in this manner, such as referring to Prince Philip as "the boss," a term he also bestowed on Charles.

It was also said that Savile acted as an informal adviser to Charles, including in the selection of key appointments such as his private secretary, and Charles would often phone Savile at his office at Stoke Mandeville. Savile even attended Charles's fortieth birthday party. When Savile was finally knighted in his mother's honors list in 1990, Charles sent his congratulations, as did Diana, Prince Philip, and Sarah, Duchess of York, who sent a homemade card. Following his death, and before the devastating revelations about his abuse, Jimmy Savile's personal effects were auctioned off for charity. These included cards and letters from Charles, Diana, Sarah Ferguson, and Princes Harry and William. It was even said that, during the 1986 London Marathon, he dropped into the palace for a shower and a cup of tea with the Queen. "I just don't know how he does it," said race organizer John Disley.

Savile had been chosen to front the campaign to promote the use of seatbelts ("Clunk, Click Every Trip"), was the face of the advertising campaign to modernize the then-nationalized British Rail (an extremely profitable gig for Savile), and had a lucrative contract promoting P&O ferries. However, there were some chinks in the armor, and that latter contract came to an abrupt end in 1978 when the parents of a fourteen-year-old girl complained to the ship's captain that Jimmy was trying to lure their daughter into his cabin on the ocean liner SS *Canberra* (not an isolated incident, as it transpired). Appalled, the captain took the rare decision to censure Savile, instructing him confined to his cabin until they reached Gibraltar, where he was to disembark permanently. The British press had gotten wind of this story, but had stopped short of printing it for fear of libel laws. This was not the first or the last time such threats had stopped Savile from being exposed, and it helps to explain, partially, how he was allowed to continue. He later got a lucrative consultancy with the Thomas Cook travel agency.

Indeed, these revelations did little to stop Savile's continued ascent as a national treasure. Despite this, and rather astonishingly to look back with hindsight, Jimmy Savile was handpicked to be on the task force assembled to revamp Broadmoor Hospital after the board was suspended in 1988. In a move signed off on by the Department of Health, Savile now had a small house and an office on site as "honorary assistant entertainments officer." Savile had other ideas, and openly told anyone who would listen, "I am the boss—it's as simple as that."

In his final years, Savile was still seen as a "national treasure," but his stock had fallen somewhat, and declining health was matched by declining public exposure. To cut costs, he scaled back his charity work, and although he still appeared on television, usually as a guest on comedy programs, he faded from the public exposure he had previously enjoyed. He took to more drastic measures to remain relevant, including appearing on reality TV show *Celebrity Big Brother*, which is how he came to appear with documentarian Louis Theroux on a special program broadcast in 2000. Louis challenged Savile on his "oddness," and his relationship with his mother and with children, attempting to get to the bottom of this public enigma. By his own admission, he failed—but he was, like so many others, beguiled by the public figure.

When Savile died in 2011, the public eulogies were numerous, and his funeral was lavish and public. However, for a man who allegedly had so many friends in public life, the funeral was attended by only a couple of celebrities. Was there something *they knew*?

The Fall

In Britain, we are known for building people up and then, just as swiftly, knocking them down. With Savile, this tactic may be forgiven, although the one complaint may be that it happened too late. When Savile did finally fall, it was swift and precipitous, but the sheer scale of this downfall shocked the country—as did the details of his sickening crimes.

Shortly after his death in October 2011, the wheels started to come off what turned out to be a speeding juggernaut. Yet the allegations had been building for years, both officially and unofficially. A planned exposé by BBC journalists was ditched after editors got cold feet, but a documentary that aired on commercial channel ITV in 2012 lit the torch paper.

People who worked with Savile knew he was "dodgy," but even back in his dance-hall days, people were also loath to do anything due to his power and influence.

Tony Calder, who went on to co-manage the Rolling Stones, described being taken to Savile's flat in 1961 on the promise of guaranteed sex. His description matches the last days of Rome, with several rooms being used for intercourse at the same time with queues of girls corralled from the Mecca ballroom in Leeds. These young girls were groomed by Savile, given instructions for who to have sex with. Savile was basically a "pimp," according to Calder's descriptions. He also had a large couch in his office at the Plaza in Manchester: "I'm just going to interview this young lady for a job," he would say, according to a colleague.

If these girls were all over the age of consent, it would still be problematic, but Savile was known to prefer them younger. He was described by some as a "weirdo," a rather tame description by today's standards, and was always seen with young girls in his Rolls-Royce. One of the young DJs at the Mecca stated that his colleagues knew about his ways and always "joked" that Savile was "either going to be a huge success" or end up in prison for his proclivity for underage girls. This was almost the case, as another colleague, Dennis Lemmon, a doorman at the Leeds Mecca, testified. Enquiring as to why his boss was in a foul mood one morning, he was told that Savile was due in court the next day to answer charges of being involved with underage girls—and not for the first time. It was suspected that he had paid the girls off. A pattern emerged of Savile using money and influence to "get away with it," and when the abused did pluck up the courage to challenge him, they would only get so far.

There was a definite power dynamic at play, something that only was exacerbated as this power grew. Another pattern emerged—accusations were made, and the accuser was not believed or the incident was covered up, something the #MeToo movement has revealed as societally endemic. These followed wherever Savile went—and he went to a lot of places. At Leeds General Infirmary, there were numerous complaints that ranged from Savile entering the nurses' chambers to groping and attempted rape. These were all ignored. When a new contract was in the offing at BBC Radio One, such was the apprehension that several journalists were contacted and asked if they were aware of the rumors about Savile. They were. Stories were not run because of his popularity and charity work. Another newspaper, famed for its investigative journalism, decided against running a story as they had just hired Savile to write a column. In 1975, the daughter of a local journalist was assaulted, but still nothing happened.

It was clear from Savile's own words that he considered fame and influence a ticket to impunity. His first taste of television was described as akin to being given the "keys to the Bank of England." When he finally achieved his knighthood, he talked of being "off the hook"—not the words of an innocent and noble Knight of the Realm. The charity work, he felt, was sufficient to balance out his crimes. He admitted to being "a great abuser of things, and bodies, and people."

Some of the worst allegations came from sick, vulnerable, disabled, and other patients recovering from serious surgery at Stoke Mandeville. Numerous complaints were made, and ignored. One poor girl was groped after she had undergone spinal surgery—she was too scared to say anything. Many came to believe they were the only ones, or that it was their own fault, especially the residents of places like Duncroft, where vulnerable girls were often sent after they had been sexually abused by others in the first place. Several victims said the same thing—Savile would suddenly force his tongue down their throats and expose himself. Another poor girl was groomed with gifts, being wheeled by a man into a room where she was abused by Savile, then wheeled back to the ward by another man. When she complained to the nurses, they allegedly laughed and walked off at the mention of Savile's name. Her father also refused to believe her.

This was another pattern—the parents of the abused often refused to believe that the man they saw on TV could have done such things. Yet on the rare occasions when they did, the police did not believe them, as with one instance from Stoke Mandeville in which a police claim was made by the father of an eleven-year-old molested by Savile while recovering from skin cancer in 1977. In fact, one of the few occasions when police summoned Savile was in connection with the famous "Yorkshire Ripper" serial killer investigation. Peter Sutcliffe operated in the Leeds area, and the body of one of his victims was found in a park near Savile's flat. Despite the fact that Savile was friendly with police, with them often popping into the flat for tea, an anonymous tip-off meant that Savile was called in to provide a cast of his teeth. Several of the sex workers had been found dead with bite marks on them. Savile was known to use prostitutes in the area.

A lot of the offending took place in Savile's ever-present motorhome— the same one he parked at Buckingham Palace or in other transient spaces that helped to allay suspicion. But the majority of the incidents were in locations where Savile had permanent residences—London, Leeds, and Scarborough. Sometimes, these came back to haunt him. In later years, he would regularly bark at girls he was abusing to ask whether they were "on the [contraceptive] pill" after he had gotten at least one of them pregnant. He refused to acknowledge this, and at least one girl was forced to undergo an illegal abortion.

One of the saddest tales at least sparked an investigation into what happened to underage girls in the dressing rooms of the BBC. Claire McAlpine was a fifteen-year-old dancer on *Top of the Pops* who took her own life in 1971. Her diary detailed abuse by key figures at the BBC, including Savile, according to her family. Although her family escalated these to police and prosecutors, the deceased girl was ultimately dismissed as a fantasist.

Operation Yewtree, the police operation established to investigate the crimes of Savile, cast its net further, and several other television presenters and high-profile figures were tried and convicted for similar crimes.

Cherished memories of childhood in the 1970s and 1980s took hit after hit as presenter Stuart Hall and beloved children's entertainer Rolf Harris were both found guilty of heinous acts against minors. Years earlier, 1970s glam rocker Gary Glitter had suffered the same fate when obscene images were found on his computer, although this wasn't enough to stop him from gaining royalties from his song "Hello, Hello, I'm Back Again" being played at American sports games and in the *Joker* film. Tellingly, Savile defended Glitter, blaming everything on a tabloid witch hunt and erroneously stating that what the pop star did was his own business. Chilling footage of Glitter on the Savile-fronted TV program *Clunk-Click* has reemerged, with them both jokingly discussing sharing out the young girls in the audience between them. Many members of the audience were invited by Savile from the Duncroft school as part of his bribery (on the BBC's expenses) and grooming techniques.

When the investigation was finished and reports were published, the results were jaw-dropping. The known offending had taken place over a period of fifty-four years, between 1955 and 2009—the youngest victim was eight and the eldest forty-seven. The peak offending years coincided with Savile's elevated status at the BBC between 1966 and 1976 (1974–1975 being the most prolific), when Savile was between forty and fifty years of age. He offended in at least fourteen schools where "the nation's favorite uncle" had been invited by children who wanted to be on *Jim'll Fix It*. He offended in fourteen hospitals and hospices, including the venerable Great Ormond Street Hospital for Children in London. He even offended at the last recording of *Top of the Pops* in 2006.

Police and institutional failures were acknowledged: "mistakes were made." These included the continued failure by various police forces to act on accusations or to coordinate and share their intelligence across forces. Savile's too-cozy relationship with police officers in Leeds and Manchester, through his connections and the "Friday Morning Club," helped him dictate the terms of anything that *did* raise suspicion. On finally being called in for interview, Savile managed to get the interview held on his own turf, at his offices at Stoke Mandeville, rather than in a police station, and at a time of his own convenience. He wriggled out of this via litigious threats as usual. The Crown Prosecution Service concluded in 2013 that he could have been brought to justice as early as 2007 if police and prosecutors had handled the allegations differently.

Perhaps as a testament to the hold that Savile continues to have, there are still some who refuse to believe he was capable of these crimes. One of the people to have known Savile at close quarters is Janet Cope, who acted as his private secretary at Stoke Mandeville for more than thirty years. In reality, she was much more than that; she did his laundry and other personal chores, and he even gave her away at her wedding. She describes a man who did not like children or any personal attachments, who was cruel and dismissive of her, and who craved "high-profile institutions." She describes a narcissistic control freak that was threatening and "quite lethal in lots of ways," including with her. When he decided to dispense with her services after all that time, he simply pointed at her and said, "She's out," before sending her a threatening legal letter. Despite this, she describes the end of their relationship as being like a "marriage" coming to an end. The allegations are "unfair," she maintains.

Pathology and Modus Operandi

Jimmy Savile's MO is all too familiar to any sex offender, serial killer, domestic abuser, or any person who has abused a position of power and trust. His was just enacted on a much larger scale—grooming an entire nation as well as his victims. He used superficial charm, humor, eccentricity, money, influence, bribes, evasion, threats, and fear as his tools. He maneuvered himself into positions where he had easy access to vulnerable people—people whose word he knew wouldn't be taken seriously. Eccentricity and oddness were a veil.

He manipulated—as at Duncroft, where he cautioned girls not to tell about his activities as it would spoil things for the other girls—or he threatened and blackmailed that he would divest his charitable services. He associated with people whom he felt were similarly untouchable, or that others wouldn't have the nerve to challenge. He boasted of his friendship with the notorious East End gangsters the Krays, through his Broadmoor connections, and of his employment of former Nazi Sonderkommandos in his clubs. (Sonderkommandos were concentration camp inmates forced to do the Nazis' work, such as retrieving bodies from the gas chambers.) He liked to think of himself as a "godfather figure" and kept the few "friends" he had at a controlled distance. In Louis Theroux's documentary, Savile takes great pleasure in telling Theroux that he has traced his home address, despite it being non-public.

Yet Savile went one further—he actively teased his true nature, in public, to trick others into thinking it couldn't possibly be true, or that his charity work could cancel out anything else. He once made a point of making a journalist wait while he had sex with a girl. One poor girl was regularly abused every Sunday at the Stoke Mandeville chapel. She said that Savile kept the door open in the back room so that he could still see the priest. She stopped attending church.

He liked to surround himself with the sick and disabled ("sub-normals" as he referred to them) in keeping with his messiah complex and deflection of suspicion. Yet when suspicion was raised, he tackled it head-on, getting his "story" out first.

Savile's opportunism was also brazen. Even his charity work was used to land lucrative contracts and paid endorsements. On awakening from heart surgery, his first impulse was to grope a nurse's breasts. As he received well-wishes from royalty, this incident, like so many worse, was glossed over. He also used his second meeting with Elvis to molest a fan club member. In good faith, she visited him at his London flat. She left minus her virginity and with some cheap merchandise.

Conclusion

One of the newspaper reports into Savile's offending describes a "rare moment of national self-revelation." Some say we were all victims—we were groomed collectively as a nation. Some suggest we were all complicit in a society that values celebrity above all other virtues and, furthermore, encourages children to grow up too fast. One thing is for certain: not only did these revelations shake and sully the view we have of people and institutions we have held dear, but it was quite another thing to look back to the warmth and comfort of cherished childhood memories and replace them with a collective shudder. In this, we can empathize at least one small modicum with those unfortunate individuals who had not only their childhoods shattered by Savile, but their subsequent lives as well.

If not a "Watergate" moment in British cultural life, then it certainly was a watershed, after which things never quite looked the same again.

GARTH DRABINSKY: THEATRICAL IMPRESARIO TO CONVICTED FRAUDSTER

ANYA WASSENBERG

The business of movies and the performing arts naturally attracts big personalities, both on stage and on camera, and behind the scenes. Canadian lawyer/businessman/theatrical impresario/convicted fraudster Garth Drabinsky hit the North American cinema and performing arts industries like a hurricane through the 1980s and 1990s, leaving both innovation and financial disaster in his wake.

Garth Drabinsky created the modern North American multiscreen cinema experience as it is known today. He was the first to innovate the perks urban moviegoers have come to expect, like plush seating and more sophisticated choices on the menu than popcorn and soft drinks. He also initiated the practice of showing ads before the main feature, something audiences appreciate less.

He made Canadian theater history with a decade-long run of *The Phantom of the Opera* and North American theater history for the most lavish production of the time, won a Tony for *Kiss of the Spider Woman* on Broadway, and, along the way, according to the courts, bilked investors to the tune of five hundred million Canadian dollars.

Renowned Broadway director Hal Prince has been a friend of Drabinsky's since his first days on the "Great White Way," so-called because of the bright marquee lights that drew audiences, as well as dreamers like him, decades ago. He told the *Toronto Star* in 2016 that he understood the controversial figure better than most. "I know both sides of Garth, I know what he did and at the same time, I know what's good about him," said Prince. "I've been the beneficiary of what's good about him and clearly, I've been on the receiving end of royalties he didn't pay (when Livent collapsed), but I have lost no sleep about that. I believe the theater needs creative producers with taste and there is no question that he is that."

Early Life

Drabinsky was born in Toronto on October 27, 1948. At age three, he contracted polio. It resulted in a string of painful operations, and the disease left him with a limp.

According to his 1995 autobiography, *Closer to the Sun*, Drabinsky was first captivated by the power of theatrical magic as a high school student while watching a production of Molière's *The Imaginary Invalid*. As a teen, he worked at the Canadian National Exhibition, a large annual carnival-style event in Toronto. He would analyze people's handwriting in a booth, and the experience taught him a thing or two about sales. "I was amazed at how credulous people were, how accepting of the most obvious con," he wrote.

Drabinsky got his law degree from the University of Toronto in 1973. Called to the bar in 1975, he became an independent producer in the entertainment business in 1978. He wrote a book titled *Motion Pictures and the Arts in Canada: The Business and the Law* (1976) that was considered an industry reference for years.

From the late 1970s, Drabinsky served as producer or executive producer on a string of movie and TV projects, including shorts, documentaries, and mini-series. Among others, he produced *The*

Changeling, a 1980 ghost story starring George C. Scott, and *The Silent Partner* (1978), a bank robbery flick starring Elliott Gould, Christopher Plummer, and Susannah York, all stars of the era.

When it came to financing, Drabinsky always had a talent for creative solutions. *The Changeling* was financed through a public film offering, the first Canadian production to take that route. The deal involved Myron Gottlieb, who would go on to become a longstanding partner and, in the end, co-defendant. At the time, eyebrows were raised at the fact that Drabinsky was serving simultaneously as producer, distributor, and lawyer for the movie. It was legal, but pushing the limits.

In an interview with *Maclean's* magazine at the time, Drabinsky justified his all-out approach. "Who's going to perpetuate the business? The actors? The gaffers? No, it's the entrepreneurs." When the interview piece came out, he sued *Maclean's* for ten million Canadian dollars for libel, later settling out of court for $75,000 and an apology. Despite the talk, the project was not a financial success for investors, who believed they weren't being given their fair share, and Drabinsky and Gottlieb were sued for fraud.

A Tangled History of Movie Theater Chains

As he worked in the movie production side of the business, Drabinsky was also getting his start in Canadian movie theater chains.

The movie theater market is relatively small in Canada, with logistical challenges posed by its geography: a population essentially clustered in a narrow margin around its southern border and spread across more than 5,700 miles. By the early twentieth century, two major players began to emerge. Famous Players began operations in Canada in 1920 with business mogul Nathan L. Nathanson as president. The Odeon chain had begun as a string of independent cinemas, but was bought by British owners in 1946 to become Canada's second-largest chain.

Cineplex was an upstart to the burgeoning Canadian movie theater business. In 1934, Toronto native Nat Taylor founded 20th Century Theatres, which became the third largest chain in the province of Ontario (Canada's largest by population). By 1941, Famous Players asked Taylor to operate twenty-five of their cinemas, in addition to his seventeen, to keep him from linking his chain with Odeon. As early as 1948, he was experimenting with multi-cinema locations on a small scale. However, by the 1970s, he'd sold most of his cinemas to Famous Players.

Taylor kept a handful of signature locations and went into partnership with Garth Drabinsky to launch a brand-new chain of their own. Taylor coined the name Cineplex, and the pair founded Cineplex Corporation in 1979.

The new chain built their flagship location at the new Eaton Centre shopping mall in downtown Toronto. As the first true multiplex, it had an unprecedented eighteen screens, making *The Guinness Book of World Records* as the largest movie theater to date. Because of existing agreements with the two largest chains, however, major American movies were not on the menu. The multiplex screened art films, second runs, and 16mm specialty flicks. Because of this, the big two distributors didn't see it as a credible threat—not at first.

Drabinsky, together with Myron Gottlieb, began to pursue continental cinema ownership. The company opened the first US Cineplex in 1982 at the new Beverly Center in Los Angeles. At the time, its fourteen screens made it the largest in the United States. That same year, the company went public.

Existing arrangements, however, limited Cineplex's ability to expand in Canada. Famous Players already had an established relationship with major American movie companies Warner Brothers, MGM-United Artists, and Walt Disney Company's Buena Vista (Canada). The company was itself owned by Gulf+Western, which in turn owned Paramount Pictures.

Cineplex, through Nat Taylor's connection, had a longstanding relationship with Twentieth Century Fox Film Corporation, Columbia

Pictures, and Universal Studios (then a division of MCA). However, the mix still resulted in about 80 percent of the top-grossing North American films screening exclusively at Famous Players.

Drabinsky dug into his legal background and went to court to break the stranglehold that Famous Players and Odeon had on the market. In 1983, he won a hearing before the Restrictive Trade Practices Commission in Ottawa. Mere hours before the hearing was scheduled to take place, six of the biggest American movie distribution companies issued a joint statement saying they would change their procedures and allow for more competition in the industry.

Buoyed by the increase in business for Cineplex, they bought out Odeon in 1984, with Montreal's prominent Bronfman family as major investors. The new company was named Cineplex Odeon and was helmed by Drabinsky, with Gottlieb in a key role.

Cineplex Odeon soon went on a buying spree, snapping up the Pitt Theatre chain in Pennsylvania, Essaness Theatres of Chicago, Neighborhood Theatres of Virginia, the RKO Century Theatres chain and RKO Stanley-Warner Theatres in New York and New Jersey, and Seattle-based Sterling Recreation Organization. Cineplex Odeon ended up as the second-largest chain in North America, with 1,630 screens in 365 locations.

In 1986, to finance that growth, Drabinsky sold just over 49 percent of Cineplex Odeon to MCA, the parent of Universal Studios.

The Movie Biz

Part of Drabinsky's strategy was to lovingly restore vintage cinemas, as well as building brand-new ones in then-innovative environments like suburban shopping malls. He combined the luxurious new look and feel of the multiplex with the utility of smaller venues in new locations. His innovations are credited, in part, with reviving a movie-going industry that had been stagnant through the 1970s. Drabinsky brought lattes and state-of-the-art sound systems to the modern moviegoer. Although he has always had many naysayers, and rivals claimed the frills he introduced didn't influence audiences' buying decisions, the standard for moviegoers had been irrevocably raised.

Through the 1980s, Cineplex Odeon and Famous Players acted out what became a notorious corporate rivalry.

The Imperial Six Theatre on Yonge Street, Toronto's iconic downtown thoroughfare, was Famous Players's flagship cinema in Canada. However, the building actually comprised three separate lots owned by different parties. Famous Players owned a portion that included the entrance on Yonge Street, along with the front half of the cinema complex. The lease on the other two lots in question was owned by a private family holding based in Michigan.

In 1986, the lease came up for renewal, and Famous Players dropped the ball on negotiations. The private company leaseholder contacted Cineplex Odeon directly to offer up the renewal, and Drabinsky hopped on a plane to Michigan to sign the deal himself. Once he held the lease, Drabinsky denied Famous Players access to the areas he controlled, which included the lobby, all of Cinema 2, four of the six projection booths, and half of two of the other cinemas. Famous Players took Cineplex to court in an attempt to force entry via an injunction, but failed at the Supreme Court level. Famous Players attempted to stay in business, but they were limited to only one screen and an alternative entrance off Yonge Street.

The loss of the movie theater exacerbated a caustic business rivalry. In 1987, when Drabinsky was set to open his Pantages Cinema with a screening of *Wall Street*, someone at Famous Players contacted the fire marshal's office with a complaint. An investigation proved that the fire exits were still under construction. This meant the opening gala had to be relocated while crews scrambled to get the exits done in time for the premiere.

Famous Players eventually sold their stake in the building to Cineplex with the stipulation that it could never again be used to screen movies. The eventual fate of the property would be tied to both Drabinsky's most high-profile successes and his spectacular downfall.

Out of Movies and into Theater

Cineplex Odeon was on an expansive high through most of the 1980s. By 1989, however, fortunes had changed. Famous Players was about to launch a major expansion (ironically, incorporating many of the innovations Drabinsky had introduced), and Drabinsky's hold on Cineplex was beginning to falter.

Cineplex was carrying a lot of debt. Along with MCA's 49.7 percent of Cineplex shares came a 33 percent voting interest. Montreal businessman Charles Bronfman owned 30 percent of the company shares. It left Drabinsky and Gottlieb with only 8 percent.

Drabinsky offered the Bronfmans a sweet buy-back deal in order to regain more control. As Cineplex's largest shareholder, MCA of California launched a legal challenge of Drabinsky's move to sell the stock. The company demanded that the same sweet deal Drabinsky offered his longtime friends the Bronfmans be offered to all the shareholders.

With the stock sale brought to a halt, Drabinsky and his partner Myron Gottlieb tried and failed to raise enough capital (about eight hundred million US dollars at the time) to buy out MCA. This set up a confrontation with the board of directors, who made moves of their own. The board created a new office of the chairman, made up of three people. That office would review all of the company's major decisions. Drabinsky would be one of the three, along with Charles Paul, a vice president with MCA, and James Raymond, representing the investment group linked to Charles Bronfman.

As an alternative, Drabinsky and Gottlieb were offered a golden parachute severance deal in the amount of $9.5 million, subject to board approval.

The end of one career launched Drabinsky's next one.

Theatrical Impresario

In the 1980s, Cineplex Odeon was developing a live theater division. As part of the gold-plated severance deal, Drabinsky retained ownership of Toronto's Imperial/Pantages Theatre building as well as the Canadian rights to the then-new musical *The Phantom of the Opera*.

After a pricey renovation of the historic Art Deco structure, the Imperial Six reopened as the Pantages Theatre for live performances. When Drabinsky inherited Cineplex's live theater division, it was a money loser. *Phantom* had already been playing at the Pantages for two months. In the revamped theater, the production went on to enormous success, and would have a run of a full ten years, from 1989 to 1999, for four thousand performances and seven million audience members. It became Canada's longest-running musical theater production. Along the way, Drabinsky founded Live Entertainment Corporation of Canada, or Livent, as it was known, in 1990, taking the company public in 1993.

In its heyday, Livent was the largest live theater company in North America. It was also the first publicly traded company in the live theater business. Drabinsky's habit of opening shows in Toronto as a test run on the road to Broadway helped raise the city's profile on the international theater circuit.

Along with *Phantom*, Livent took big Broadway shows like *Show Boat*, *Kiss of the Spider Woman*, and *Ragtime* on the road across North America, often playing in period theaters Drabinsky himself had lovingly refurbished. In addition to the Pantages in Toronto, he had a hand in renovating New York City's legendary Apollo and the Oriental Theatre in Chicago. Livent also built a brand-new theater, the Ford Center for the Performing Arts, to house *Ragtime* in Toronto.

Drabinsky's shows became known for their lavish production values. Renowned soprano Dame Kiri Te Kanawa starred in his revival of *Show Boat*. *Kiss of the Spider Woman* won a Tony Award for Best Musical. He was known to treat the talent well.

Drabinsky put his personal stamp on everything, from sets to costume fabric. *Show Boat* cost about USD $700,000 per week to run, the most expensive Broadway show ever at that point. The show ran three hours, incorporating twenty scenes, five hundred costumes, and a crew of 170. Eight computers were required to run the sound and lights. Tickets started at seventy-five dollars, but the math just didn't hold up. Despite the buzz, it was obvious the show was not making money.

In an interview with *N'Digo* magazine in June 2021, Drabinsky talked about the kinds of projects he was drawn to. "I have always produced musical work that is supportive to the sympathies and disenfranchised concerns with the issues of America's systematic racism. I produced *Ragtime* in 1996 and *Show Boat* in 1993. I am attracted to the story of the racial struggles of Black America, and I am deeply supportive of provoking audiences to understand the struggles and raising the issues, and having conversations. The theater is to provoke thought with relevant and profound conversations about those affected so dramatically."

Even at his height of fame and influence in that world, however, there were rumors of ill-treatment and bullying of his staff, and other misdeeds. There was also talk that his shows weren't the profitable powerhouses he claimed they were.

It's probable that Drabinsky's well-known willingness to sue put a damper on the speculation that was growing about Livent and its finances. Back in 1985, Drabinsky was interviewed in a piece for *Forbes* magazine. In response, Alex Winch, a Toronto investment analyst, wrote a letter to the editor that was critical of Livent and its finances. The company fired back with a ten-million-Canadian-dollar suit for libel that cost Winch about $350,000 and an apology.

"He never allowed anything to get in the way to stop him, which is the only way he could ever have accomplished what he accomplished," says film producer Robert Lantos in a 2009 interview with *Maclean's*. "There was no obstacle that couldn't be climbed or torn down or barreled through."

An anonymous source quoted in *Maclean's* describes a man who was more than driven. "He must win. He will not brook interference. He won't tolerate anyone who fails to get it or see it or agree. If they don't, they're not just wrong, but ignorant and stupid and dismissed."

The Collapse of Livent

In 1998, Drabinsky secured additional financing from Hollywood super-agent Michael Ovitz, who at the time had recently stepped down from his position as president of The Walt Disney Company to the tune of twenty million US dollars. That move, however, is what triggered the opening of the company's books and the discovery of accounting irregularities. That year, just as *Fosse: A Celebration in Song and Dance* opened in Toronto, Drabinsky and Gottlieb were called to a meeting with the Livent board of directors.

The scene was reportedly dramatic. Drabinsky and Gottlieb, who had emerged from the sale to Ovitz as vice chairman and vice president of Canadian administration respectively, were summoned to a meeting with the board in which they were accused of hiding the company's true financial status. Their offices were sealed, the two were suspended from their posts, and they were barred from Livent's premises.

Both denied the accusations publicly.

The board accused the pair of keeping two sets of books. One, which showed profitable operations, was made to show to the board of directors and shareholders. The other set documented the real state of the company's volatile finances.

In particular, the board alleged that the board-ready set of books used what is called "capitalizing expenses," or recording costs that should have been subtracted as profits and shifting them to the statement of assets. It made the losses look like capital gains. Costs from one show were shifted around to another's books, and some of the massive theatrical production costs for Livent's lavish shows were posted to construction projects instead. It served to disguise the true financial status of the shows, and made them look profitable even if they bled money.

In 1999, US authorities charged Drabinsky with fraud. Among the accusations was the charge that he'd appropriated $4.6 million of company money for personal use.

In total, Drabinsky and Gottlieb faced sixteen counts of securities fraud and conspiracy in the United States, charges that could have resulted in up to 140 years in prison and sixteen million dollars in fines. The Securities and Exchange Commission filed a civil suit. The 1999 litigation by the SEC against Drabinsky, Gottlieb, and seven others details the damage, including the following:

> For fiscal 1996, Livent reported pre-tax earnings of $14.2 million when, in fact, the company incurred a loss of more than $20 million in that year. For fiscal 1997, Livent reported a pre-tax loss of $62.1 million when, in fact, the company's true loss in fiscal 1997 was at least $83.6 million. The Complaint alleges that as a further result of the scheme, Livent reported preproduction costs or fixed assets that were fraudulently overstated for fiscal years 1994 through 1997.

As for Livent, the company never recovered from the highly public scandal, and filed for bankruptcy protection in both Canada and the US, claiming debts of about CAD $334 million. Its assets were sold to Los Angeles-based SFX Entertainment in 1999.

After the grand jury indictment, Drabinsky and Gottlieb left for Canada, where charges proceeded much more slowly. The RCMP charged Drabinsky with "fraud affecting the public market" after a four-year investigation in 2002. The charges included Drabinsky as well as Gottlieb and two others.

Drabinsky hired high-profile defense lawyer Edward Greenspan, who immediately issued a statement refuting the charges and insisting on his client's innocence. While the charges forced him to miss the US opening of the Fosse show, along with *Seussical* and *Parade*, Drabinsky stayed active on the other side of the border even as the Canadian investigation proceeded.

As the fallout began to materialize, Drabinsky kept working. He brought a production of the South African play *The Island* to Toronto in 2001, and in the same year brought boxing legend Muhammad Ali to Toronto for an appearance as part of a Parkinson's disease fundraising effort.

Just as he was finally facing charges in Canada in 2002, Drabinsky, along with Gottlieb, was working on a stage revival of *The Dresser* on Broadway.

Crime and Punishment

After years of bail and legal wrangling, Drabinsky was convicted after a nine-month trial in 2009. His sentence initially called for seven years' imprisonment. In her judgment, Justice Mary Lou Benotto wrote that Drabinsky and partner Myron Gottlieb "systemically manipulated the books."

The sentence was later reduced to five years on appeal; in the end, Drabinsky got out in 2012 on parole. He actually only spent seventeen months behind bars, with the balance of his sentence completed on probation and day parole. He lived in a halfway house for most of that period.

Drabinsky describes that period—from police probe to incarceration—in a *Toronto Star* interview as "the most painful episode" of his life.

In 2014, the then sixty-four-year-old was granted full parole and allowed to return to his family home with his wife and two children. As part of the conditions of his release, he was barred from contacting Gottlieb or any of the others accused.

When questioned during his final parole board hearing about his crimes, Drabinsky blamed the whole debacle on a fear of failure. "I didn't want to fail and I didn't want my company to fail," he said. He went on to explain that he was no longer driven by that fear, and that he'd never repeat the pattern that led to his downfall and, essentially, he'd learned his lesson. "They are indelible and will haunt me for the rest of my days," he said.

The Legal Residue

After his full release in 2014, the US charges were dropped.

Imprisonment, however, wasn't the only price Drabinsky would pay for his financial wrongdoing. In 2017, the Ontario Securities Commission succeeded in imposing a permanent ban on his participation in any capital markets in the province. In their twenty-one-page judgment, the court noted: "These sanctions follow from the need to deter Mr. Drabinsky and others from the misconduct reflected in his criminal convictions." The OSC ruling prohibits him from trading securities or promoting investments, or serving on any company boards.

Drabinsky was permanently disbarred as a lawyer in 2014, and lost his membership in the Order of Canada, a prestigious public honor he'd been awarded in 1995. He fought every step of the way, including appealing the ruling that stripped him of the Order of Canada, but lost at every turn.

The man who was known to be quick to litigate has found himself embroiled in court on multiple fronts. Drabinsky found himself in a legal tussle with Toronto's Ryerson University. After his disgrace, and while out on an appeal of his original conviction, in 2010, Ryerson had negotiated what the university's administration thought was a deal for Drabinsky to donate his personal archives to its performing arts school. When the deal fell through, Ryerson threatened to ditch the entire archive. Drabinsky had brokered the deal just after his conviction in order to score a substantial tax credit. Instead, his archive ended up at the city's York University.

The trail of retribution extended to accounting firm Deloitte, which, in 2017, was subjected to a CAD $118-million civil damages award, later reduced to $40 million on appeal, for their role as auditors of Livent from 1989 to 1998. The company was sued based on the allegation that they had either failed to detect the financial wrongdoing, or did so and ignored it. In addition, the judge found that Deloitte had a duty to warn the company's creditors of the fraud they should have found.

Even after serving his prison sentence, Drabinsky is still on the hook for the money the court says he owes due to his fraud. In 2020, an Ontario court ruled against Drabinsky on charges that he had transferred the title of a Toronto home worth $2.6 million to his wife in an attempt to avoid creditors. The transfer took place in 2015, just after his release from prison. The legal action was initiated by a securities lawyer who was looking to reverse the title change, and who claimed more than $50,000 in legal fees from the former business mogul.

"To all appearances, the transfer can only be explained as an effort to put the property beyond the reach of Mr. Drabinsky's creditors. The transaction is replete with the badges of this kind of surreptitious creditor-proofing," the court wrote in its judgment.

"Mr. Drabinsky offers no other explanation that makes sense. While he insists under oath that he had not turned his mind to the effect of the transfer on his creditors, the objective indicia are such that he could hardly have been thinking of anything else," the court found.

In court testimony, Drabinsky revealed that he'd borrowed seven million dollars from friends to keep his legal battles going.

Denouement

In his autobiography, *Closer to the Sun*, Drabinsky talks about the Icarus analogy—the boy who flew too close to the sun and melted his wings of wax. "I think the bastard just gave up too soon," he wrote. "He should have gotten himself another set of wings and taken off again!"

In a 2016 interview with a Toronto newspaper, Drabinsky talked about the costs, both financial and otherwise, of his actions, while avoiding any statement of responsibility. "The entire past eighteen years was [sic] emotionally ruinous to my family first, to me second," he said. "They had to endure. My wife, my children had to endure. Obviously, it was incredibly destructive to me."

Drabinsky said the prison experience had done nothing to damp his passion for live theater. "Whether in motion picture form or television form or musical form or even poetic form, that is my life. I've always been an artistic person.... Nothing in one's darkest moments—and here have been many—is going to destroy my optimism for life and the need to express myself artistically."

He kept as active in the industry as he could, even during the years of trials and appeals. In 2011, while out on bail for his appeal, Drabinsky produced the non-musical show *Barrymore*, starring longtime friend Christopher Plummer, and he also served as artistic consultant to a massive, ambitious outdoor music festival north of Toronto that became an enormous financial disaster.

After leaving prison, Drabinsky went back to the only trade he had left: live theater. On contract to Teatro Proscenium Limited Partnership, he produced a musical called *Sousatzka*. Directed by Adrian Noble, *Sousatzka* was based on the novel *Madame Sousatzka* by Welsh author Bernice Rubens; it revolved around the relationship between a Holocaust survivor working as a music teacher and a talented student from South Africa. It opened in Toronto in 2017 to unenthusiastic reviews.

Drabinsky's involvement in Teatro Proscenium Limited Partnership came with some restrictions, as CEO Richard Stursberg elaborated in a 2016 interview with the *Toronto Star*: "Garth has no control over any money."

In March 2022, Drabinsky opened a new show on Broadway. *Paradise Square*, set in a New York saloon during the Civil War, was vaunted as the first new musical to reopen Broadway after the long COVID-19 pandemic-related closure. Directed by Tony Award nominee Moisés Kaufman, and with choreography by the legendary Bill T. Jones, the production makes clear that Drabinsky's sights are still set on big theatrical spectacle. The story is set in Lower Manhattan's Five Points neighborhood. The production first opened in November 2021, in Chicago, for a month-long premiere run before taking on Broadway, to largely good reviews.

In a 2021 interview, Drabinsky was asked what he did for fun.

"I have a beautiful Four Seasons home on a lake north of Toronto. It functions as a reset, as a getaway where I do great thinking and savor life. I enjoy the sweetness of the air and living a slower pace of life. I cherish music. I spend time listening to music. My taste is eclectic. I like Frank Sinatra, Stan Getz, and Quincy Jones. I am a fan of Joan Baez and Peter, Paul, and Mary. I like Harry Belafonte and gospel music. I like Burt Bacharach," he said.

"I have had a fascinating life."

Despite a Tony award for best leading actress for Joaquina Kalukango, Drabinsky's production of *Paradise Square* closed after a three-month run, to be followed by multiple lawsuits over contractual breaches, including a federal case filed by Actors Equity to the tune of $174,000.

THE BLOOD COUNTESS

KHADIJA TAUSEEF

In the village of Čachtice in modern-day Slovakia lie the ruins of a centuries-old castle, isolated high up in the mountains. In 1611, four hundred years earlier, a woman had been condemned to death by being walled up within a single room. Countess Erzsébet Báthory belonged to one of the most powerful aristocratic families in Hungary. Accused, tried, and convicted of murdering approximately six hundred innocent young women, these horrific acts would earn her the title "Countess Dracula" and a reputation as one of the most prolific female serial killers in history.

Erzsébet Báthory was born on August 7, 1560, at the Ecsed (Nagyecsed) family estate at Nyírbátor, Hungary. Her parents, György (a baron) and Anna, belonged to two separate branches of the Báthory clan, and their marriage merged the two households, creating a powerful union. Thus, Erzsébet was born into a world of power and privilege that came from belonging to one of the most prestigious families in Central Europe. Among her relatives were princes and kings. Her uncle István was the king of Poland, and her cousins András, Gábor, and Zsigmond would become Transylvanian princes. Born with a silver spoon in her mouth, Erzsébet believed she was beyond reproach.

The world at the time was full of conflict and chaos. Sixteenth-century Hungary was divided into three parts. Western Hungary fell under the control of the Habsburg, which caused clashes with Hungarian nobles who tried to regain power. The north, and a large portion of Transdanubia, was controlled by the Turks; and lastly, Transylvania remained independent. The rulers of Transylvania would often side with either the Turks or the Habsburgs, depending on who would benefit them the most. There was always an uneasy tension between the three ruling powers governing Hungary.

The Christian Europeans were clashing with the Islamic Turks; thus, a war was always raging. Unfortunately, this was not the only fight plaguing the country; an ideological battle was also brewing among the people. There was a struggle between the Catholic and Protestant Europeans. Protestantism was popular in Transylvania among the common people and some of the nobles; however, the kings and other lords of the region continued to maintain the Catholic faith. Erzsébet and her parents were Protestants, yet there were members of her family that chose to follow the Catholic faith, such as her uncle István, the king of Poland.

When Erzsébet turned six in 1566, Sultan Süleyman passed away, which led to a temporary lull in the fight between the Hungarians and the Turks. There were still raids, but otherwise there was peace; this was a much-needed reprieve for the Hungarian people. The constant fighting had led to food shortages and famines, as well as a decrease in the male population. At the same time, the world was beginning to emerge from the medieval era, and the Renaissance was ushered into Europe. Erzsébet Báthory was growing up in a time when the arts and science were flourishing. The world was dynamic, complex, revolutionary, bloody, and brilliant; as a member of the nobility, Erzsébet would get to experience it all.

Although the Báthorys were an illustrious clan, they had a darker side. It's believed that Erzsébet suffered from epileptic fits and insanity, and she would display increasing sexual sadism as she got older. The cause of the dysfunctional behavior might have been the inbreeding that took place. The saying "keep it in the family" was often taken very seriously, to ensure that outsiders didn't get their hands on property and riches. Because of this, there were some negative claims regarding Erzsébet's family. For example, her brother, also named István, was accused of being a sadistic, lecherous sex fiend and a drunkard who often ran around naked in marketplaces when drunk. Another family member who might have had a negative impact upon the young Erzsébet was her aunt, Klára. It's possible that Klára had poisoned or killed her husbands, and she was even accused of practicing witchcraft. Klára was the one who might have taught Erzsébet how to torture.

Among the stories of her youth is one in which some Romani people were invited to the Báthory family seat at Ecsed Castle to provide entertainment. One was accused of selling his child to the Turks and, being enemies of the Turks, the Báthorys decided to make an example of him. The man was sewn up in a dying horse's stomach, where he would stay until his death. Observers claimed that young Erzsébet was seen to have been amused by the event and had even laughed uncontrollably.

It wasn't unusual for servants or peasants to be dealt with harshly; therefore, it's very possible that Erzsébet witnessed several peasants being tortured or executed. The reason for this treatment lies in the peasant revolt of 1514, known as the Dózsa Rebellion. The revolt caused the nobles to drastically change the laws of the kingdom. In 1517, Hungarian statesman István Werböczy's *Tripartitum* was introduced. The *Tripartitum* basically reduced the local workforce to "property" status. Growing up, Erzsébet was likely reminded again and again of her status and power, even seeing that peasants were nothing more than tools to be used. All these factors could have shaped the mindset of the young countess.

Unlike most females at the time, Erzsébet received an outstanding education. Her family was very progressive, allowing their daughter to receive the same education as her brothers. Erzsébet learned to read and write in Hungarian, Greek, Latin, German, and Slovak. She learned the classics and mathematics, and showed an interest in religion, sciences, astronomy, botany, biology, and anatomy. Her thirst for knowledge inspired her to collect books. However, as a woman, she was also taught how to run the household, manage the estate, and take care of the servants who worked for her.

Erzsébet's life changed drastically at the age of ten, when her father died. With the protector and provider of the family gone, now Anna had to ensure that her children found good matches in marriage. In 1571, Erzsébet became engaged to the young Count Ferenc Nádasdy. Ferenc's mother, Orsolya, believed that Erzsébet's superior intelligence would help her son in the running of the estate. The marriage also brought prestige and status to the Nádasdy family.

With the wedding contract finalized, Erzsébet would have to leave her family home and move to the Nádasdy estate at Sárvár, as tradition dictated. This was intended to help a young bride become accustomed to living with her in-laws and get to know the life of her husband's family. Being alone in an unfamiliar environment would have had a profound effect on the mind of the then-eleven-year-old. It's believed that at some point Erzsébet's future mother-in-law died, and with her fiancé always away from home due to his military duties, she was cursed with unlimited free time. Therefore, it's no surprise that she sought comfort in the arms of another.

Unsupervised, Erzsébet was allowed to move around as she pleased. It was during this time, according to gossip, that she met a young man by the name of László Bende, who worked on the property. As a result of their affair, Erzsébet became pregnant, eventually giving birth to a baby girl. When word of the affair reached her family and fiancé, they tried to sweep the whole situation under the rug. The baby was taken from Erzsébet, and she would never see her daughter again. As for László, Ferenc castrated him and threw his severed parts to the dogs. There are no records that tell what sort of an impact this episode had on the young countess.

Another version of the story exists, in which a pregnant Erzsébet went to the priests at the Cathedral Chapter of Esztergom to lodge a formal complaint that she had been forcibly abducted by László and raped. Whether she did this due to family pressure or for her own self-preservation is unclear. But she saw László as expendable and, by "throwing him under the bus" so to speak, she was ensuring that her wedding contract wouldn't be broken.

The wedding between Erzsébet and Ferenc took place in 1575 at the palace of Varannó in Vranov. The marriage united two powerful families, and collectively the couple inherited vast riches and property. In public, the two seemed happy, but no one knows what lies beneath the surface. Although she had children later in the marriage, during the first ten years, Erzsébet did not. Historians believe that Ferenc might have kept his distance from his wife due to the affair she'd had.

However, everything began to unravel in 1591, when people began to notice the number of deaths occurring at Nádasdy Castle.

Normally, the death of a servant wasn't something that would warrant closer inspection. Therefore, when the local Lutheran minister, István Magyari, was summoned to the castle because a young servant had died, it appeared to be a routine situation. But behind this seemingly normal death, Magyari saw that the girl's body had been placed inside a sealed coffin. When he confronted the countess as to the unusual practice, she explained that the girl had died of cholera and, in order to prevent a panic, the coffin had been sealed. Accepting her explanation, the minister conducted the funeral proceedings, and the girl was buried.

A few days later, the clergy were again summoned to the castle about a death. Since the minister wasn't available, his assistant went in his place. To his surprise, the servants showed him a sealed coffin. Unlike before, this time a rumor was going around that the bodies of three girls had been nailed inside one coffin. The minister's assistant asked the servants to wait while he went to confront Erzsébet. She fiercely denied the accusation, saying there were two women in the coffin, not three, once again claiming that cholera was the cause of death.

No one took much notice of a few deaths among the domestic staff; it wasn't considered unusual due to all the disease at the time. But as time went on, more and more girls were ending up dead. A singular incident was turning into an ever-increasing stream of dead bodies that followed the countess everywhere she went. The rise in the death toll began to concern the clergy, who were becoming more aware of the rumors that servant girls were being tortured to death. Funerals and burials were taking place at an alarming rate. Eventually, when the complaints against the countess piled up, István Magyari decided to confront Erzsébet when his conscience could no longer keep silent.

Magyari reported the strange rumors to Count Ferenc Nádasdy on his return. To avoid a scandal, Ferenc paid the relevant authorities to make sure they would stay silent. Although he might have been annoyed and angry with Erzsébet, as the saying goes, "Let those without sin cast the first stone." Ferenc also enjoyed torturing servants, and it's believed he taught his wife various methods of "disciplining" them.

Despite Ferenc's flaws, he cared very much about his image, and he was furious with Erzsébet regarding the attention she'd drawn by killing so often. While he was alive, he was able to control her, ensuring that the number of dead girls was limited. Ferenc would continue to protect his wife until his death in 1604. However, once he was gone, the number of deaths increased even more dramatically. No longer was anyone there to keep a check on Erzsébet's actions; now she could do as she pleased. Her killing spree took on a much darker tone as she was accompanied by four servants who helped with the torture.

As time went on, the countess became obsessed with her age and beauty. She would often sit in front of the mirror for hours. One day, as she sat before her mirror, she noticed the effects of age catching up with her. At the time, a servant had upset her, and an angry Erzsébet lashed out, hitting the girl so hard that she bled. When Erzsébet wiped her hand, she imagined that the one smeared with blood looked more youthful than the other. And so, according to legend, began the countess's obsession with blood. She believed she had found the fountain of youth.

According to the testimony of accomplices such as her servant Ilona Jó, Erzsébet would beat and kill the girls in such a way that she would be drenched in blood, after which she would change her stained clothes. The punishments would often be conducted in the kitchen or bathroom, where evidence of the torture could be washed away. Perhaps the obsession with blood is something later writers and historians added on, but no one can dispute the savagery with which the girls were killed.

As rumors continued to spread, Erzsébet found herself desperate for money. She even appeared at court while in mourning to request that the king pay back the debt he owed her late husband, but the crown refused. As her finances began to dry up, she put her Dévény castle up for sale. All the pressures that were piling up after her husband's death might have triggered a mental breakdown; she even suffered a theological crisis. Ultimately, Erzsébet no longer cared what happened to her. Since she believed she was already destined for hell, she no longer needed to hold back.

Another major trigger for the countess was the death of her brother, István Báthory, in 1605. She traveled to Ecsed to attend the funeral, accompanied by a group of servant girls. The strain of another loss might have been too much to bear for Erzsébet. Witnesses reported that three of the girls had been tortured so severely during the journey they later died. One, who was of high lineage, had also traveled with the countess to Ecsed, where she was later killed. When the girl's family arrived, they were informed that she had died of cholera. A squire from the village of Dénesfalva also reported that he'd heard that the daughters of two men of lower nobility had been cruelly tortured and put to death as well. The girls were buried en route to Ecsed.

Free from her husband's restraints, Erzsébet went on a killing spree. She had already murdered up to two hundred victims within the few years since Ferenc's death. Losing all interest in her regular duties, she chose to settle down in the quiet country castle at Čachtice.

Count György Thurzó, who would later arrest Erzsébet when he became palatine of the kingdom of Hungary, was her cousin, and he had promised her husband he would look after her. In 1607, Thurzó was celebrating the marriage of his daughter, and of course Erzsébet was invited to the happy occasion. But it seems the stress of attending another social gathering proved too much. On the journey home, one of the maids tried to flee. Erzsébet was enraged by this, which meant that the girl had essentially signed her own death warrant. Male servants reported that the servant girl was taken to a nearby village, where she was stripped naked and made to stand up to her neck in freezing water; she was repeatedly doused until she had frozen to death.

Erzsébet would seek darker ways of punishing the crimes committed by her maids. For instance, if a servant girl was accused of stealing a coin, the countess would heat it until it was red-hot, then press the coin into the maid's hand. Despite everything that occurred, few nobles took notice; Erzsébet was even invited to King Matthias's coronation in 1608. The nobles paid little attention to lower-class gossip, and since Erzsébet came from a powerful aristocratic family, few were eager to make an enemy of her. On the way home from the coronation, the countess stopped at one of her castles, where she burned her attendants with molten iron, nearly torturing them to death.

A pattern had now emerged; whenever Erzsébet attended high-profile gatherings, they had a profound psychological effect on her. The amount of torture she inflicted always increased when she traveled—and the more uncomfortable the event, the worse the fate inflicted upon her victims.

Erzsébet had help in managing the household. Anna Darvolya and Dorottya Szentes supervised the staff, which included János Újváry, Ilona Jó, and Katalin Beneczky. These five servants assisted the countess in the torture of her victims. They were even responsible for bringing more girls to the castle when the number of maids began to decrease.

Erzsébet once pierced a girl's lips with needles, in effect fastening her mouth shut; if she tried to move her tongue between her lips, the countess would pierce her tongue with a needle. Some servant girls were beaten so badly that blood splattered the floor and walls, even scattering chunks of flesh. Sometimes the victims passed out from the pain, only to be revived and made to endure more torture until they finally died.

Many of the male servants tried to help these girls, but Erzsébet wouldn't stop until someone finally stopped her. A servant named Benedikt Deseo was a witness to many of the countess's crimes, and he would beg her to stop, though to no avail. By late 1610, he'd had enough and threatened to leave, only to be stopped by Imre Megyeri (tutor to Erzsébet's son), who asked him to stay for a few more weeks. Maybe Megyeri knew that the countess's end was fast approaching.

As rumors of her violence spread through the villages, many people began hiding their daughters whenever Erzsébet's servants came looking for new maids. Even the clergy began to refuse proper burials for the ever-increasing number of dead girls. So in order to hide the bodies, the countess secretly buried them in the local cemetery. She would even hide the bodies in the gardens, drainage ditches, grains bins, and fruit pits on the castle grounds.

Among her accomplices, the worst was Anna Darvolya, who had taught the other four servants how to torture. She would bind the arms and legs of the victims so tightly they turned a deathly pale. She was even reported to have beaten victims repeatedly—up to five hundred times, or until they finally died. Dorottya Szentes and Ilona Jó had the same reputation for cruelty, as did János Újváry, who had the protection of the countess, which allowed him to do as he pleased. Katalin Beneczky was the only one who tried to help some of the girls, such as giving them food when they were being starved.

Perhaps if Erzsébet had continued to torture low-born girls, no one would have taken notice. But in 1609, Anna Darvolya suffered a stroke, which might have caused her death. During this time, Erzsébet turned more and more to Erzsi Majorova, a forest witch, for advice. The countess's dealings with the witch might have been her undoing, since it was Erzsi who advised Erzsébet that the blood of noble girls was more powerful than the blood of commoners, especially when it came to magic.

It was at this point that Erzsébet established a sort of finishing school for high-born young women known as a gynaeceum. Some of these young women were even related to Erzsébet by blood. This project provided her not only with income, but also with a fresh supply of young maidens. Nobles were eager to send their daughters to the countess. Either the rumors hadn't reached their ears, or they believed that only low-born girls were dealt with harshly by the countess.

It wasn't long before the nobles' daughters started going missing, or their families were forbidden from seeing them. In one incident, Janós Belanczky, accompanied by a friend, arrived at Erzsébet Báthory's court. At first, Belanczky wanted his sister to return home, but Erzsébet refused. Belanczky then demanded he at least be allowed to see her before he left. After he was kept waiting for an hour, his sister was finally brought out. Crying and whining and severely weakened from torture and torment, she could barely hold out her hands. Despite seeing his sister's condition, Belanczky returned home without her. Why he did so is unknown. Once her brother was gone, the girl was tortured still further until she died.

Many aristocratic families lost their daughters and sisters to the countess. They formally lodged complaints with King Matthias, who in turn ordered György Thurzó to conduct an inquiry regarding the numerous allegations against Erzsébet Báthory. Thurzó, who was both the palatine and a cousin to Erzsébet Báthory, was now struggling between duty and family. In the end, he followed through with his duty and began investigating the horrible tragedies that had been taking place everywhere the countess went.

Thurzó sent letters to the proper authorities, reading: "You know how, both in the past and present time, several serious complaints have come to us regarding the noble ... Lady Erzsébet Báthory ...; namely, that [she], through some sort of evil spirit, has set aside her reverence for God and man, and has killed in cruel and various ways many girls and virgins and other women who lived in her Gynaeceum."

Within the letters, Thurzó instructed the authorities to question everyone who might have any knowledge of the countess, including members of the church, nobility, and all other classes. Slowly, they began collecting evidence. From March to July 1610, the chief notary interrogated thirty-four people. Up until the time of her arrest, people were still frightened of the countess and her power, and many hesitated to open up about the goings-on in the castle. A break finally came when a tortured servant girl managed to escape. She made her way to the nearest town, a knife still stuck in her foot. Information in hand, Thurzó made his way to Čachtice to confront his cousin.

Erzsébet's downfall came on December 29, 1610, when a party of armed men arrived at Čachtice Castle, with György Thurzó at the head. With him were two nobles, Count Miklós Zrínyi and György Drugeth de Homonna, and lastly, the tutor Imre Megyeri. Upon entering, they were greeted by a gruesome sight. The bruised body of a young girl lay sprawled near the entryway. As they continued forward, they found the bodies of two more girls, stabbed and beaten to death. Moving through the castle, they heard screams. Following the noise, the men reached a room where four servants (under Erzsébet's orders) were in the process of torturing a girl. In one corner, they found another sobbing as she waited to be taken next. Apprehending the servants and liberating the girls, Thurzó made his way to the countess's bedchamber. Erzsébet was enraged that the men had entered her private quarters. After a fiery confrontation, she was arrested, bringing an end to her reign of terror.

At the trial, the four servants who had served her were tortured. In the end, they finally provided testimony against the countess. János Újváry, Ilona Jó, and Dorottya Szentes were executed, while Katarina Beneczky was spared. Although Erzsébet had been convicted, Thurzó did his best to ensure that she would not be executed. Ultimately, she was imprisoned within her own castle. She was confined to one room, where her daughter brought her food until her death in 1614.

THE BOY WHO THRIVED

CATHY PICKENS

Every year, a select few US athletes leave college in their early twenties with multimillion-dollar contracts to play pro football. Even their signing bonuses can be in the millions. And the bottom of the pay scale isn't shabby either: $660,000 in 2021. A minimum six-figure salary the first year out of college? Add the "fame" factor and the macho culture, and the real surprise might be that more of these fame-worthy few don't go wrong.

The most recognizable name on that gone-wrong list is O. J. Simpson, tried and acquitted in 1995 for killing his ex-wife Nicole Brown Simpson and her friend Ron Goldman. Simpson later lost a $33.5 million civil lawsuit by the victims' families, and in 2008, he was imprisoned on a list of charges involving a sports memorabilia robbery.

Most recent on the list was All-American Aaron Hernandez, who hanged himself in jail after being convicted of murder. A postmortem brain study showed he suffered from CTE (chronic traumatic encephalopathy), a degenerative disease associated with violence in those who've suffered too many hard hits to the head. He was the second player still active on the National Football League roster to be charged with murder.

The first still-active football player accused of murder was Rae Carruth. The murder seemed so misguided and the lives destroyed so promising that the city where it happened can't forget—especially because of one shining, happy reminder of the best of those involved, and plenty of questions about what fame and "the big time" really mean.

Joining the Big Leagues

When businessman Jerry Richardson—famous for playing pro football and starting food franchises—met with a group determined to bring an NFL team to Charlotte, North Carolina, most experts put that bid in the really-long-shot column. Even with partners like Hugh McColl—the CEO building a local bank into national powerhouse Bank of America and the city into the second-largest US financial center—the betting line was against them. But Richardson would be unique among team owners as the only one who had played in the NFL.

The city's first professional sports team—the Hornets NBA basketball team—set league records for fan attendance in its 1988 inaugural year. In 1996, the new Panthers football team began playing in its new stadium, with aerial shots showcasing the city's skyline on nationally televised games. Charlotte felt it had arrived, getting a taste of big-city fame, prosperous enough for the professional sports gods to smile.

Sports teams were only a symbol, not a cause, of the city's tremendous growth spurt in the coming years. But in November 1999, the dark side of high-profile professional sports cast its shadow over Charlotte. What should have been quietly handled in a domestic support agreement became a case that makes several "top-ten" lists of NFL players gone wrong.

New Arrivals in Charlotte

In 1997, for its third season, the Carolina Panthers football team got pick number twenty-seven in the first round of the draft. True, the draft is set up so the worst teams get the best new players. A wide receiver with Rae Carruth's stats was big news for the Panthers. Twenty-three-year-old Carruth signed a four-year deal with a $1.3 million signing bonus as part of his $3.7 million contract—small amounts compared to contracts today, but this was twenty-five years ago.

In 1983, when I moved to Charlotte, it was best known for three things: televangelists Jim and Tammy Faye Bakker and their PTL Club (which would fall in disgrace thanks to a sex-and-money scandal starting in 1987); as regional headquarters for two national motorcycle gangs—Hell's Angels and the Outlaws, plus several violent local bike clubs; and its homegrown sports franchise, professional wrestling (which family-owned Jim Crockett Promotions sold to Ted Turner in Atlanta in 1988). As entertaining (or embarrassing) as those televangelists, motorcycle gangsters, and men wearing tights while leaping from rope rings were, things were changing in Charlotte. Even those who cared nothing for football knew big-league sports marked an important shift.

In 2012, ESPN reporter Shaun Assael interviewed Big Gus Panos, a convicted bookie described as a "philosopher-king" who had plenty of perspective on athletics in Charlotte. Big, good-looking guys with at least the aura of money attract attention, and in the clubs and restaurants around Charlotte, people took note of the city's new celebrities. Gus felt the city "wasn't used to the demands of pro personalities. A traditional college sports center, it was more familiar with athletes who were humble and willing to sip sweet tea at charity functions."

Amid so many bright lights and so much hustle, who could forecast the effects of one inconvenient pregnancy?

The Emergency Call

Around 11:45 p.m. on November 15, 1999, Rae Carruth left the movie theater at StoneCrest shopping center with his date, Cherica Adams, who was eight months pregnant with their child.

Twenty-four-year-old Cherica was a slender, attractive, motivated young woman who easily drew attention. News reports often identified her as an exotic dancer. Sure, she had danced at an adult entertainment club, but that was a side job, the kind that could pay for her BMW. And even in that environment, she found ways to help others and encourage them toward better lives. Her primary job was selling real estate, and she had dreams of being a music promoter. She'd grown up in a Charlotte with its share of wealthy athletes, and she'd figured out how to travel in those circles. Much like Rae Carruth, she knew she'd make her mark.

Those who knew Rae in his growing-up years in California and his college time at the University of Colorado describe a quiet, reserved guy. He was personable, approachable, funny, and flirty. He had lots of women friends—some with benefits. His mother, Theodry Carruth, pushed him about grades, pushed him to go to college. Rae wasn't a hulk; he was less than six feet tall and less than two hundred pounds. But he could run really fast, and that's important for a wide receiver.

Cherica met Rae when they both showed up with friends at a pool party in June 1998. They again crossed paths in November, at a teammate's birthday party at the club where she worked. According to Carruth, they had a few consensual sexual encounters. He'd given her a cell phone as a gift—not something everyone had in 1998.

Dating a professional football player, especially one with the marquee value of Rae Carruth, was a plus. Rae was not pushy or aggressive, and he had an obvious appeal to women. But he also knew he had a big field to play on and, in the game of love, he wasn't ready to sign any contracts. Too much fun to be had, too easily.

Cherica became pregnant in the spring of 1999, and she planned to keep her baby. Rae asked her about an abortion, but she refused. He already had a child, born when he was a sophomore at Colorado and for whom he paid three thousand dollars a month in child support. But Cherica was ready to start her family, and she knew her mother and family would be the support she needed to raise it. According to a friend, she'd already picked out names for a boy and a girl: Chancellor and Chase.

After the couple watched the late movie together at the upscale suburban theater, they picked up her BMW sedan at his house in Blakeney, a few miles south of StoneCrest, and she followed him back to her house.

About a mile after Rea Road crossed busy Highway 51, the narrow two-lane road dipped into a hollow shadowed by trees. Rae's Ford Expedition slowed, forcing Cherica to stop. Before she had time to process what was happening, a Nissan Maxima pulled alongside her car. From the back seat, someone fired five bullets into her driver-side door and window.

She tried to turn and lean away from the shots, but she was hit once in the neck and three times in the back. A crime scene photo shows the open driver's door, the window glass crazed around four tightly grouped round holes. One of the last bullets did all the damage.

Despite the shock and pain, she managed to drive her car a few yards, turn onto MacAndrew Drive, and into the yard of the first house on the right. She repeatedly honked her car horn, hoping to wake someone who could help. At 12:31 a.m., 911 received her cell phone call.

In the twelve minutes she talked to the dispatcher and then to the officer who came to the scene, she delivered a lot of information, interrupted at times with gasping moans of pain. She'd been following her baby's daddy, the football player, and he'd called somebody from his house before they left. She told how Carruth slowed and another car pulled up, how Carruth "just left" after she was shot. "I think he did it," she said. "I don't know what to think."

At the hospital seven hours after her baby was taken, Cherica's mother brought her a picture of Chancellor Lee Adams. By this time, she had a breathing tube down her throat and couldn't speak, but she squeezed her mother's hand.

When homicide detective Darrell Price and a nurse asked her questions, she gestured for a pen and paper and scrawled answers. Rae was there. Price asked, "Do you think Rae had anything to do with it?" She drew a question mark. She asked for Chapstick and repeated the information she'd told the dispatcher.

Soon after she wrote those words, Cherica went into a coma.

Charlotte was in the early stages of establishing a forensics collaborative to train those involved with crime victims how to collect and handle evidence: emergency physicians and nurses, SANE (sexual assault nurse examiners), fire, MEDIC (Mobile Diagnosis for Improved Care), crime lab, police, district attorneys—anyone involved in the process. Cases against perpetrators would be easier to bring if everyone shared the same protocols.

Not-so-funny jokes circulated—not just in Charlotte, but at crime scenes everywhere—about where would be the best place to start cutting the clothes off a gunshot victim. The bullet hole, of course. A ready-made opening.

District attorneys were often stymied in prosecuting cases because a bullet or casing had been discarded, along with the bloodstained clothing the victim wore into the ER, or the clothing and other evidence had been thrown onto the floor and potentially contaminated. Either no photographs were taken of the injuries, or no sexual assault kit was utilized. Medical personnel were, rightly, focused on saving a life, not on saving evidence. But with an awareness of the importance of those items, small changes in protocol might save the victim and get justice.

An emergency room physician led the push for change, but others quickly joined her. I served with then-Deputy Chief Darrell Price and others on the Mecklenburg Forensic Medicine Program board, which established procedures, coordinated supplies and reporting, and set up training sessions. The two large hospital systems in the county, first responders, police, the judicial system, and educational institutions all put aside any competitiveness to work on this joint effort.

Cherica Adams was shot on a dark road before these efforts were fully realized, but awareness of the need to capture whatever details they could was already evident in the hospital trauma unit that night.

A defense appeal sought a new trial based in part on Cherica's handwritten answers. The state argued that excluding her notes because the defense couldn't cross-examine her "would, in effect, reward him for participating in her murder," but the state appeals court agreed with the defense and held that the notes shouldn't have been admitted. However, information in the notes was corroborated by witnesses who did testify, so the notes did no harm and no new trial was granted.

Cherica's baby boy was delivered that night, but his brain suffered from loss of oxygen during the seventy minutes between the shooting and the emergency C-section delivery at the hospital. Grandmother Saundra Adams had the joyful and heartbreaking task of seeing that her new grandson was properly named as she watched her only daughter fight to live.

As an attorney, I'd spent several years working obstetrical malpractice cases. News reports didn't give details about the baby's prognosis, but such a traumatic birth was a bad omen. Like so much happening in those early days, though, that part of the story remained the family's private struggle.

Hospital hallways and waiting rooms have a brightly lit, hard-edged sameness. Once you've kept vigil for a loved one in such a space, you don't forget it. You grieve for others who must do the same.

While Cherica's family held vigil during the early-morning hours at the hospital, Rae was playing video games at a teammate's house and not responding to repeated phone calls and pages from Cherica's mother.

Tensions were high when he arrived just before dawn, accompanied by what was described as an entourage. Saundra Adams confronted him, convinced from what she'd learned from Cherica that he was somehow involved.

Thanks to Cherica pointing investigators toward Carruth, they weren't investigating a random drive-by shooting, and they quickly found links to the three men in the Nissan: Van Brett Watkins, Michael Kennedy, and Stanley Abraham.

Ten days after the shooting, Carruth was arrested, but quickly bonded out.

A month after the shooting, Cherica was removed from life support.

Immediately after her death, police got an arrest warrant for Rae Lamar Wiggins—his legal name—now wanted for murder.

Trouble was, he'd taken off as soon as he heard the news, and no one was saying where he'd gone.

Local police and the bail bondsmen on the hook for Carruth's three-million-dollar bond were following every lead, trying to find him. His mother, worried her son might be shot, provided the tip.

The next day, FBI agents surrounded Carruth in the parking lot of a Tennessee motel, curled into the trunk of a lady friend's car with food supplies, $3,900 in cash, and bottles of his own urine.

Rae later became the Mecklenburg County Jail's celebrity inmate.

The Defense Attorney

David Rudolf wasn't Theodry Carruth's first choice for her son's defense attorney. She lived in California, so naturally she contacted the office of O. J.'s attorney, Johnnie Cochran. They referred her to Rudolf. He proved a good choice.

In addition to a string of multimillion-dollar verdicts in wrongful conviction and product-liability cases, Rudolf had posted a big win in a 1995 Charlotte murder case. A local doctor was charged with stabbing his wife to death in their home before he left for work one morning. In a pretrial hearing, Rudolf argued that the district attorney's office withheld evidence about a handyman who had worked at the house. In addition, prosecution witness Dr. Michael Baden, famed forensic pathologist and former chief medical examiner for New York City, was unable to state with a reasonable degree of medical certainty (the evidentiary standard in North Carolina) that the wife was dead before the doctor left the house. Thanks to Rudolf's arguments, the criminal charges were dismissed and never refiled.

Two years later, in a civil trial, Rudolf won for the doctor husband an $8.5 million verdict in a wrongful death suit against Marion Gales, the handyman who'd acted strangely on the day of the murder. The standard of proof in a civil case—by a preponderance of the evidence—is easier to meet than the standard in a criminal case: beyond a reasonable doubt. But an indigent civil defendant is not provided counsel by the state as he would be in a criminal case, so questions were raised about the fairness of the fight, given the handyman's volunteer lawyer going up against Rudolf and a well-to-do plaintiff.

Still, the evidence Rudolf presented convinced many outside the courtroom who took the time to sift through it. Even though the defendant had no means to pay even a portion of the large judgment, it was a win.

Gales, reportedly a nice guy unless he was using drugs, later ended up in prison for murdering another woman. Gales maintained that he did not kill the doctor's wife and leave her in the house with her baby, though he did plead guilty to involuntary manslaughter in the death of LaCoya Monique Martin.

After the civil court win in 1997, David Rudolf's next big criminal case in Charlotte was defending Rae Carruth.

Thanks to a French film producer and Netflix's documentary series *The Staircase*, Rudolf's reputation got even bigger in 2003, when he defended novelist Michael Peterson in Durham, North Carolina, for the 2001 murder of his wife, Kathleen. Peterson was convicted after a five-month trial—then the longest in Durham's history—and sentenced to life without parole. Following a newspaper exposé and audit of the North Carolina State Bureau of Investigation's crime lab and its agent's questionable blood-spatter testimony, Peterson's sentence was overturned in 2011. Rather than face another trial, Peterson accepted an Alford plea, which meant acknowledging that the state had enough evidence to convict him and accepting the punishment without pleading guilty. He was released for time served.

The Trial

In the weeks following October 23, 2000, I didn't need to drive the four miles to the county courthouse to watch the trial. *Court TV* televised it.

Rae Carruth was the first—and only—defendant tried. He faced a first-degree murder charge, which meant a possible death penalty. Additional charges were conspiracy to commit murder, using an instrument with intent to destroy an unborn child, and discharging a firearm into occupied property. Interestingly absent from the list was second-degree murder, but the judge felt the evidence showed the intent necessary for first-degree.

Every case has two sides, and every good trial lawyer must have a theory of the case that plausibly links all the evidence and points to the conclusion that serves the client's interests. Rudolf built a case that the shooting was retaliation for a drug deal Carruth backed out of financing.

Prosecutor J. Gentry Caudill said it was murder for hire. Carruth paid to get Cherica out of the way because he didn't want to be saddled with more child support. But Caudill needed someone involved in the plot to tell the jury about the details and provide the crucial link to Carruth.

Van Brett Watkins, the gunman, confessed early. He took a plea deal for second-degree murder when it was offered, which removed the risk of the death penalty for him. When he agreed to testify, Caudill had his witness.

However, during jury selection, Michael Kennedy's attorney approached Caudill. Kennedy had driven the car and was ready to testify against Carruth—and he would do it without benefit of a plea deal.

That never happens.

A defendant understandably wants something in return for testifying against someone he once called a friend. In this case, Kennedy's offer made him and his family the target of death threats. But as a co-conspirator who has gotten nothing in return, his testimony was credible. A defense attorney couldn't accuse him of telling a story only because he got a sweet deal. He had no reason to lie.

Carruth got to know Michael Kennedy, age twenty-three, while talking about car modifications at a shop one day. Kennedy also dealt drugs, and through him, Carruth met Stanley Abraham, Kennedy's eighteen-year-old friend.

On the stand for the prosecution, Kennedy outlined the planned hit, the players, and what they did that night. He was believable and not swayed on cross-examination. Later, even Rudolf admitted that he hadn't shaken him. "It doesn't mean he wasn't lying," Rudolf told *Charlotte Observer* sports columnist Scott Fowler. "It just means that he was a good liar."

Prosecutor Caudill, a tall, languid man, methodically presented evidence that Carruth did not want another baby. Two ex-girlfriends described his reaction to their baby news in ways a jury couldn't ignore. While in college, his girlfriend had his baby. Now he paid three thousand dollars a month in child support, which Carruth had negotiated down from more than five thousand dollars—and he didn't want another obligation. When she told him that she might bring their son to Charlotte for a visit, he'd said, "Don't be surprised if you get in a car accident." She'd known him a long time, and she couldn't quite pass that off as a joke.

Another girlfriend testified that she got an abortion after Carruth threatened to send someone to kill her. "You know I can do it. You can't have this baby."

Some testified that he seemed pleased about Cherica's baby, but he had distanced himself from her and made it clear they weren't going to be a family. Others said he clearly *wasn't* pleased.

What those of us watching from home on *Court TV* didn't see was the parade of attractive young women who came every day to support Rae.

The Hit Man

Years later, *Court TV* placed the testimony of confessed shooter Van Brett Watkins on its list of top courtroom moments.

With Kennedy's testimony, the prosecution decided its case was strong enough without calling Watkins, that he was too unpredictable.

So David Rudolf called Van Brett Watkins as part of the defense case—an admittedly unusual gamble. And he used an unusual tactic: he just let Watkins talk. Rudolf wanted the jury to see him for the arrogant, aggressive man he was.

Watkins was a big man—six-foot-three and almost three hundred pounds—with an impressive criminal record. On the stand, he wore a dark suit, starched white shirt, and red tie. What was only partially visible in the TV shot was the pair of sheriff's deputies the judge had stationed on either side of Watkins, separating him from the judge on one side and the jury on the other. No one quite knew what to expect from this man.

Rae, meanwhile, sat at the defense table with his eyes downcast, his demeanor calm and gentle.

Rudolf kept Watkins on the stand for two days, goading him, challenging him. Watkins admitted he'd been overheard saying, "I hope the bitch dies." Had he been talking about Cherica? No, he said, he wasn't wishing Cherica would die.

Watkins leaned toward the defense table, his arm outstretched, his finger pointing straight at Rae, his voice emphasizing each word. "That's the bitch I was talking about—Rae Carruth."

In another exchange, Rudolf ridiculed the notion that this was a hit, that no hit man would show up without a gun.

Watkins bellowed. "I didn't need a gun, okay? Can't you look and see?" In his rant, he delivered the last sentence directly at David Rudolf: "I could rip you like a rag doll." The menace was palpable, even on a TV screen.

The most memorable part of Watkins's time on the stand came at the end, without him saying a word. It started routinely enough. David Rudolf had no further questions, signaling the witness was dismissed.

On the TV screen, I watched as Watkins put his hands on the arms of the chair and moved to stand up. He filled the screen—except for a glimpse of the deputy standing behind him, near the judge's right shoulder.

The next sound was a gavel banging furiously and a voice yelling for him to *sit down, sit down.* The camera stayed on Watkins. The deputy behind him tensed, ready for action.

Van Brett Watkins's expression showed genuine surprise. He thought he was supposed to leave the stand. Then he got a little smile at the corner of his mouth as he eased back into the witness chair. He didn't intend to cause a panic—but he enjoyed it.

———————————

Later, jurors said they believed Watkins's testimony. One told Scott Fowler, "His story was powerful, nasty, and evil as you can get." And convincing. The jury believed Carruth was involved. But in what? In a drug deal? In arranging a hit? And how did the facts fit the elements required in the charges he faced?

What the jury didn't hear—what wasn't made public until Watkins spoke years later to Scott Fowler in Raleigh's Central Prison—was that Watkins had killed other people. He worked legitimate jobs in construction and as a bouncer at a club, but he also sold drugs and did whatever someone would pay him to do. He told Fowler he'd worked as a hit man, hired by four wives to kill their husbands, in New York, Miami, and Atlanta. Some had been abused, others just wanted their husbands gone. He wouldn't give any other details because he didn't want the women to go to prison. But he also pointed out that those hits had done the job: "I got away with it. They died right there on the spot."

Carruth had visited the club where Watkins worked as a bouncer, though Watkins didn't get to know him there. They were introduced by a friend when Carruth wanted a quote on building a fence. Watkins sometimes detailed Carruth's cars, and the press frequently described him as Carruth's handyman.

Watkins said Carruth asked how much he would charge to beat up a girl and make her abort. Watkins told him, "I don't beat up a girl. I kill people."

And thus, the plot was hatched.

What Happened That Night

The public watched the story unfold in three stages: the early news reports following the shooting, the trial coverage, and the interviews long after the trial, when those involved had more perspective and felt more comfortable talking. At trial, we saw the players for the first time, heard their stories, and began to understand how the pieces fit together.

That November night, Watkins, Kennedy, and Abraham were at Carruth's home when Cherica arrived for what she expected to be a "wonderful first date" after a long time apart. Cherica then called her mom, saying she wasn't sure what was going on. Her mom told her to just leave, though Saundra could hear Rae in the background, convincing Cherica to come along, he was ready. Cherica ended up leaving with Rae.

With the couple at the movie theater, the three men left the house and drove around, drinking beer. First, though, they had to go buy a gun for a hundred dollars. Watkins hadn't brought one because, he said later, even though he'd agreed to do this hit for six thousand dollars, he still wasn't sure about it.

Attorney David Rudolf pointed out that this didn't sound like a well-planned contract hit. This sounded like what Rae said it was: a drug deal gone bad. Rae told his lawyer he'd agreed to finance a drug buy for Watkins, who'd brought a load of marijuana from Atlanta in a U-Haul that a buddy let him rent cheap. Watkins drove the truck as his regular transportation, even parked it near Carruth's house that night. Rae reneged on the deal and said the shooting was to teach him that Watkins meant business.

Rudolf said Rae got scared when he saw the Nissan pull around Cherica's car. He thought Watkins was coming for him. "He was scared, and he took off," Rudolf said in an interview. "And he's not particularly proud of that. It's not sort of a heroic thing to do—big football player, you know, running. But that's what he did."

To support the contention that Carruth had taken off in fear for his own life, Rudolf called expert witness Henry Lee. An experienced forensic scientist and head of Connecticut's state crime lab, Dr. Lee hosted a cable network show featuring his cases, and testified in high-profile cases around the country, including O. J. Simpson's. Dr. Lee would later testify in another of attorney Rudolf's cases as a blood-spatter expert for Michael Peterson.

In Carruth's defense, Lee testified that three of the bullets went into Cherica's car at a ninety-degree angle, but two went in at a slant. He said those slanted shots meant that Cherica's car wasn't stopped but may have moved forward, so Rae Carruth's vehicle wasn't in front of her. Otherwise, the cars would show damage.

Kennedy testified that he drove the nondescript Nissan sedan he'd been renting for a while, and Abraham sat in front with him. Watkins sat in the back seat alone, and fired the five shots.

Afterward, as Kennedy turned his car around and sped away from Cherica's car, he didn't tell the others what he saw in his rearview mirror. He told police later he'd seen her brake lights "blink on. So I didn't think she was dead." But he didn't tell the others.

After they left the scene, Watkins pulled off his sweatshirt, wiped himself with gasoline to eliminate any gunshot residue, and was ready to go to Waffle House. He was hungry.

After the trial, jurors and court-watchers commented on Cherica's strength and her presence of mind. Without the details she gave on the recorded 911 call, the investigation and prosecution would have been much more difficult. Caudill said the piece of evidence linking Carruth to the crime was Cherica's own voice, which was so powerful he opened his case with those twelve minutes of anguished audio. "She was the strongest witness for herself—to her own murder."

Without her words, would that very early morning on that little road be anything but a tragic, unexplained drive-by shooting?

The jury deliberated for twenty-four hours over four days and convicted Carruth of the three lesser charges, but not of first-degree murder. The defense arguments may have saved Rae Carruth's life—which, in the world of a criminal defense lawyer, counts as a win.

In a later interview, given with Carruth's permission, Rudolf said of course Carruth felt guilty about Cherica's death—not because he planned the shooting, but because he'd agreed to the drug deal that led to the retaliation.

His sentence was a maximum of twenty-four years and four months.

To a trial full of the unexpected, Saundra Adams added a graceful coda. After the verdict, she pulled the prosecution team and her family into a room, and gathered them in a circle. Caudill said, "And she prayed. Prayed for Rae Carruth. Prayed for Van Brett Watkins. It was an incredibly moving moment I'll never forget."

Afterward

Watkins was sentenced to between forty and fifty years. He became a practicing Muslim and has accumulated a remarkable number of prison infractions, many involving violence or threats. But he is also the defendant who reached out to Saundra Adams, the one she said she feels the most connection with, the one who has shown remorse. Watkins could be released in 2046.

Michael Kennedy served almost eleven years and was released in 2011. Stanley Abraham, who ended up in the car because his friend Kennedy was worried and wanted him along, served two years and was released in 2001.

This was Gentry Caudill's last big case before he donned a robe for a newly created position as superior court judge.

On David Rudolf's law firm website, among an impressive string of his criminal and civil court successes, a heading reads: "North Carolina Panther Rae Carruth Found Not Guilty of Murder." Technically, that was correct. The jury did not convict him on the charge of murder.

Rae was released in October 2018, after serving eighteen years. He moved to Pennsylvania to live with a friend.

Before his release, Rae replied to Scott Fowler's persistent requests for interviews. In his letter, the former English major identified himself as the story's antagonist. "That's something that will never change. There's absolutely nothing that I could ever say or do to right my wrongs... to no longer be the bad guy."

In October 2018, Fowler wrote what became an eight-part series and a podcast on the case, with detailed interviews gathered during a year of research. His reporting, illustrated with photos by Jeff Siner, remains the most comprehensive account of this case.

In those retrospective interviews, almost twenty years after the shooting, Fowler learned that the investigators were surprised by how the case came together. They questioned Watkins, let him hear Kennedy's confession naming Watkins as the shooter, and then shared their Thanksgiving dinner with him. At that point, detective Darrell Price said, Watkins "gave it up—and it really blew my mind." They knew he was telling the truth "because his story fit everything that we knew."

Fowler ended his series with a question Carruth posed in one of his emails: "Do you think that it's possible for a generally good person to get him/herself involved in a situation as heart-wrenchingly horrible as the one I was in, or is it your belief that such a person could only be cut from the worst of molds?"

Saundra and Chancellor Adams were awarded $5.8 million in a civil lawsuit in 2003. Of course, she won't collect any of that unless Carruth finds a post-prison way to make a lot of money. But the money would come in handy, providing for Chancellor. Fowler reported that a charitable group at Carruth's Colorado alma mater helped the Adamses get a house that accommodates his physical limitations—and the grandmother and the one she calls her "miracle" child have become regulars at the group's charity golf tournament in Colorado.

A news camera followed a teenaged Chancellor Lee Adams during a physical therapy session as he worked to walk on his own. He's done far more than seemed possible when he was born, and his grandmother sees both Carruth's physical strength and her daughter's determination and joy in him.

As I watched the televised video and saw how hard he concentrated, how his muscles quivered from the effort, I wondered if any athlete puts in the work that young man does as he struggles with the simplest tasks. And do they smile as broadly as he does with his victories?

Today, the Panthers have moved on to other stories, and the movie theater at StoneCrest still shows movies and serves popcorn. The two-lane stretch of Rea Road (pronounced "ray," coincidentally, just as Rae's name is pronounced) has been widened to add bike lanes and broad sidewalks now filled with neighborhood walkers. Though the trees no longer shelter a cool, dark spot and the dip in the road isn't as noticeable, I still think about Cherica whenever I drive along that section, about how hard she fought for herself and for her baby.

Chancellor Lee Adams graduated from a special high school program in 2021, at the age of twenty-one. The news media in Charlotte have documented his life, so we've come to recognize his huge beaming smile, his good spirit—and his struggles. His grandmother Saundra—"G-Mom," he calls her—raised him.

Saundra feels blessed and grateful—not the reaction many have to challenges and heartbreak. "In some ways, as ironic as it may sound, if this hadn't happened, I would have never stepped into the greatness that God had for me." Her joy, her big heart, and the genuine devotion between her and her grandson are obvious as their milestones and celebrations are reported to a city that wants to share a small part of their very personal victories.

Those who've covered the case talk in terms unusual for seasoned journalists—they talk about how one special aspect of this case changed their lives. In a *Washington Post* interview, veteran *Charlotte Observer* sports reporter Scott Fowler, who followed Carruth's professional career and the murder case from their beginnings, said, "The takeaway for me and what has changed my life for the better is being around Saundra Adams.... She would never want someone to say she's a saint. She's still feisty. She's still mad at Carruth in ways. But she has forgiven him.... And she has stirred some emotions in me that I didn't know I had."

By all reports, Chancellor is a very happy guy. Thomas Lake echoed that when talking about his *Sports Illustrated* article, "The Boy They Couldn't Kill." Forgiveness is hard, he said, and Saundra's happiness seemed far beyond possible. "It's almost like there's no word in the English language that properly describes it. The way she's been able to let go of that anger and just love her grandson is something truly astonishing and appears to have made all the difference," Lake said. Maybe this is what the whole story is about: Forgiveness. And joy.

In the end, is that what being famous really is? The ability to affect other people, to make them consider their own lives and want to be better? For those who've been in the orbit of one remarkable young man and his G-Mom, forgiveness and joy are lasting testaments that eclipse more ephemeral images of fame.

THE DEVIL'S PROPHET

MITZI SZERETO

I first heard of Lostprophets via a guy in Birmingham. He absolutely loved them, even going on to make the lofty claim that he was supposed to be in the band, but something happened to scupper his chances of rock stardom. I assumed he was trying to impress me. I had my doubts as to why a group of musicians from Pontypridd, Wales, would seek out the purported musical talents of some random Brummie. In the meantime, said Brummie kept sending me their songs. I thought the band was pretty good.

But in 2013, I got rid of every Lostprophets music track I had, as did many other people in Britain and elsewhere.

Sex and drugs and rock-and-roll. The music business has long been known for its excesses, especially regarding sex. The men performing on stage have an extensive history of illegal and barely legal activities. Taking the candy on offer is nothing new. Whether they wield a microphone, play a guitar, or sit at a piano or behind a set of drums, they've had young women and girls flocking backstage and to their hotel rooms ever since the first vinyl records were pressed. Granted, it was a bit more restrained in the days before rock-and-roll. Back then, a man might think twice before risking his career on "forbidden fruit."

The supposedly squeaky-clean 1950s began to leave restraint behind, particularly when it came to famous musicians who now had no qualms when it came to sexual encounters with underage females. Some of the biggest names in rock music history did it. When twenty-two-year-old Jerry Lee Lewis married his thirteen-year-old cousin, it caused such a scandal that his British tour was canceled. Little Richard likewise had a reputation for pursuing underage girls, and Chuck Berry (at age thirty-three) actually served prison time for transporting a fourteen-year-old girl across state lines for "immoral purposes." Even Elvis Presley was known to like them young (his future wife Priscilla was only fourteen and he twenty-four when they began dating).

By the time the 1970s rolled around, rock stars were determined to outdo their predecessors, not just flaunting it, but playing games with the law in order to save their own backsides. Has-been rocker turned far-right spokesperson Ted Nugent skirted possible charges of statutory rape and a possible stay in jail by becoming the legal guardian of his seventeen-year-old "girlfriend." In addition to openly admitting to having sexual relations with underage girls, Nugent was so proud of it that he released a song called "Jailbait." Rock legends such as Led Zeppelin's Jimmy Page and David Bowie were known to have very young girls in their beds, particularly those who were part of the "Baby Groupies" scene in Los Angeles, some of whom were as young as twelve. Page reportedly kept his favored groupie locked in a hotel room so she'd be there whenever he wanted her. Iggy Pop also availed himself of the Baby Groupies, one being a tender thirteen when he bedded her. He too would brag about his exploits in his song "Look Away."

In the 1980s, Bill Wyman of the Rolling Stones began a sexual relationship with a fourteen-year-old girl when he was in his thirties. Aerosmith's Stephen Tyler became involved with a sixteen-year-old girl, even taking her on tour with him. In the 1990s, R&B star R. Kelly's illegal marriage to a fifteen-year-old girl backfired on him, busting open a stew of predatory activity with underage girls and young women that in June 2022 resulted in a prison sentence of thirty years for sex trafficking.

And the list goes on.

With the rare exception, the majority of these famous men continued with their careers and did not *face the music*. Those in the industry, as well as fans, appear to have been content to turn a blind eye to what was, in some cases, borderline pedophilia. Regardless of whether these girls agreed to or even initiated the encounters, there is still what's known as the "age of consent." Sexual activity with someone who hasn't reached a specific age is considered statutory rape and/or child abuse, and is therefore prosecutable. Even if some of these men later married their "girlfriends," it doesn't erase the fact that they were having sex with underage females.

Did these girls have the intellectual and emotional maturity to enter into sexual encounters with adult males many years older than themselves? The sexuality of young adolescents and children is an uncomfortable subject for many, but nevertheless, it exists. One might argue that these girls were willing participants, budding Lolitas dazzled by stardom and grappling with their newly emerging hormones—girls who were eager to service the famous rock gods whose records they listened to and whose concerts they attended. Like the infamous Baby Groupies, maybe they saw these men as notches on their belts. Never mind that some of these girls had barely begun to menstruate (assuming they'd begun at all) or, for that matter, weren't old enough to drive a car, let alone drink alcohol, apply for a credit card, or vote in an election.

Were these men sexual predators? Even Vladimir Nabokov's notorious protagonist Humbert Humbert eventually understood the enormity of what he'd done after his sexual relationship with his young "nymphet" was over. One can only wonder if any of the rock stars who indulged themselves so freely with their own nymphets experienced a similar epiphany.

Perhaps we can attribute this lack of accountability to the decades in which these events took place and, even more so, to an industry culture that normalized grown men having sex with underage girls. It was all just rock-and-roll, right? Today, this behavior would elicit somewhat more than a raised eyebrow, particularly in light of the #MeToo movement. Yet even in the more aware twenty-first century, the sexual dynamic between male rock star and female fan is still a powerful one, and no amount of #MeToo is likely to change that. Which begs the question: just how far is a fan willing to go to please her idol?

In 1997, Ian Watkins (vocals), Mike Lewis (guitar), Lee Gaze (guitar), Stuart Richardson (bass), and Mike Chiplin (drums) burst out of the suburban wilds of Pontypridd, Wales, entering the Cardiff music scene as Lostprophets. But their journey to professional rock-band status began years earlier, when Watkins met Lewis in high school. In 1991, the two teens formed their first band, Aftermath. A chance introduction brought Gaze into the picture. Abandoning Aftermath, Watkins and Gaze formed Fleshbind. Although short-lived, Fleshbind earned enough kudos to be a supporting band for Feeder at a London gig. Watkins then reunited with his friend Lewis, forming Public Disturbance in 1995. Meanwhile, he and Gaze had also formed another band called Lost Prophets, featuring Watkins as lead vocalist—and that heralded the beginning of rock music stardom. Watkins ditched Public Disturbance to focus his energy on the newly christened Lostprophets.

The band's mix of musical genres, blending alternative metal, heavy metal, nu metal, post-grunge, and hard rock, struck a chord with listeners. In 2000, Lostprophets landed their first album deal with UK independent label Visible Noise, resulting in *The Fake Sound of Progress*. Shortly afterward, keyboardist Jamie Oliver came on board. In 2001, Sony Records in the US signed the band, releasing for American ears a remixed and rejigged version of their UK album, with famed producer Michael Barbiero at the helm. In 2004, *Start Something* was released, landing on the charts, including every musician's dream, *Billboard*. In 2005, departing drummer Chiplin was replaced by Josh Freese. Around the same time, the band changed album producers, recruiting Canadian producer and musician Bob Rock, who'd worked with Metallica, the Cult, Bryan Adams, and other big names. This led to their 2006 album, *Liberation Transmission*, which was followed by *The Betrayed* in 2010 and *Weapons* in 2012. Other musicians came and went, though the main band members stayed the same, with Watkins always front and center as lead vocalist. Lostprophets would be graced with silver, gold, and platinum albums, including a UK number one, top-ten singles, and *NME* and *Kerrang!* awards, the latter for best British band two years in a row.

Collectively, Lostprophets could do no wrong. Individually, however, was another matter.

Ian Watkins, with his floppy dark hair, slim build, tattoos, and emo persona made female fans sit up and take notice. Young women and girls liked what they saw, and Watkins liked what he saw too. Of course, this story could have been just another account of rock star sexual excess, with Watkins following in the footsteps of his predecessors with occasional (or frequent) dalliances with female fans whose ages were ambiguous at best, illegal at worst. But that would have been too tame for him, too pedestrian. He was far more interested in something else they had to offer.

"it u belong to me so does ur baby"

—Text message from Ian Watkins to a female fan

Born July 30, 1977, Ian Watkins grew up north of Cardiff in the Welsh valley town of Merthyr Tydfil, near the edge of the Brecon Beacons. His father died when he was five, and his mother remarried three years later. Now the stepson of a church minister, Watkins was raised in a Baptist manse, though his parents say they didn't push religion on him. Drawn to music from an early age, young Ian earned good grades in school and even went on to study graphic design, earning a first-class honors degree from the University of

Wales, Newport. His future looked bright. However, music was his true calling—and Lostprophets would change Watkins's life.

Lostprophets had earned a reputation as a "straight-edge band," a term given to bands whose members aren't into alcohol and drugs. In the beginning, front man Watkins shunned these negative trappings of the rock music scene, preferring a clean lifestyle to the wild excesses the business was known for. His parents couldn't have been prouder.

But in 2007, things changed.

Something dark was taking over Ian Watkins's life—and this darkness began to consume him. He developed an obsessive interest in extreme pornography. He also had taken to filming himself engaging in sexual activity, even participating in "extreme sex" sessions, uploading his photos to the internet. He was using drugs, specifically crack cocaine and crystal meth. He spoke openly and unashamedly to female fans who'd entered his inner circle about his interest in having sex with children. More significantly, he was cultivating relationships with female fans who *had* young children.

How did Ian Watkins go from a normal lad from South Wales to a convicted pedophile? "It's the first thing a parent asks themselves—where did we go wrong? What happened?" the singer's devastated stepfather said in a *Daily Mail* interview.

To look at him, no one would have guessed. Watkins's public persona was every bit the successful rock star, replete with attractive women on his arm and, one might assume, in his bed. At one point he'd even dated BBC presenter Fearne Cotton and model and TV personality Alexa Chung. He certainly didn't look like the kind of young man a mother would hide her children from. Though perhaps that depended on the mother.

Watkins celebrated the release of the band's 2012 album *Weapons* by filming himself for seventeen minutes sexually abusing a female fan's baby boy only hours after he'd appeared on BBC Radio One. In a Skype video call lasting forty-five minutes, he watched another young mother sexually abusing her own infant as they discussed plans for further abuse, with the singer referring to mother and baby as his "sex duo."

An unconnected drug bust at Watkins's Pontypridd home in September 2012 blew the lid off his "secret" life. Aside from crystal meth, cocaine, and GHB, police uncovered evidence of the singer's history of sexual abuse. A significant number of indecent photos of children were discovered, the victims ranging in age from two to fourteen. Images and videos of extreme pornography were also found, as well as images of bestiality. Also damning were camcorder tapes showing Watkins involved in sex acts with underage female fans in the United States. In one tape dating back to March 2007, a sixteen-year-old girl was made to dress in a school uniform; Watkins then filmed himself taking her virginity. In a tape from August 2008, another sixteen-year-old girl was filmed performing a sex act on Watkins and snorting a substance he told her was cocaine.

Evidence had been seized from computers, laptops, and mobile phones. Watkins had been tech-savvy enough to encrypt files and store them in cloud servers. One of his passwords, which GCHQ (the UK's intelligence, security, and cyber agency) was eventually able to crack, was I FUK KIDZ. According to Detective Chief Inspector Peter Doyle of South Wales Police, officers recovered a total of twenty-seven terabytes of data storage from computers and devices in Watkins's possession— almost five times more data storage than the police force itself had. To put that into perspective, one terabyte can hold on average 250,000 photos (taken with a twelve-megapixel camera), 250 movies, or 500 hours of high-definition video.

Suspecting the rock star had underage victims in multiple countries, police expanded their investigation, liaising with Interpol and the US Department of Homeland Security. "Operation Globe" was the name given to the investigation, which was led by a team of roughly twenty-five detectives, including from the US and Germany, and headed by DCI Doyle. "There is no doubt in my mind that Ian Watkins exploited his celebrity status in order to abuse young children," the detective told reporters.

Watkins strongly denied the allegations and continued to proclaim his innocence despite the evidence against him. He portrayed himself as the victim of a malicious campaign, claiming he was being stalked by a "crazed fan" who had access to his computer.

In November 2013, thirty-six-year-old Ian Watkins, now with graying hair and looking very much unlike a rock star, finally pleaded guilty in Cardiff Crown Court to multiple sexual offenses, including the attempted rape and sexual assault of a child, conspiring to rape a child, sexual assault involving children, counts involving taking, making, or possessing indecent images of children, and possessing extreme pornographic images involving sex acts on an animal.

Watkins didn't appear particularly upset or remorseful about his crimes until the very last minute. According to his barrister, Sally O'Neill QC, her client was "deeply deeply sorry" and hadn't initially understood the gravity of what he'd done. She explained how Watkins had developed an obsession with filming himself having sex and that he'd become addicted to drugs at the age of thirty, which had dulled his ability to confront the reality of his actions, let alone remember them.

Two women in their twenties were also held to account for the roles they played in the sexual abuse of their own infants. Yet, despite their participation, they were still looked upon as victims and therefore given the unique protection that category allows. "It's likely the offender has normalized the sexual abuse of children, has rationalized it, minimized it for these females, and therefore the psychological barriers that had stopped those females abusing in the past were then eroded and they took the steps of abusing the children," Helen Whittle from the UK's National Crime Agency told reporters. In other words, these women were groomed.

Not everyone felt so charitable toward the singer's co-defendants, both of whom were adults, not adolescent star-struck fans. Nevertheless, their identities were legally cloaked. In one twist that quickly backfired, the women's names were posted on Twitter by British model and TV presenter Peaches Geldof, daughter of activist Sir Bob Geldof of the Boomtown Rats. She claimed she first saw them on an American website. In Britain, victims of sexual offenses have automatic lifetime anonymity; providing details that can lead to their identification is a criminal offense under the Sexual

Offenses Act and carries a fine of up to five thousand pounds. (Note that it
was also discovered that the names had mistakenly appeared on the court
service's listing site.) Aside from concerns about releasing the women's
names, there was a risk that doing so could result in the identification
of their children, which the authorities wished to avoid at all costs. Like
others who also thought Watkins's co-defendants were criminals rather
than victims, Geldof, who faced criminal charges for her actions, felt the
names should be made known to the public. "The babies will... probably
be given new identities to protect them," she said in a tweet. "These women
and Watkins will be gettings [sic] three-meals a day, a double bed, cable
TV etc.—all funded by the tax payer alongside not being named...." In the
end, she apologized and deleted the tweets.

However, in reading the thirteen-page sentencing document
describing what these young mothers not only allowed to be done to their
infants but did themselves, it's hard to summon up much sympathy for
Watkins's co-defendants.

So who were these women known only as "B" and "P"?

B met Ian Watkins in late 2011. Soon afterward, the two were in
regular communication as they planned the sexual abuse of her baby boy,
which began in spring 2012 and lasted for several months. She pleaded
guilty to the offenses she'd been charged with. In her defense, her barrister
Jonathan Fuller QC singled out Watkins as having "corrupted" his client
(though the singer claimed B was equally as guilty as he). Fuller went on
to state that Watkins had given her drugs, including heroin, and she'd
become obsessed with him due to his fame and was willing to do anything
to keep the relationship going. Indeed, it's difficult to buy into the victim
factor when Fuller's client is not only seen and heard in Watkins' sex tape
encouraging the singer to sodomize her ten-month-old infant, but she can
be seen using the infant for her own sexual gratification. She also abused
her infant when Watkins wasn't present, sending him a photo. According
to B's psychiatric assessment, she was not considered to be suffering from
mental illness during the time in which she carried out the abuse and,
though she appeared genuinely remorseful for her actions, the assessment

indicated that she still posed a high risk of causing serious harm to children and others. B was twenty-one at the time of sentencing.

P met Watkins in August 2012. Almost immediately, she proved eager to offer up her baby girl for their mutual sexual abuse, and had even discussed moving in with the singer. As if to further dehumanize her child, she told Watkins (in more graphic terms) that the infant needed to know she wasn't loved and was just there to be used by them. The pair communicated regularly, coming up with increasingly depraved plans for the infant. P also abused her infant without Watkins being present, sending him photos as well as performing the abuse while they were video calling on Skype. Despite compelling evidence that she took her baby to meet Watkins at a hotel for their planned abuse, there was no video footage to corroborate it; therefore, some of the charges against them were reduced to conspiring to rape and conspiring to sexually assault. In P's psychiatric assessment, it was concluded that she had a mixed personality disorder and had used her daughter as a tool in order to secure Watkins's acceptance of her. She was deemed to pose a medium risk of harm to children. P was twenty-five at the time of sentencing.

The three perpetrators' admissions of guilt meant that the prosecution would not be seeking a trial, thereby sparing a jury from having to watch what the judge called "extremely graphic and distressing material."

In sentencing Watkins, Mr. Justice Royce said, "You, Watkins, achieved fame and success as the lead singer of the Lostprophets. You had many fawning fans. That gave you power. You knew you could use that power to induce young female fans to help satisfy your apparently insatiable lust and to take part in the sexual abuse of their young children. Away from the highlights of your public performances lay a dark and sinister side." The judge then added, "I am satisfied that you are a deeply corrupting influence; you are highly manipulative; you are a sexual predator; you are dangerous. The public and in particular young females and children need protection from you."

Watkins received a twenty-nine-year custodial prison term, which was increased to a total of thirty-five years, with six of those on license (released under supervision). Therefore, he would be eligible for parole after serving only two-thirds of his term—which means he could be released when he's in his fifties. Co-defendant B was sentenced to fourteen years, and P seventeen years. Both women would be eligible for release after serving half their sentence, after which they'd also be on license.

Watkins's new home was the maximum-security prison HMP Wakefield in West Yorkshire, which houses the country's most high-risk prisoners. Dubbed "Monster Mansion" due to the notoriety of some of its residents, the disgraced Lostprophets front man would be following in the prison footsteps of serial-killer doctor Harold Shipman and "Hannibal the cannibal" serial killer Robert Maudsley.

A few weeks after his conviction, Watkins, believing his sentence to be too harsh, lodged a bid to take his case to the Court of Appeal. The man who'd called his child sex offenses "megalolz" claimed he hadn't realized that by pleading guilty to avoid a trial he had, in effect, made himself "look guilty." Not surprisingly, judges threw out the appeal.

How could Ian Watkins offend for so long without anyone noticing?

For nearly four years, fans who'd been befriended by the singer had reached out for help, posting warnings about him on internet forums and warning police. Yet it seemed as if Watkins was invincible. He'd even created an online profile featuring photos of himself involved in sex acts, also subscribing to groups on the site that contained images of child abuse. Although his profile had been viewed by 40,000 people, nothing was done about it.

A former girlfriend tried to get help from police as early as 2008. Joanne Mjadzelics, who worked as an escort, said Watkins had boasted repeatedly about how he used his fame to prey upon female fans, turning them into what he called "Superfans"—women willing to offer him their children for sex. Mjadzelics was put under a gag order after Watkins learned what she was up to; nevertheless, he felt certain that police wouldn't touch him, bragging that he had the same lawyers as Madonna. "I've always said to the police, there's hundreds of victims out there and you're never going to find them because the mothers are in on it," Mjadzelics told reporters, but police refused to investigate. She even reached out to a former detective and investigative TV reporter who had helped expose Jimmy Savile as a serial pedophile. Seeing that police weren't taking her seriously and, in fact, viewed her as a "nuisance" who was harassing and stalking a famous rock star, Mjadzelics said she took matters into her own hands by going into escort mode, swapping indecent images with him and engaging in explicit online conversations in an effort to entrap him. Instead, she found herself in court for possession of child pornography. A former drug user herself, Mjadzelics admitted she'd been in love with the singer and, at least in the beginning, was merely going along with him to please him until she realized how wrong it was, especially after he reportedly told her of his fantasies about murdering a baby—something she believed he was capable of. "He even wanted to get me pregnant so he could rape our baby. How does anyone become that sick?" she said in an interview. In January 2015, Mjadzelics was found not guilty of the charges against her.

With Watkins finally in custody, the litany of police missteps and incompetence began to come out. At the center of the investigation was a detective sergeant who reportedly worked in child protective services in Watkins's hometown of Pontypridd. Police forces in different parts of England had also received information about Watkins. In two separate reports published by the IPCC (Independent Police Complaints Commission) in 2016 and 2017, it was found that South Wales Police had failed to act on numerous allegations of abuse relating to Watkins dating between 2008 and 2012. The reports state that in some instances rudimentary investigations were not even carried out, and that errors and omissions had allowed Watkins to continue offending when he could have been brought to justice much sooner. Several people had come forward with allegations against Watkins to South Wales Police and other forces, but since complaints came from fans and/or ex-girlfriends, this rendered them less "believable," just as it had for Joanne Mjadzelics.

According to IPCC investigators, one detective had been concerned that any actions brought against the rock star would attract "huge publicity;" another stated that fans and ex-girlfriends were making allegations due to Watkins's "fame," which, when investigated, were false. The 2017 report contained a recommendation that South Wales Police's safeguarding procedures be amended to give "specific consideration" to suspects who may pose "additional risk by virtue of their profile, which may be elevated due to their profession, wealth, celebrity, or good standing in the community."

Yet the question remains: If police hadn't acted on information that Watkins regularly smuggled in drugs from the States and gone to raid his home, would he have been caught at all? The possibility of finding illegal drugs certainly seems to have taken precedence over investigating multiple allegations against a celebrity of sexual abuse and pedophilia.

Where did it all go wrong for Ian Watkins? Can drugs be blamed for turning him into a depraved monster who groomed and preyed upon others? The singer had developed an addiction to crack cocaine and methamphetamine, both psychostimulants and personality-altering. Although these substances surely intensified his desires, maybe there was something inside him all along, and he set that something free after he'd achieved fame. Research shows that child sex offenders usually develop an interest in children during their own sexual development, so it seems unlikely that Watkins suddenly became sexually aroused by children in adulthood. Nonetheless, his fame played an integral role in the attainment of his desires, as did his narcissistic tendencies, which made him believe he could do anything he wanted without consequence. It's clear from his own words that he minimized his actions—to him, it was all just "megalolz." Maybe we'll never know when it began, or how many victims there are, or how far back in time they go.

Watkins's parents (since divorced) were left in a state of shock, disbelief, and horror by the news that their son was a serial pedophile. His mother, who underwent a kidney transplant in 2007, suffered from deteriorating health after learning of her son's crimes. "He was a normal happy young lad who grew up in the Valleys in a loving family," Watkins' stepfather told the *Daily Mail*. "It was devastating. We thought, 'there must be some mistake here. There must be some reason for this. There's no way that this is true,' " adding that he hoped his stepson wouldn't forever be remembered as another Jimmy Savile.

As it happens, the Savile reference wasn't too far off the mark. Four years before he was charged with his crimes, Watkins had been named Kidney Wales Foundation's ambassador for young people and, like the "charity-minded" Savile, had visited sick children while he was actively abusing. He'd even taken part in a special New Year's Eve fundraising concert for the foundation in 2008, at which he urged fans to sign up on the NHS Organ Donor Register. Watkins had become involved with the cause because of his mother. That same year, at a fundraising visit to University Hospital of Wales in Cardiff (accompanied by his mother), photos show Watkins smiling and posing with children, and even being greeted by then-Labour Health Minister Edwina Hart. The fundraiser was to raise awareness of organ donation. "Lots of the children are waiting for a kidney transplant, but there's a desperate shortage of donors," said Watkins. It beggars belief that he could have a genuine concern about the welfare of these children and yet sexually abuse children for fun or *megalolz*. Watkins has since been stripped of his ambassador title for the charity.

Band members say they would've killed him on the spot had they known.

Aside from Watkins's legacy of abuse, he destroyed the band he was instrumental in creating. It's hard to imagine that your colleague, your friend, the man with whom you've created music, could be guilty of such heinous and unthinkable crimes. With the exception of their front man, all the band members had children, with one even referring to the singer as "Uncle Ian." Aside from being shocked and sickened by the news, band members were made to feel like pariahs. Social media was filled with death threats against them and their families. Not surprisingly, they hurried to distance themselves from Lostprophets and its disgraced lead singer, going on to form a new band called No Devotion. But the specter of Ian Watkins wasn't one they could erase from their professional, or even their personal, lives. "We are heartbroken, angry, and disgusted at what has been revealed. This is something that will haunt us for the rest of our lives," band members posted on their Facebook page.

How could they not have known? was the question everyone was asking. Granted, it's a fair question, and one that is always asked of those who are closest to someone who has committed a terrible crime. Disillusioned and angry fans refused to believe that the band members couldn't have known that Ian Watkins the rock star was, in reality, Ian Watkins the pedophile.

In reality, the band didn't live in one another's pockets. On the contrary, Watkins was living in Wales while the other band members lived in the States; they didn't see him nine months out of a year.

"Ian was incredibly charming and manipulative—he could win anybody over. It was a powerful tool of his. We knew he had a different woman in every city, but with pedophiles, you don't assume them having relationships with adult women," guitarist Lee Gaze told *The Guardian.* "A guy who'd been in prison with Ian did an interview when he came out, and said that he [Watkins] had said: 'How could I be attracted to children? Because they don't have features.' I think he was just attracted to what was bad, and to being in control."

"Up until the final second he said he was innocent. He destroyed his family's life, giving them a glimpse of hope every time he said he was innocent. His mum thought he was innocent. What a fucking cunt," added bassist Stuart Richardson. When referring to the aftermath of these events, Richardson said, "That's on my fucking gravestone."

One thing his fellow band members *did* know: Watkins had developed a serious drug addiction, first to coke, then meth. After being issued an ultimatum, he got clean in 2012. It didn't last. Instead, he became increasingly nasty, arrogant, and difficult to deal with (worse than usual, apparently, since by then Watkins had earned a reputation as a "douchebag"), delivering substandard performances onstage or not showing up at all. His erratic and irresponsible behavior so enraged the other band members that Richardson was provoked to the point of assaulting Watkins during the Warped Tour, punching him repeatedly and smashing a can of energy drink into his head.

By this time, Lostprophets band members had little in common with their lead singer other than the band itself. Watkins was no longer the person they used to know; he'd become someone they didn't even want to be around. Others had noticed the changes too, including a British music journalist who said that Watkins had started staying in separate hotels from his bandmates, even traveling in separate cars, as if he had "something to hide."

Lostprophets officially disbanded in October 2013, just before Watkins was sentenced. Their CDs quickly disappeared from store shelves.

———————

It was reported in 2015 that Watkins was moved to HMP Rye Hill in Warwickshire, a lower-security prison that houses sex offenders. He'd been moved previously to HMP Long Lartin, causing outrage among inmates who didn't want a convicted pedophile in their prison, which led to concerns about Watkins' safety. This time it was the public who was outraged, especially child safety campaigners. Joanne Mjadzelics launched a petition calling for the justice secretary to reverse the move, calling Rye Hill "a haven for pedophiles" and likening the facility to a stay in a hotel. The Ministry of Justice's rationale behind housing sex offenders in one place is so they can receive specialist interventions and services not available to them in more general prison populations. However, it remains to be seen whether Watkins has been cooperating with his sex offenders' treatment, or has even admitted to the seriousness of his crimes.

Despite being locked up, Watkins hasn't stopped cultivating new "relationships" with mothers of young children. He receives hundreds of letters from smitten female fans, to which he has replied, asking for explicit selfies and phone numbers, addressing the women as "Minx," "Princess," and "Pretty One," signing off with XXXXs and epithets such as "Trouble," "The King of Dancers," and "The Boy Wonder." Despite the cutesy nicknames, the tone of his letters as he urges the women to offer up explicit photos and videos of themselves can be construed as bullying and condescending as he tries to get the less forthcoming ones to do what he wants. "Read this letter a few times so it sinks into your pretty little head."

The fact that Watkins is once again up to his old tricks from his prison cell, and doing so in a place where availing himself on a regular basis to crack cocaine and meth isn't as easy as when he was a free man, seems to invalidate his courtroom defense that he'd been so out of his head on drugs he didn't know what he was doing, indicating that any last-minute remorse he displayed at his sentencing hearing was nothing but hot air. It seems that he's just as interested in exploiting and abusing young women and children when sober.

In 2017, a twenty-one-year-old fan had her two-year-old daughter taken into care after exchanging letters with Watkins. Not only did she visit him in prison, but she also wore an "engagement" ring at his request. That same year, Watkins entered into lengthy correspondence with a young mother in her thirties. When it was discovered that she had a six-year-old daughter, she and Watkins were banned from having any further contact with each other. There are numerous reports of still more young females visiting him in prison and cozying up to him as if he's their boyfriend. It brings to mind the Ted Bundy groupies, who not only sent him fan mail and nude photos of themselves, but attended the serial killer's trial in 1979, even dressing like his victims. Despite being fully aware of the viciousness of Bundy's crimes (which were committed against young women like themselves), they were still enamored of him. Observers note that Watkins, who's now put on a few pounds, gone gray, and has rotting teeth (according to at least one visitor), bears little resemblance to the swaggering rock star he once was. Yet he gives every indication that he hasn't got a care in the world as he laughs and jokes and holds hands with his female visitors.

In a video interview from 2007, Watkins and fellow band members can be seen chatting amiably with an interviewer. The singer's pleasing accent, easy smile, and youthful features are a far cry from the infamous bearded mugshot he's become associated with, let alone the descriptions from observers of Ian Watkins, the prisoner.

In August 2019, Watkins found himself back in the courtroom, this time at Leeds Crown Court, where he received a further ten months tacked onto his prison term for possessing a mobile phone in prison, which he'd kept hidden in his rectum. He was caught when he texted an ex-girlfriend, who reported him to the police. Watkins denied the phone was for his own use, claiming he was being threatened by "known murderers" who'd forced him to hide the phone or they would slit his throat. He told the court that some inmates had ordered him to use the phone to contact fans who wrote to him as part of an extortion scheme, though he refused to identify these inmates out of fear for his life. He added that he shared a wing with "murderers, mass murderers, serial killers, rapists, pedophiles. The worst of the worst," and the conditions were so alien to him that he was on medication for anxiety and depression. One can only wonder how much sympathy he elicited in the courtroom as he pleaded his case.

Like the proverbial bad penny, Ian Watkins has continued to pop up in the news over the years, including reports of a newly active verified Twitter account dating back to November 2016 (possibly hacked, since his last tweet was in December 2012, before his arrest). The tweets contained links not only to his *L'Amour La Morgue* Soundcloud account (which had been a side project of his), but another account named *Megalelz* (perhaps a play on his favored catch phrase "megalolz"), fueling speculation about possible new music releases from prison.

Two years earlier, rumors went viral on social media that he'd committed suicide by hanging himself in his prison cell. No doubt there are some who hope that one day those rumors will be true.

BARETTA IN COLD BLOOD

GRANT BUTLER

When a famous crime happens, it not only becomes a fixture of media coverage, but it can also set legal precedents that affect other cases for years to come. When actor Robert Blake was put on trial for the murder of his wife, Bonnie Lee Bakley, it was not just the latest big celebrity murder trial or a fascinating tale of a dysfunctional marriage—it was part of a larger pattern of interwoven Hollywood criminal cases stretching from the 1980s into the 2000s. The trial of Robert Blake for the murder of Bonnie Lee Bakley was influenced by several prominent trials and crimes it was directly connected to, and the trial and its aftermath had an unexpected impact on American society.

Born in 1956, Bonnie (sometimes spelled Bonny) was raised by her grandmother in New Jersey. Her sister would later state that the two grew up near a nudist colony. When she was twenty-one, Bakley married her first cousin, Paul Gawron, and they had a son and a daughter. She eventually left her children for Gawron to raise, though she sent money from time to time. Bakley's daughter, Holly, would later say that her mother was her best friend, who supported her in whatever she wanted to do, and was also a shrewd businesswoman. But she also conceded that her mother "did do things that most people would not approve of."

If there was one thing people agreed on, it was that Bakley wanted to be either famous, or connected to those who were famous. At first, she attempted to make it big through performing, once advertising her availability for acting jobs on a billboard above the Sunset Strip. When that didn't pan out, she resorted to other means. In addition to selling nude photographs of herself, she would place personal ads in newspapers and ask men for rent money or money for travel. Her half-brother, Peter Carlyon, said that Bakley could be called a con artist.

In the late 1980s, Bonnie moved to Memphis, Tennessee, in an attempt to get close to rock-and-roll icon Jerry Lee Lewis. In the words of his tour manager, Bonnie was "very, very determined" and "she just had her way of working her way in." When she became pregnant, Bonnie claimed that Lewis was the father of the child, until a DNA test proved otherwise. Then she tried stalking Dean Martin, the "Rat Pack" veteran, who was by this time seventy-eight years old. When Martin died in 1995, she moved on to other men.

As part of more elaborate schemes, Bonnie would steal credit cards and forge driver's licenses to construct aliases. Charged with drug and fraud-related offenses during the 1980s and 1990s in the American South, Bakley's trial on her third and final charge took place in Arkansas in 1998, when she was convicted of fraud. One year later, she met actor Robert Blake at a jazz club.

Blake was born in New Jersey on September 18, 1933, as Michael Gubitosi. The child of two vaudeville performers, he moved with his parents to Hollywood, and by the age of six had achieved a starring role in the *Our Gang* shorts, also known as *The Little Rascals*. Blake would later say that he was subjected to a highly abusive childhood. Referring to his father, he said, "I was his punching bag."

The studio that produced *The Little Rascals* was Metro-Goldwyn-Mayer, the biggest and most revered studio in Hollywood at the time, its name synonymous with quality and home to the biggest stars of the film era. By the time Blake arrived at the studio, it had produced and released *The Wizard of Oz*, one of the most iconic films in history. But the studio also had a dark side. MGM was home to Judy Garland, and her well-publicized struggles have always been connected to the studio's notoriously demanding management style. As an employee of MGM, there's no telling what Blake would have seen and been subjected to at such a young age.

By 1940, he was acting alongside film stars Myrna Loy and William Powell. Throughout the decade, he would make appearances in some of the most acclaimed films of the era, acting in *The Treasure of the Sierra Madre* with Humphrey Bogart and *Humoresque* with Joan Crawford. In the early 1960s, Blake married actress Sondra Kerr, with whom he would have two children before their divorce twenty years later. After acting in Oscar-winner George Stevens's biblical epic *The Greatest Story Ever Told* alongside Max Von Sydow, Charlton Heston, and Telly Savalas, Blake made his most famous cinema appearance as convicted killer Perry Smith in the film adaptation of Truman Capote's true crime classic *In Cold Blood*. Noting the irony of the film and Blake's real-life legal troubles, film critic Roger Ebert thought Blake's troubled childhood was what connected Blake to Perry Smith more than anything else. Although Blake worked steadily in television and film during his career, his most famous role was the title character in the 1970s TV detective series *Baretta*, which would win him an Emmy Award. His final film credit was in David Lynch's 1997 film *Lost Highway*. In total, Blake had a film and TV career that lasted almost sixty years. It was at this point in his life that he met Bonnie Lee Bakley.

In June 2000, Bakley gave birth to a girl she named Christian Shannon Brando, since she'd been involved with Christian Brando at the same time as Robert Blake. When a paternity test revealed that Blake was the biological father, she renamed the girl Rose Lenore Sophia Blake. In November of that year, Bonnie Lee Bakley and Robert Blake got married, and Blake became Bakley's final husband, after nine previous marriages. But the marriage was far from a happy one. After the wedding, the couple didn't even share the same house; Bakley lived in a small house behind her husband's ranch house. By all reports, the two never got along well. Despite being married, Bakley still kept pursuing men for money, renting a mail drop in Studio City for this purpose.

On the night of May 4, 2001, Blake and Bakley went to dinner at Vitello's in Studio City. Blake was a well-known regular at the restaurant; Vitello's even had a dish on the menu called "The Robert Blake Pasta Special." Later, when the couple left the restaurant and got into Blake's car, he discovered he'd left his gun inside the restaurant and went back to get it. When he returned to the car, he found Bakley had been shot dead. The murder weapon, an unusual revolver later found in a dumpster, did not belong to Blake or anyone else the authorities could link it to. When questioned, Blake told the police he believed someone from his wife's murky past was stalking her, and that was why he was carrying a gun.

In death, Bonnie Lee Bakley finally achieved the fame that had escaped her in life.

On April 18, 2002, Blake was arrested at his sister's house in connection with his wife's murder. His chauffeur and bodyguard, Earle Caldwell, was also taken into custody. On April 22, Blake was formally charged with one count of murder with special circumstances, two counts of solicitation of murder, and one count of conspiracy to murder. At first, he was denied bail and kept in custody, but he was eventually freed on $1.5 million bail. While in jail, and despite being encouraged by his lawyers not to speak to the press, he did a television interview with Barbara Walters, during which he described Bakley as someone who was a lost soul from a very young age. In the interview, which was later admitted as evidence during the trial since he didn't testify, Blake denied that he bore any resemblance to the tough-guy characters he often played. His lawyers ended up being pleased by the interview, since he also spoke lovingly of his daughter; it portrayed him as an honest and emotional man. Blake would later thank Barbara Walters, saying he would have never gotten out of jail without her.

While Bakley's daughter Holly testified at the trial that Blake would phone her mother when the two were living in Arkansas together, and that when she answered the phone, Blake would sometimes start "yelling" and "cursing obscenities" when he thought Bakley was on the line, there was nothing to link him directly to the killing. There were no eyewitnesses, and no gunshot residue had been found on Blake's hands. The heart of the prosecution's case was their two main witnesses: stuntmen Ronald Hambleton and Gary McLarty. The men had worked on the *Baretta* series and claimed Blake had hired them to kill Bakley. It wasn't McLarty's first time testifying in a high-profile trial; he had served as a witness during the trial regarding the tragic helicopter accident that took place on the set of the 1983 film *Twilight Zone: The Movie*. He was in the helicopter that crashed, causing the deaths of several actors involved in the film.

McLarty testified that Blake offered him ten thousand dollars to kill Bakley and had discussed multiple scenarios with him. He claimed that at first he thought Blake was just blowing off steam, but when the actor called him several days later, the stuntman refused, as did Hambleton. It soon came out that McLarty admitted to suffering delusions caused by drug use. Blake's defense team presented medical records showing McLarty had used marijuana and cocaine in the weeks leading up to his alleged encounter with Blake. The defense also found McLarty's son, Cole, was willing to testify that his father was once so addled by drugs he was convinced the Los Angeles Police Department was tunneling under his house. Hambleton fared no better. It came out that he once thought there were twenty armed men in his house when, in fact, no one was there.

Both stuntmen also had documented run-ins with the law. In 1991, McLarty shot and killed a man living on his property who was wanted for the rape of a twenty-one-year-old woman, who happened to be a friend of McLarty and his wife's. McLarty shot the man six times. The district attorney's office later classified it as self-defense. In 1999, Hambleton called the police, saying that people were stealing from his property. When officers arrived, they saw nothing; yet Hambleton, who was still on the line with the dispatcher, said the theft was in progress at that moment. The officers approached the house and asked Hambleton to come out, which he did while toting a .22-caliber rifle. He was eventually charged with resisting arrest and brandishing a firearm.

Aside from testimony, all Hambleton could offer the prosecution were some records from a prepaid phone card that documented calls from Blake's home to the stuntmen. So the prosecution was in effect claiming that Blake had hired someone to murder Bakley, though they didn't know who that someone was.

As the trial progressed, Blake acquired a reputation for being a difficult client. Aside from his media presence, he had gone through several attorneys. Because of this, people began to speculate that his next lawyer would be Gerry Spence. A famed defense attorney with a reputation for winning cases against giants, Spence had successfully defended Imelda Marcos when the former first lady of the Philippines was indicted in New York in 1988 on fraud and racketeering charges. Not only does the graft and corruption of the Marcos regime hold a spot in *The Guinness Book of Records*, but Imelda Marcos has also become infamous specifically for her vast collection of shoes, so it's not hard to see why Blake would want Spence to defend him. Although Spence never joined the defense team, they did a good job without him. Blake's lawyers wasted no time in pointing to Bonnie's past as being full of people who might've wished her harm. They even had another suspect who could've done the killing: Christian Brando, the man Bakley first claimed had fathered her daughter.

The son of cinema legend Marlon Brando and his first wife, Anna Kashfi, Christian grew up in a different world from Bakley as far as status and money went, though he was no stranger to parental acrimony, as the battle between Brando and Kashfi over custody of their son lasted more than a decade. At one of many court appearances, Kashfi slapped Brando in the face in front of reporters and photographers. When Christian was a child, his mother kidnapped him and took him to Mexico, where he was found with a group of hippies living in a tent. To feel safe from being kidnapped again, Christian began buying guns. He also became involved with drugs, dropping out of school at sixteen. In the words of one Brando biographer, "Christian led a very self-abusive life."

On May 16, 1990, Christian arrived at his father's Hollywood Hills residence on Mulholland Drive, which shared a driveway with actor Jack Nicholson's home. While there, he encountered Dag Drollet, the twenty-six-year-old boyfriend of his twenty-year-old half-sister Cheyenne, and shot him with a pistol. When the police arrived, Christian told them that during dinner earlier that night, Cheyenne said to him that Drollet was slapping her around. At the time, she was eight months pregnant, and Christian had been drinking.

While there was never any doubt that Christian shot and killed Drollet, he claimed he merely pointed the gun at Drollet to scare him, and it accidentally went off. But that didn't match the crime scene. Drollet was found on the couch, with a cigarette lighter in one hand and a TV remote in the other, a single gunshot to the face. Later, Cheyenne, who had a long history of mental problems and possible schizophrenia, admitted that Drollet hadn't been hurting her. In response, Marlon Brando made sure his daughter was taken out of the country and checked into a psychiatric hospital. Cheyenne committed suicide in 1995 and is buried next to Drollet in Tahiti.

To help his son, Marlon Brando not only put up his estate for bail, but he also took the witness stand. In a manner straight out of his movies, he rambled and pleaded for his son to be shown mercy. Brando had long ceased to look like the legendary movie star everyone knew. By that point he was morbidly obese, and the sight of the man known to people in the courtroom as Stanley Kowalski, Terry Malloy, Don Vito Corleone, and Colonel Walter Kurtz, reduced to pleading for his son and saying, "I think perhaps that I failed as a father" would have been sad to see.

Upon hearing of his sister's mental problems, Christian said, "I feel like a complete chump for believing her"—words that could've easily been said by any number of men about Bonnie Lee Bakley. Christian Brando pled guilty to voluntary manslaughter in February 1991, and spent five years of a ten-year sentence in prison. One of the attorneys for Christian Brando was none other than Robert Shapiro, who would later rise to fame as one of the members of O. J. Simpson's legal defense team.

While Christian was in jail, he corresponded with Bakley, who sent him nude pictures of herself via FedEx. During the trial, Robert Blake's defense team submitted a recorded phone call between Christian Brando and Bakley that took place in fall 2000. During the call, in which Christian is described as being angry, he told Bakley, "You're lucky somebody ain't out there to put a bullet in your head," and "You have no idea what you do to people with this shit." Christian Brando died of pneumonia on January 26, 2008, at age forty-nine.

Christian Brando's was just one of several famous cases the Blake case was connected to. The fact that these trials all took place in the same area is significant. Despite its massive size and world renown, Los Angeles is a company town like countless others, the difference being that, instead of being home to people who work in a mine or factory, the company is the entertainment industry. It's not surprising that lawyers involved in celebrity cases tend to overlap.

Blake's first attorney, Harland Braun, successfully defended film producer George Folsey Jr. on manslaughter charges stemming from the *Twilight Zone* film in which McLarty had been a stuntman. Braun even briefly represented the film's director, John Landis, until the manslaughter trial began. He also represented Ted Briseno, one of the police officers involved in the 1991 beating of Rodney King. When the officers in question were acquitted in 1992, it set off massive riots in Los Angeles. These events were still strong in the public consciousness when O. J. Simpson was charged with murder two years later, and the conduct of the LAPD became a focal point of the Simpson defense team.

The Robert Blake trial was the first big celebrity trial to take place after the O. J. Simpson trial. While countless trials have been slapped with the label "trial of the century," Simpson's is worthy of the title. In 1995, more than 150 million viewers, which amounted to 57 percent of the country, tuned in to watch the verdict. For many, the Simpson case was their first real experience watching a trial or seeing a courtroom environment.

As the Blake case went to trial, the pressure to win would have been high, as memories of O. J. Simpson's acquittal would have been strong in everyone's mind. Los Angeles District Attorney Stephen Cooley, a Republican, assumed the post in 2000 after defeating Gil Garcetti, who had held the office during the Simpson trial. One might wonder if the unsuccessful prosecution of Simpson was a root cause for Garcetti's defeat. Since Cooley was a strong critic of Garcetti, he no doubt didn't want a repeat of the failure to convict a high-profile celebrity accused of murder. Blake's attorney told the news media that the Los Angeles Police Department "wanted to make up for the public perception that the LAPD and Los Angeles district attorney's office had blown the O. J. Simpson case." There's no question that the police officers involved would've bent over backward to make sure everything was done by the book. Ron Ito, the LAPD homicide officer in charge of the investigation, agreed that the case against Blake was far from perfect, but said they had a very good circumstantial case, despite the lack of eyewitnesses or DNA evidence. During the trial, Detective Ito admitted to Blake's lawyer, Thomas Mesereau, that he had also worked on the Simpson case for a year, though he'd received no publicity for it.

The Blake case wasn't the only big murder case involving a husband happening at the time. In 2003, Scott Peterson became a household name. A few hours away in Modesto, the disappearance of pregnant Laci Peterson became a huge national story. Robert Blake's trial began on December 20, 2004, only a month after Scott Peterson was convicted of the murder of his wife Laci and unborn son Conner. Blake's trial took place ten years after O. J. Simpson had been charged with murder, and much had changed since then. Virtually every criminal lawyer in the city would've carefully watched the Simpson trial and applied what they'd learned accordingly. Mindful of the way the Simpson trial had become a media circus, Blake's lawyer,

Harland Braun, moved to have cameras banned from the courtroom during his client's 2002 arraignment.

Trial by jury is one of the most basic elements of the modern legal system. But what happens when the jury not only knows who the defendant is, but has grown up with the image of the defendant as a beloved icon? For better or worse, people have a hard time reconciling the image of a widely liked performer with them committing a crime like murder. Robert Blake, who first became famous as part of *The Little Rascals* and had a decades-long career lasting into the 1990s, would have been a familiar face to potential jurors. Members of the jury who had watched *Baretta* in the 1970s would've seen Blake and immediately thought of him as the cop on TV. That's a powerful impulse for any prosecutor to overcome.

A criminal trial is an attempt by the prosecution to convince a jury that the defendant is guilty of a crime and deserves a certain punishment. This is far more difficult if the jury already has an established image of the defendant in their minds. When a prosecutor puts a famous person on trial, they are not just putting that person on trial, they're putting their image on trial as well. This is what makes celebrity trials so different from those of an average person the public doesn't recognize. The prosecution has to persuade a jury that the defendant not only is *not* the person they know from movies or TV, but they're someone who deserves to face some kind of consequence for their actions.

If the district attorney's office hoped to redeem itself by winning a conviction against a celebrity on murder charges, the Blake case was going to disappoint them. Considering the lack of physical evidence, Bakley's criminal record, coupled with the fact that she openly associated with at least one other person who'd done prison time for manslaughter with a firearm, and Blake's lack of connection to the murder weapon, the case was a no-win for the prosecution. Therefore, it wasn't surprising when jury foreman Thomas Nicholson said, "They couldn't put the gun in his hand," with Blake being acquitted of all charges on March 16, 2005.

After hearing the verdict, District Attorney Cooley called the jurors "incredibly stupid" for acquitting Blake and described him as "guilty as sin" and "a miserable human being." The jury rejected Cooley's comments, with one juror saying, "They didn't have a good case. Their case was built around witnesses who weren't truthful," and another expressing disgust at the DA's comments.

After the murder, Blake and Bakley's daughter, Rose Lenore, was adopted by Blake's daughter from his first marriage. Although Blake was acquitted of murder, the jury in a subsequent civil suit found him liable for Bakley's murder and ordered him to pay her family approximately thirty million dollars. The amount was later cut down to fifteen million dollars.

Like the criminal trial, those involved in Blake's civil trial also remembered that O. J. Simpson had been found liable for murder in 1997 by a civil jury, not a criminal one. Blake's appeal of the 2005 civil trial decision claimed that the jury had mentioned both O. J. Simpson and Michael Jackson, stating: "Jurors discussed setting the damage figure high enough to 'send a message' that celebrities and rich people cannot get away with murder," and that "O. J. Simpson and Michael Jackson had escaped punishment." The Blake murder trial had links to Michael Jackson's second trial for sexual abuse in that Blake defense team member Thomas Mesereau represented the pop superstar shortly after working on Blake's team. Michael Jackson was acquitted in June 2005, just three months after Blake.

With Blake's acquittal, the pressure would have been even higher on the LA district attorney's office for the next high-profile murder case: the trial of music producer Phil Spector, who was found guilty in 2009.

In 2017, Blake married his third wife, Pamela Hudak. Now eighty-three years old, Blake had known the fifty-five-year-old Hudak for decades. But, not only had he known Hudak before Bakley, she testified on his behalf during the trial.

Scott Ross, a private investigator who worked for Blake's defense team, spoke to the media in 2016. Ross explained that, while he didn't think Blake pulled the trigger, he did believe the actor was involved. Ross also said he believed that the prosecution could have convicted Blake had they given his bodyguard Earle Caldwell immunity, instead of charging him with conspiracy to commit murder, in 2002. The charge was dismissed, and the jury that found Blake liable in the civil case also found Caldwell not responsible.

Ross is right to speculate on what the prosecution was thinking when conducting the trial, since they simply didn't have a case against Blake. It's hard to know exactly how much losing the Simpson case affected this trial, or the motivations involved, but there is no doubt that it strongly affected what happened. Had O. J. Simpson been found guilty, it's likely the case against Blake would have gone differently.

The Blake trial also had consequences that went far beyond the case. In 2010, District Attorney Cooley ran as the Republican candidate for California Attorney General. In November of that year, he was defeated by the Democratic nominee, San Francisco District Attorney Kamala Harris, in what was described as one of the closest statewide races in California history. Had Cooley not made those comments attacking the jurors in the Blake trial, it's possible he might have become California's attorney general instead of Harris, who went on to become the first female Vice President of the United States ten years after defeating Cooley.

ALFREDO CODONA: THE DARING YOUNG MAN ON THE FLYING TRAPEZE

MORGAN BARBOUR

On average, twenty people per minute will be abused by an intimate partner in the United States alone. One in four women and one in nine men will experience intimate partner violence, be it physical or sexual, in their lifetime. Intimate domestic violence accounts for 15 percent of all violent crime, yet only 34 percent of victims will receive medical aid for their injuries. Seventy-four percent of all murder-suicides involve an intimate partner. Ninety-four percent of those murdered are women.

———————

Alfredo Codona is an icon of flying trapeze history. Some go so far as to call him the greatest flying trapeze artist who has ever lived. He was the first man to consistently perform and catch the triple back somersault in front of a live audience (though not the first artist to perform it—that mantle belongs to female flying trapeze artist Lena Jordan, who successfully completed the first recorded triple back somersault in 1897, as acknowledged by *The Guinness Book of World Records*). Codona and his second wife, Polish acrobat and circus star Lillian Leitzel, took the world by storm when they performed together under the big top. His family troupe, the Flying

Codonas, wowed audiences as they traveled and performed daredevil aerial stunts with Ringling Brothers, The Greatest Show on Earth. Alfredo was a shining star who has been memorialized in the industry's history. His brilliance so often outshines his darkness.

On the surface, Alfredo had it all. He was young, strong, handsome, and absolutely dripping with talent and potential. The circus ran in his blood. Born in Mexico to Italian performer Eduardo Codona (originally Codoni) and French aerialist Hortensia Buislay, Alfredo made his circus debut at just seven and a half months old, perched stoically atop his father's upstretched hand. His parents groomed all their children for a life in the spotlight, rearing siblings Victoria, Abelardo ("Lalo"), Joe, Hortense, and Rosa to match their brother's aptitude in the ring. Sister Hortense and Alfredo spent two seasons at Barnum and Bailey from 1910 to 1911, performing slack wire and static trapeze acts respectively. When they returned from their American stint, Eduardo set to work readying Alfredo, Lalo, and Victoria for a flying trapeze act that would go on to be known as the Flying Codonas.

Alfredo wasn't just a skilled flyer. He possessed an otherworldly grace in the air. Flying trapeze legend Art Concello said, "If Alfredo had been run over by a truck, he'd have done it so gracefully that your first instinct might have been to applaud." He was as natural in the air as a bird flying south. He passed through the air with a sense of precision and beauty that was unparalleled.

From 1913 to 1915, the Flying Codonas made their first big international debut on contract with Wirth's Circus in Australia. Alfredo and Lalo represented their family, joining Australian flyers Steve Outch and Ruth Farris to round out the troupe. When they returned at the end of the contract, with Steve tagging along, they were approached by the inimitable Siegrist-Silbon Troupe, a flying trapeze act comprised of two flying trapezes arranged to form a crucifix, an innovative and boundary-pushing act that is still performed today, most famously by the Flying Royals in the United States. It was on this contract that Alfredo met the first of three women to forever shape the course of his life: Clara Groves, a dashing young aerialist married to fellow performer Indian Groves of the Valentinos act.

If gravity was no mistress to Alfredo, Clara certainly was. The two were drawn together by some unseen magnetism. She left her husband swiftly, joining Alfredo both in the bedroom and in the air. Sex and companionship aside, Alfredo saw another opportunity in young Clara: the ability to replicate the fly act performed previously in Australia. Three dashing young men and a feminine beauty as the symbolic icing on top of their act—they would be unstoppable. In 1917, the Flying Codonas departed for Cuba to perform in *Circo Pubillones*, where they tumbled through the air to amazed and cheering crowds. That winter, Alfredo and Clara made their love official by joining hands in marriage.

The Flying Codonas were on fire. Alfredo set his sights across the pond, on Ernest Clarke of the Clarkonians, one of the few flyers attempting (with nominal consistency) the triple back somersault in front of a crowd. Alfredo was younger than old Ernie, who didn't master the trick until the ripe old age of thirty-six—practically a geriatric in Alfredo's eyes. If Ernie could do it, Alfredo certainly could. In 1919, Alfredo began working the elusive triple, and by 1920, he and Lalo were catching often enough to debut it in the Chicago Coliseum with the Sells-Floto Circus. For every ten Alfredo threw, Lalo caught nine. They were a force to be reckoned with, writing circus history with every swing.

The Flying Codonas—whittled down to a trio, but with no less astonishing talent, thanks in part to Alfredo's nonstop pursuit of flying perfection—soon became an international sensation. They traveled to Europe, where they began to tick off countries and notable circus theaters like college kids on a Euro trip: Portugal, at the *Coliseu dos Recreios*; Spain, flying with the French show *Palisse*; Germany, with Hagenbeck-Wallace Circus; and then to Berlin to perform in *Wintergarten*, where their act was filmed and would end up in the film *Varieté* (1925). Then they were off to Denmark to perform in Circus Schumann; England, with Bertram Mills Circus; and then finally to the homeland of flying trapeze itself: Paris, with *Cirque d'Hiver,* where Alfredo cemented himself as a living legend in the minds of the circus-educated Parisian audiences, who, above all else, recognized the astonishing feat that was Alfredo and Lalo's unmissable triple.

Men wanted to be him, women wanted to be with him, and Alfredo knew it. This self-assured belief in his own ability, pumped full of adrenaline-fueled mental steroids to the point of grandiosity, has been passed down the lineage of male trapeze artists ever since. A solemn nod, a scoff, or an eye roll might follow a woman flying trapeze artist bemoaning the unfaithfulness or inflated ego of the male flyer she was pursuing. "Trapeze men," her fellow flyers might respond knowingly. #NotAllMenButProbablyAllTrapezeMen.

Which is why it came as little surprise when—upon returning to the US to perform once again with the Ringling Bros. and Barnum & Bailey show in 1927—Alfredo, young-flyer-turned-international-circus-star, found himself stopped in his tracks when he met his match in the form of the Queen of the Air herself, Lillian Leitzel.

When he met Lillian, it was as if the stars had aligned, and he could do no wrong. The pair were a force to be reckoned with, brilliant young daredevils high on the pheromones of their own success. The drama and trauma that surrounded them during their rise to the top made them all the more mysterious, and all the more inviting for audiences from all walks of life to steal away for a couple of hours to the big top, shrouded in air thick with sawdust and sweat, and allow the rules of the world to pause. It was titillating to watch the pair enter the ring each night, asking gravity to kindly fuck off for the ten minutes of their act while they swung through the air with nary a care in the world.

Wedding vows meant little when the electricity sparked so strongly. When Clara later injured herself—an injury that would end her career—she departed the show and filed for divorce. Alfredo, eager to move on with his sights set on his newfound muse and obsession, supported this perhaps a bit too eagerly. Clara, on the other hand, was willing to leave the circus and her husband, but would cling to the Codona name until the end of her days.

But, for all the reports of his ego, bravado, and adulterous nature, the man loved Lillian Leitzel more than anything in the world. More than flying, more than the pedestrian women who fanned themselves emphatically at the sight of the raw sexuality, the taboo tango danced under the big top, fawning in a moment of stolen societal reprieve. Lillian, born of the unfettered and unregulated depths of the circus, was his match in both skill and temperament. A star in her own right, Lillian's anger was only exceeded by her notoriously daring skill on the Roman rings. (Her poor assistant Mabel Cummings was said to be fired, rehired, and then fired again many times a day, a passing leap of explosively perceived shortcomings juggled over the duration of a show.) This spitfire attitude, deemed either diva-esque or star-worthy depending on who was peddling the gossip, bled into the couple's relationship. It was tumultuous, dramatic, a constant ebb and flow of *I-love-you-I-hate-you-I-need-you-Fuck-you* played in perpetuity. But surely this was love, this intensity bordering on codependency, this straight-out-of-a-Hollywood-picture romance.

Upon Clara's official departure, Lillian recommended that the Flying Codonas take on one Vera Bruce, a young Australian acrobat and equestrienne to whom Lillian had taken a shine. A quick learner, Vera soon joined the ranks as a full-fledged Flying Codona, just as Alfredo and Clara's divorce was finalized. Joining their flying family, Vera stood witness to one of the greatest weddings in circus history: the union of the king and queen of Ringling, Alfredo and Lillian, unstoppable, inimitable, and the hottest item of the twentieth century.

Alfredo may not have been the perfect husband, Lillian not the stalwart and timid wife, but they were well matched, and in the quiet moments when they could settle and feel their breath fall into an even and steady rhythm, two hearts beating to the same drum, it was the perfect marriage. Even as Alfredo's eyes began to wander to the bodies of other women, those in the air and gravity-bound, even as the two began to accept contracts in different troupes, cities, countries—it was a fact that he loved her, and she him, more than anything else in the world.

The Flying Codonas, and Lillian, returned to Europe. The pair remained an item as they returned to Paris's *Cirque d'Hiver*, but when it came time to move to Berlin to once again perform in *Wintergarten*, Lillian was absent from the bill. Instead, she had departed for Copenhagen, where she was to perform Roman rings at the Valencia. This would be a turning point for both of their lives.

Separated and rumored to be on the fritz, but nonetheless still publicly engaged in the greatest love story of their time, the two continued to do what they did best: fling themselves through the air, defying death.

Young aerialists today have the importance of rigging safety drilled into their heads before they ever step onto a stage. It doesn't matter how strong you are, how springy, how lithe, how catlike you can be as you twist and grapple through the air—if the very machinery holding you up fails, nothing can save you. And so it came to pass, on February 13, 1931, cruelly on a Friday, the swivel—a piece of rigging that allows for the attached apparatus to spin endlessly—failed and broke. Lillian, mid-performance, plummeted to the ground below. As an aerialist, there was no net to greet her like the one her husband had beneath his flying trapeze. She was instead met with the hardness of the earth, unwavering and unyielding, death waiting patiently to collect the tax all aerialists so boldly evaded.

Alfredo rushed to Copenhagen, Nellie Pelikan, Lillian's mother, at his side. Lillian was badly injured, having sustained spinal and internal injuries, but she was alive and hopeful. She would be okay, she assured her husband. His troupe needed him. There was no point in staying with her while she was grounded, she insisted, not when he was needed in the air. Return to *Wintergarten*, I'll be fine; fly high for the both of us while I recover.

There was no arguing with Lillian; this was common knowledge, known best of all by her dear husband. So Alfredo went back to Berlin, back to the air, back to his brother and young Vera Bruce and the safety of his net below. And Lillian, kept company by her mother, the Queen of the Air dethroned and exiled to the ground, died two days later, at age thirty-nine.

If our story ended here—with Lillian dead, and Alfredo heartbroken—it would be tragic, but it would not belong in this book. Perhaps you would never know Alfredo's name at all, so niche is the history of the flying trapeze greats to anyone happily gravity-bound. I certainly would be recounting Alfredo's legacy differently had it ended here, with less conflict, less disconcertment, less internalized disgust and confusion at crucifying a man who paved the way for the thing I love most in this world.

If we have learned anything from the #MeToo movement, it is that sometimes great artists commit unspeakable crimes. Some can disassociate the crimes of the man from the art; others cannot bear to think of work created by hands capable of causing such harm. For so many of us in the flying trapeze world, Alfredo is both icon and stain, savant and villain. How do you reckon with a grandfather who left you so much, whose legacy paved the way for opportunity and privilege for his wee baby flying descendants, but whose actions simultaneously stamped out greatness in a selfish attempt to quiet pain?

But I am getting ahead of myself. At this moment, Alfredo is still purely a hero in this story—full of faults, surely; an inability to keep it in his pants; an ego that, quite irritatingly, his talent could back up; but not a criminal, not a murderer. He was instead a widower wracked with grief, a performer expected to keep on performing flips for paying audiences while his mind and heart were enveloped in the unimaginable trauma that comes with losing a spouse too young, too unexpectedly, too unfairly.

On February 19, 1931, Lillian's funeral was held in Copenhagen, her body cremated, reduced to portable ashes. Upon returning to the United States, Alfredo had her remains interred in Inglewood Park Cemetery in Los Angeles, buried beneath *Reunion*, a seventeen-foot marble statue of an angel embracing a woman. Engraved on the pedestal:

In everlasting memory of my beloved LEITZEL CODONA—
Copenhagen Denmark Feb. 15, 1931—erected by her devoted husband
ALFREDO CODONA.

Alfredo became reckless following his beloved Lillian's death. His flying became angrier, more erratic, far more dangerous. He lacked the self-preservation and consistency necessary for safe and reliable flying. While the Codonas continued to rise to the top, bodying for several Hollywood films including *Tarzan the Ape Man*, *Polly of the Circus*, and *Swing High* (all 1932 releases), Alfredo's recklessness only grew. In April 1932, Lalo failed to hold onto Alfredo's triple and Alfredo, landing sub-optimally in the net, injured his shoulder.

While he was grounded and recovering, young Vera Bruce became increasingly appealing to the trapeze star. In September 1932, a year and a half after Lillian's untimely death, Vera and Alfredo tied the knot, marking his third marriage. A marriage of convenience, the two continued to tour and perform together until April 1933, when Alfredo once again sustained a significant shoulder injury while performing at Madison Square Garden, after missing the safety net and striking a steel cable, abruptly and unceremoniously ending his fly career.

Accustomed to the spotlight, Alfredo did not take his grounding in stride. For the remainder of the season, he was replaced by Bert Doss. At the end of the season, the Flying Codonas moved to a side ring to make way for the up-and-coming Flying Concellos, swooping in for the chance to take center stage with Alfredo out of the picture.

From 1934 to 1935, Alfredo worked as the performance director for Hagenbeck-Wallace Circus. The Flying Codonas hired Clayton Behee, whom Alfredo went on to coach to perform the elusive triple somersault. While Clayton proved adept—perhaps frustratingly so for Alfredo, who struggled seeing his protégé soaking up the spotlight and life-force-fueling applause—he could never hold a candle to the shadow of Alfredo's career. Nonetheless, Alfredo grew moody, a jealous teenager unable to channel his feelings of grief—for himself, for his career, and for the love of his life, sweet Lillian. His marriage to Vera grew rockier by the day.

In 1936, Vera departed the Flying Codonas to work with her brother, Clarence Bruce. Alfredo, working as the equestrian director at the Tom

Mix Circus and Wild West, did not follow her. Vera was replaced by Rose Sullivan, who debuted with the Flying Codonas in England's Tower Circus. Clayton was now throwing triples with regular consistency, but the Flying Codonas, with Lalo the only Codona remaining, were like a Frankensteined shell of the act they had once been.

In 1937, Alfredo left the circus and went to work in a garage run by his sister Hortense's husband in Long Beach, California. That June, Clara filed for divorce. The marriage was cruel, she claimed. She wanted out. Alfredo might be ready to throw it all away, but she certainly was not.

Alfredo did not contest her claims. Instead, he asked to meet her, alongside her attorney James E. Pawson and her mother Annie Bruce, to finalize the proceedings. No one had any reason to fret. While the marriage had been tumultuous, the divorce thus far had been amicable, and bordering on friendly. Alfredo meant no harm, surely; he was a broken man, a shell of his former self, doing Clara a kindness to release her from whatever self-constructed prison he had chosen to spend the rest of his days.

The meeting went down without a hitch. Vera could be free of her husband; Alfredo would not fight her wishes. She had requested half of the couple's valued $34,000 property and $200 alimony per month. That was fine, Alfredo said. Then, calmly, he requested a moment alone with his wife. Pawson agreed to leave to give them privacy, but Vera's mother refused; it was best if she stayed present. Alfredo shrugged it off. At this point, both in life and in love, he was used to not getting exactly what he wanted.

Women are more likely to be murdered by an intimate partner than by anyone else. In fact, 74 percent of all murder-suicides involve an intimate partner. Of those, 94 percent of the intimate partners murdered are female. These are cold facts we now know to be true. Perhaps Annie Bruce had an inkling.

When the lawyer departed, it was reported that Alfredo calmly told Vera that this was "the last thing he could do for her," a bitter resentment and satirical irony dripping from his tongue. Vera reached for a cigarette, a cool armor to shield her from any last desperate cruelties flung her way by her husband. Alfredo reached for a gun.

He fired four successive shots into Vera's body, a man on a mission. He did not aim for Annie; she wasn't the target, just a bystander, a nosy mother-in-law trying to insert herself into a narrative in which she had no business meddling. Then Alfredo turned the gun on himself, firing a bullet into his brain, killing himself. He was forty-three.

Vera died the next day, her body giving up its fight in Seaside Hospital. She was thirty-two.

Per his wishes, Alfredo was interred next to Lillian. Vera was buried in Calvary Cemetery in East Los Angeles. Her epitaph:

Peace at Last

I do not begrudge Alfredo's heartbreak. I mercifully cannot relate to the pain one must undergo, the transformation the trauma must wreak down to every last atom of one's body when one loses a life partner. The closest I can come to relating to it is the absolute agony I experienced when one of my dearest friends, American trapeze artist Charles-Ryan Barber, was struck by a drunk driver on Christmas Day 2018, losing his leg, and almost his life, in the process. He survived, but I still remember the pain, the anger, the uncertainty that followed. And so I empathize fully with how heart-wrenching loss can be, especially in an industry where performers must trust one another so strongly, literally putting their lives in the hands of their colleagues, friends, and lovers on a nightly basis. God, I feel for him.

Suicide is complex; and had Alfredo chosen to end his own life, and his alone, it would not be my place to pass any judgment. Far be it from me to dictate how someone chooses to cope with their own inner turmoil—provided the buck stops with them.

But to take someone else's life, the life of a woman, as these familicides often play out, is unforgiveable. And that is why, for me—a woman immersed in the world of flying trapeze but also a fierce advocate for victims of domestic and sexual violence—Alfredo's legacy is so complex. He was an indisputable genius in the air, and he paved the way for the industry I love so dearly today. But he isn't the only one. We can pay thanks to those who came before us while still acknowledging their flaws and cruelties. To call the selfishness of a murder-suicide a flaw grossly understates the case. I so wish that Alfredo's genius in the air could have been transposed to the ground.

Eighty-eight percent of murder-suicides are committed with a firearm. What a bitter irony that a man who prided himself on being so unique ended his life in so utterly basic and cowardly a way. David Adams, author of *Why Do They Kill? Men Who Murder Their Intimate Partners*, posits that the use of a firearm is "low-hanging fruit," and the prevalence of gun-related murder-suicide in the United States is due to the ease of firearm access, in contrast to other industrialized countries.

Dr. Jane Monckton-Smith says that, in most male-on-female intimate homicides, an eight-stage pattern is followed:

1. A pre-relationship history of stalking or abuse by the perpetrator
2. The romance developing quickly into a serious relationship
3. The relationship becoming dominated by coercive control
4. A trigger to threaten the perpetrator's control—for example, the relationship ends, or the perpetrator gets into financial difficulty
5. Escalation—an increase in the intensity or frequency of the partner's control tactics, such as by stalking or threatening suicide
6. The perpetrator has a change in thinking—choosing to move on, either through revenge or by homicide
7. Planning—the perpetrator might buy weapons, or seek opportunities to get the victim alone
8. Homicide—the perpetrator kills his or her partner, and possibly hurts others, such as the victim's children

———————————

Monckton-Smith says it is important to note these patterns, that they refute the narrative that such evils are "crimes of passion" committed in the heat of the moment—the sort of narratives that tend to absolve the abusers of any sort of genuine accountability. For men such as Alfredo Codona, who are revered and talented and have a legacy so much bigger than the cruel and selfish act of stamping out the life of a lover before snuffing out their own, it is easy to view the crimes through rose-tinted glasses. Poor Alfredo, broken in both mind and body, driven to the depths of depravity and gone too soon. Never poor Vera, married in a rebound of grief to a man who was ostensibly her boss and a decade her senior, a conciliation prize, an object to be done away with at will.

May Vera and all the women who have followed rest in power, and find peace, at last.

ABOUT THE EDITOR

Mitzi Szereto (mitziszereto.com) is an author and anthology editor whose books span multiple genres. Her popular true crime series, The Best New True Crime Stories, features the volumes *Unsolved Crimes & Mysteries*; *Partners in Crime*; *Crimes of Passion, Obsession & Revenge*; *Well-Mannered Crooks, Rogues & Criminals*; *Small Towns*; and *Serial Killers*. She's also written crime fiction, gothic fiction, horror, cozy mystery, satire, erotic fiction, and general fiction and nonfiction. She has the added distinction of being the editor of the first anthology of erotic fiction to include a Fellow of the Royal Society of Literature. Her books and short stories have been translated into multiple languages. Mitzi has appeared internationally on radio and television and at literature festivals, and has taught creative writing courses around the world, including at university level. She produced and presented the London-based web TV channel *Mitzi TV* and portrayed herself in the pseudo-documentary British film, *Lint: The Movie*. Her (oft-neglected) blog of personal essays can be found at *Errant Ramblings: Mitzi Szereto's Weblog*. She's currently working on a crime novel. Follow her on Twitter, Instagram, Facebook, and TikTok @mitziszereto.

ABOUT THE CONTRIBUTORS

Morgan Barbour (morganbarbour.com) is a model, writer, movement director, and circus artist. Her work has been featured in *Insider*, *Al Jazeera English*, *APC*, *GenderIT*, *The Journal.ie*, *Circus Talk*, *HuffPost*, and in two previous volumes of The Best New True Crime Stories series. She's a vocal advocate for victims of sexual abuse and has publicly criticized the justice systems in the US, the UK, and the Republic of Ireland. Her European debut play, *By the Bi*, was recognized by Amnesty International UK as a production inspiring audiences to think about human rights. She's a former professor at University of Nebraska-Lincoln and a visiting special lecturer at Central St. Martins.

Grant Butler is the author of the novel *The Heroin Heiress*, and his short fiction has been published in *Sick Cruising* and *Mardi Gras Mysteries*. Some of his literary influences include Stephen King, Ira Levin, Agatha Christie, and Thomas Harris. Cinema is also a big influence on his storytelling, and some of his favorite films are *Jaws*, *The Godfather*, *Goodfellas*, and *Psycho*. His piece on the Red Ripper was selected as an online bonus story for *The Best New True Crime Stories: Serial Killers*. He was born and raised in Ohio.

Janel Comeau is a writer, blogger, podcaster, comedian, and human services worker currently residing in Halifax, Nova Scotia, Canada. She's a regular contributor to the satire news website *The Beaverton* and cohost of the true crime podcast *Histories and Mysteries with Jessica and Janel*. Her work has previously appeared in *The Best New True Crime Stories: Well-*

Mannered Crooks, Rogues & Criminals and *The Best New True Crime Stories: Unsolved Crimes & Mysteries.*

Anthony Ferguson is an author and editor living in Perth, Australia. He has published more than seventy short stories and nonfiction articles in Australia, Britain, and the US. He wrote the novel *Protégé*, the nonfiction books *The Sex Doll: A History* and *Murder Down Under*, edited the short-story collection *Devil Dolls and Duplicates in Australian Horror*, and contributed to several previous volumes of The Best New True Crime Stories. He's a committee member of the Australasian Horror Writers Association (AHWA), and a submissions editor for *Andromeda Spaceways Magazine* (ASM). He won the Australian Shadows Award for Short Fiction in 2020.

Dr. Mark Fryers (markfryerswriterresearcher.wordpress.com) is a freelance writer and scholar who has also worked in the film and TV industries, including conducting research for true crime documentaries. He is the author of numerous books, journal articles, and chapters, including for Routledge and I. B. Tauris. A specialist in true crime and horror, he's the recipient of several Book Authority Awards through his previous contributions in the bestselling The Best New True Crime Stories series. He lives in England.

Jill Hand is a former crime reporter. She's the author of the Southern Gothic thrillers *White Oaks* and *Black Willows*. Her work has appeared in many anthologies, including *Hymns of Abomination*, *A Walk in a Darker Wood*, and *The Corona Book of Ghost Stories*, among others. She lives in New Jersey.

Alisha Holland lives in Troutdale, Oregon, with her magnificent partner Josh, her adorable pups Rosie and Bokku, and her playful kitty Dexter. Besides contributing to books, Alisha hosts a true crime podcast (*Murder* *in the Rain*) and a *Golden Girls* podcast (*Always Be My Sisters*). When not working on these shows, she can be found overly engaged in an episode of *Jeopardy!* or dancing around the house to The Beatles.

Cathy Pickens (cathypickens.com) has written crime fiction, starting with the award-winning *Southern Fried* (St. Martin's), and a regional series on historic true crime, starting with *Charlotte True Crime Stories* (History Press). The latest is *Upstate South Carolina True Crime Stories*. She's also contributed to previous volumes in The Best New True Crime Stories series. She's served as national president of Sisters in Crime, on the national board of Mystery Writers of America, and as true crime columnist for *Mystery Readers Journal* since 2004. A recovering lawyer and former college professor, she is also the author of *CREATE! Developing Your Creative Process* (create-update.com), works with prison inmates, and coaches writers and others in creativity workshops.

Charlotte Platt (charlotteplattwriter.co.uk) is a speculative writer based in the (very) far north of Scotland. She subsists on tea and sarcasm, and is often found walking near rivers and cliffs, as there are many of those nearby. She has most recently had works in *Factor Four Magazine* and *The Future Looms*, and previously contributed to *The Best New True Crime Stories: Small Towns*. Find her on Twitter @Chazzaroo and on Instagram @chaz. platt (though she warns this is mostly dog pictures).

Khadija Tauseef is a student of history. She completed her master's in 2019 and has since been writing for several historical magazines, including *Ancient Origins*. Along with history, she's a true crime fan; the nature of humans always fascinates her. She keeps looking to expand her knowledge and better her writing. History holds many lessons that need to be closely learned from, and she wants to try making history interesting enough for people to enjoy. She divides her time between Pakistan and the US.

Joe Turner (joeturnerbooks.com) is a true crime writer from Shropshire, England. He's the author of an upcoming book on the strange story of Daniel LaPlante entitled *The Boy in The Walls*, and has appeared in three previous volumes of The Best New True Crime Stories. He also works for a number of true crime websites, magazines, and podcasts. He spends most of his time researching and writing about bizarre crime stories from across the world, all of which can be read on his blog.

Anya Wassenberg, a contributor to *The Best New True Crime Stories: Unsolved Crimes & Mysteries*, is a freelance writer with a wide-ranging background, and a specialty in arts, culture writing, and journalism. In addition to freelancing as a writer and editor, she's a college-level writing instructor in her native Canada, and runs a longstanding arts blog. It's the intersection of facts, events, and culture that have fueled her writing over a career spanning nearly three decades. Many of Anya's pieces, including posts from her blog, have been cited and appear in the bibliographies of academic publications, periodicals, and other media.

Mango Publishing, established in 2014, publishes an eclectic list of books by diverse authors—both new and established voices—on topics ranging from business, personal growth, women's empowerment, LGBTQ+ studies, health, and spirituality to history, popular culture, time management, decluttering, lifestyle, mental wellness, aging, and sustainable living. We were recently named 2019 *and* 2020's #1 fastest-growing independent publisher by *Publishers Weekly*. Our success is driven by our main goal, which is to publish high-quality books that will entertain readers as well as make a positive difference in their lives.

Our readers are our most important resource; we value your input, suggestions, and ideas. We'd love to hear from you—after all, we are publishing books for you!

Please stay in touch with us and follow us at:

Facebook: Mango Publishing
Twitter: @MangoPublishing
Instagram: @MangoPublishing
LinkedIn: Mango Publishing
Pinterest: Mango Publishing
Newsletter: mangopublishinggroup.com/newsletter

Join us on Mango's journey to reinvent publishing, one book at a time.